AF394305

PRAISE FOR GREGG OLSEN

Out of the Woods

"Novelist and true crime author Olsen (*The Amish Wife*) paints a heartbreaking portrait of a woman haunted by her narrow escape from a serial killer . . . As in Olsen's previous works of nonfiction, there's plenty of rigorous research on display, but it's his empathetic consideration of what happens to high-profile victims after news cameras stop rolling that sets this apart . . . It's moving stuff."

—*Publishers Weekly*

"Prolific true-crime author Olsen offers another exemplary narrative of unimaginable trauma that packs an emotional punch."

—*Booklist*

"An unflinching look at the aftermath of unimaginable trauma and a testament to the human spirit's capacity for strength and healing."

—*Oprah Daily*

"This book makes a significant contribution to the literature of trauma. It's masterfully structured for emotional impact, while also urging us into better-informed discussions."

—*Psychology Today*

"Victims of the most heinous crimes aren't always at the center of the story when the news cameras, podcasts, and true crime aficionados rush in to document the case. Often these victims are never the ones telling their story and when everyone moves [on] they are forgotten while their perpetrators live in infamy. Author Gregg Olsen seeks to remedy this situation in his newest work which considers what happens to those victims once everyone else moves on. *Out of the Woods: A Girl, a Killer, and a Lifelong Struggle to Find the Way Home*, is a heartbreaking tale that forces readers to confront the unbearably grim reality of survival. More than just the graphic details that happened to Shasta Groene in the Montana woods, Olsen takes readers through the aftermath of what it actually means to have survived the unimaginable . . . An honest story of what it means to be a survivor. A story of trauma and survival that will send true crime devotees through a roller coaster of emotions and leave them shocked to their core."

—Associated Press

"*Out of the Woods* takes you into the dark nightmare world of eight-year-old Shasta. Gregg Olsen portrays her ordeal with compassion, understanding, and hope, providing an intense look at trauma and its effect on victims and those who love them. *Out of the Woods* is a remarkable, heartbreaking story told well."

—Diane Fanning, author of *Lizzie*

"In *Out of the Woods*, Gregg Olsen unravels the horrific story of Shasta Groene, the survivor of a serial killer who lived to tell her darkest secrets, exclusively to him. This tale is so outlandish and shocking, it will haunt you forever. True crime fans, you have a roller coaster ride waiting for you, so be prepared to be glued to your seat. Olsen has written a masterpiece!"

—Aphrodite Jones, *New York Times* bestselling author of *Cruel Sacrifice*

The Amish Wife

"The details of the case are gripping enough, but Olsen elevates them with sturdy prose, meticulous research, and admirable journalistic tenacity. This addendum to a once-settled story lands as much more than a footnote."

—*Publishers Weekly* (starred review)

"Olsen has a gift for taking mountains of paperwork and interview material and weaving them into a cohesive narrative that is often difficult to put down, especially for die-hard true-crime fans. Because he frames the book as a step-by-step process of discovery, readers will feel like they're right there with him as he's knocking on doors and spinning out on the Midwestern ice. An engaging, well-researched historical excavation . . ."

—*Kirkus Reviews*

"The story is riveting . . . Folks interested in that peek behind the curtain will love this."

—*Booklist*

"While Olsen's extensive written character analysis is built with avid descriptors of human characteristics and quirks, fed by a black oddball sense of humor, his work is also imbued with great compassion—for human foibles, human loves and losses, and even for those who take human life . . . *The Amish Wife* is an absorbing and praiseworthy contribution to the understanding of murder."

—*Splash Magazines*

If You Tell

"This riveting account will leave readers questioning every odd relative they've known."

—*Publishers Weekly* (starred review)

"Olsen presents the story chronologically and in a simple, straightforward style, which works well: it is chilling enough as is."

—*Booklist*

"An unsettling stunner about sibling love, courage, and resilience."

—*People* magazine (Book of the Week)

"*If You Tell* accomplishes what it sets out to do. The result is a compelling portrait of terror and a powerfully honest, yet still sensitive, look at survival."

—*Bookreporter*

"This disturbing book recounts the unimaginable abuse and torture three sisters Nikki, Sami, and Tori Knotek endured from their own mother, Shelly . . . The strong bond they form to survive and defy their mother's sadistic tendencies is inspiring."

—*BuzzFeed*

"A true crime tour de force."

—Steve Jackson, *New York Times* bestselling author of *No Stone Unturned*

"Even the most devoted true crime reader will be shocked by the maddening and mind-boggling acts of horror that Gregg Olsen chronicles in this book. Olsen has done it again, giving readers a glimpse into a murderous duo that's so chilling, it will have your head spinning. I could not put this book down!"
—Aphrodite Jones, *New York Times* bestselling author

"A suspenseful, horrific, and yet fascinating character study of an incredibly dysfunctional and dangerous family by Gregg Olsen, one of today's true crime masters."
—Caitlin Rother, *New York Times* bestselling author

"There's only one writer who can tell such an intensely horrifying, psychotic tale of unspeakable abuse, grotesque torture, and horrendous serial murder with grace, sensitivity, and class . . . A riveting, taut, real-life psychological suspense thrill ride . . . All at once compelling and original, Gregg Olsen's *If You Tell* is an instant true crime classic."
—M. William Phelps, *New York Times* bestselling author

"We all start life with immense promise, but in our first minute, we cannot know who'll ultimately have the greatest impact on our lives, for better or worse. Here, Gregg Olsen—the heir apparent to legendary crime writers Jack Olsen and Ann Rule—explores the dark side of that question in his usual chilling, heartbreaking prose. Superb and creepy storytelling from a true crime master."
—Ron Franscell, author of *Alice & Gerald: A Homicidal Love Story*

"A master of true crime returns with a vengeance. After a decade detour into novels, Gregg Olsen is back with a dark tale of nonfiction from the Pacific Northwest that will keep you awake long after the lights have gone out. The monster at the heart of *If You Tell* is not your typical boogeyman, not some wandering drifter or man in a van. No. In fact, they called her . . . mother. And yet this story is about hope and renewal in the face of evil and how three sisters can find the goodness in the world after surviving the worst it has to offer. Classic true crime in the tradition of *In Cold Blood* and *The Stranger Beside Me*."
—James Renner, author of *True Crime Addict*

"This nightmare walked on two legs and some of her victims called her mom. In *If You Tell*, Gregg Olsen documents the horrific mental and physical torture Shelly Knotek inflicted on everyone in her household. A powerful story of cruelty that will haunt you for a long time."
—Diane Fanning, author of *Treason in the Secret City*

"Bristling with tension, gripping from the first pages, Gregg Olsen's masterful portrait of children caught in the web of a coldly calculating killer fascinates. A read so compelling it kept me up late into the night, *If You Tell* exposes incredible evil that lived quietly in small-town America. That the book is fact, not fiction, terrifies."
—Kathryn Casey, bestselling author of *In Plain Sight*

I Know Where You Live

"In *I Know Where You Live*, master of suspense Gregg Olsen peels back layer after layer to reveal an ugly underbelly of family secrets and revenge. This unbearably tense, serpentine tale probes the darkest corners of the heart and mind. The suspense never wavers in this electrifying page-turner, guaranteed to keep your heart pounding until the very last page."
—Heather Gudenkauf, *New York Times* bestselling author

The Hive

An Amazon Best Book of the Month: Mystery, Thriller & Suspense

"Readers who relish the aftershocks of cult exploitation will turn every page with keen anticipation."

—*Kirkus Reviews*

"*The Hive* is Gregg Olsen at his finest. Exciting, anxiety provoking, and twisty . . . You will stay up all night reading . . . not wanting to put it down until the final and shocking conclusion. This book will take you right down a rabbit hole you never suspected."

—*Mystery and Suspense Magazine*

"Mesmerizing! Gregg Olsen tautly reveals layer after layer of lies, secrets, and betrayals in an increasingly horrifying exposé of one cult leader and her terrible sway over others. Forget the evil men do. These women will have you fearing for your life."

—Lisa Gardner, #1 *New York Times* bestselling author

"*The Hive* is a riveting thriller, a tsunami of a story that starts out strong and absolutely knocks you over at the end. The characters are fascinating, their world so real and absorbing—I was transfixed from the very start. Gregg Olsen is such a compelling writer."

—Luanne Rice, *New York Times* bestselling author

"In this gripping thriller, everything is not as it seems, and beauty is only skin deep. *The Hive* is a brilliantly engrossing read—exactly what we have come to expect from Gregg Olsen."

—Karin Slaughter, *New York Times* and
internationally bestselling author

"A charismatic wellness guru, a dead young journalist, and a slew of secrets are the ingredients that make up this fiendishly fun thriller. *The Hive* will have readers buzzing."
—Greer Hendricks, #1 *New York Times* bestselling coauthor of *The Wife Between Us*

"Gregg Olsen's *The Hive* is a fast-paced, intriguing, intense, and suspenseful read that is as creepy as it is fantastic. Brilliant, thought-provoking, heartbreaking, and original, *The Hive* will keep you up at night and leave you reeling long after you've finished it. Every page carries weight in this novel. There are plenty of twists and turns to satisfy even the most seasoned crime fiction reader, and the characters feel authentic and alive in ways that only Olsen can achieve."
—Lisa Regan, #1 *Wall Street Journal* bestselling author of the Detective Josie Quinn series

"Die-hard Gregg Olsen fans will love *The Hive*; new readers will become fans. Olsen deftly guides the reader through the pages, cranking up the suspense as long-held secrets rise to the surface. The result is compulsively page turning as Olsen keeps the reader's mind buzzing in suspense. He hooks the reader as a dark crime from the past collides with a crime from the present."
—Kendra Elliot, *Wall Street Journal* bestselling author

"Gregg Olsen's *The Hive* begins with a fascinating premise and a spellbinding opening scene that held me in its grip as I flew through the pages. Olsen expertly weaves together a multilayered tale told by a complex array of unforgettable characters in his latest jaw-dropping thriller. In this dark and dangerously addictive read buzzing with secrets, betrayal, and murder, queen bees and wannabes take on a whole new meaning. Not to be missed."
—Heather Gudenkauf, *New York Times* bestselling author of *This Is How I Lied*

Lying Next to Me

"*Lying Next to Me* is a clever, chilling puzzle of a tale. A riveting, sharp-edged page-turner, it's Gregg Olsen's best book yet."

—A. J. Banner, *USA Today* bestselling author

"A dark, claustrophobic thriller filled with twists and turns. A brilliant book."

—Caroline Mitchell, #1 international bestselling author

"In *Lying Next to Me*, [Olsen] has given us a first-rate work of psychological complexity as well as a mystery that is full of twists and is quite a grabber."

—Popular Culture Association

The Last Thing She Ever Did

"Gregg Olsen pens brilliant, creepy, page-turning, heart-pounding novels of suspense that always keep me up at night. In *The Last Thing She Ever Did*, he topped himself."

—Allison Brennan, *New York Times* bestselling author

"Beguiling, wicked, and taut with suspense and paranoia, *The Last Thing She Ever Did* delivers scenes as devastating as any I've ever read with a startling, pitch-perfect finale. A reminder that evil may reside in one's actions, but tragedy often spawns from one's inaction."

—Eric Rickstad, *New York Times* bestselling author of *The Silent Girls*

"Olsen's latest examines how a terrible, split-second decision has lingering effects, and the past echoes the present. Full of unexpected twists, *The Last Thing She Ever Did* will keep you guessing to the last line."

—J.T. Ellison, *New York Times* bestselling author of *Lie to Me*

"Master storyteller Gregg Olsen continues to take readers hostage with another spellbinding tale of relentless, pulse-pounding suspense."

—Rick Mofina, international bestselling author of *Last Seen*

"Tense. Well-crafted. Gripping."

—Mary Burton, *New York Times* bestselling author

"With *The Last Thing She Ever Did*, Gregg Olsen delivers an edgy, tension-filled, roller-coaster ride of a novel that will thrill and devastate in equal measure."

—Linda Castillo, *New York Times* bestselling author

BY THE
RIVER'S
EDGE

ALSO BY GREGG OLSEN

Fiction

I Know Where You Live
The Hive
Silent Ridge
Water's Edge
Snow Creek
Cougar Point
Final Victim
Lying Next to Me
The Weight of Silence
The Last Thing She Ever Did
The Sound of Rain
Just Try to Stop Me
Now That She's Gone
The Girl in the Woods
The Girl on the Run
The Boy She Left Behind
Shocking True Story
Fear Collector
Beneath Her Skin
The Bone Box (novella)
Dying to Be Her
Closer Than Blood
Victim Six
Heart of Ice
A Wicked Snow
A Cold Dark Place

Nonfiction

Out of the Woods: A Girl, a Killer, and a Lifelong
Struggle to Find the Way Home

The Amish Wife: Unraveling the Lies, Secrets,
and Conspiracy That Let a Killer Go Free

If You Tell: A True Story of Murder, Family Secrets,
and the Unbreakable Bond of Sisterhood

A Killing in Amish Country: Sex, Betrayal, and a Cold-Blooded Murder

A Twisted Faith: A Minister's Obsession
and the Murder That Destroyed a Church

The Deep Dark: Disaster and Redemption in America's Richest Silver Mine

Starvation Heights: A True Story of Murder
and Malice in the Woods of the Pacific Northwest

Cruel Deception: A True Story of Murder and a Mother's Deadly Game

If Loving You Is Wrong: The Teacher
and Student Sex Case That Shocked the World

Abandoned Prayers: An Incredible True Story of Murder,
Obsession, and Amish Secrets

Bitter Almonds: The True Story of Mothers, Daughters,
and the Seattle Cyanide Murders

*If I Can't Have You: Susan Powell, Her Mysterious Disappearance,
and the Murder of Her Children*

*American Black Widow: The Shocking
True Story of a Preacher's Wife Turned Killer*

BY THE RIVER'S EDGE

A TRUE STORY OF IDENTITY AND SERIAL MURDER

GREGG OLSEN

THOMAS & MERCER

Text copyright © 2026 by Gregg Olsen

All rights reserved.

No part of this book may be reproduced, or stored in a retrieval system, or transmitted in any form or by any means, electronic, mechanical, photocopying, recording, or otherwise, without express written permission of the publisher.

Published by Thomas & Mercer, Seattle

www.apub.com

Amazon, the Amazon logo, and Thomas & Mercer are trademarks of Amazon.com, Inc., or its affiliates.

EU product safety contact:
Amazon Media EU S. à r.l.
38 avenue John F. Kennedy, L-1855 Luxembourg
amazonpublishing-gpsr@amazon.com

ISBN-13: 9781662534874 (hardcover)
ISBN-13: 9781662522444 (paperback)
ISBN-13: 9781662522437 (digital)

Cover design by Jarrod Taylor
Cover image: © Tomas Nevesely / Shutterstock; © Kokia & Sawyer / Unsplash

Printed in the United States of America

First edition

For the Circle
Yolanda, Nickie, and Kathy

PROLOGUE

He had been dressing as a woman off and on for a while by the time he slid into a window seat for the eighteen-hour flight from Seattle to Bangkok in the winter of 2000. The journey that started in rural Omak, then Spokane, Washington, had been a lifetime in coming. Mental health counselors said he needed to prepare for at least a year before they'd approve any surgical alterations to his anatomy, which, they all agreed, was the only real solution to his dire situation.

So, he had been good.

Very good.

Passengers and crew likely barely noticed him. Odd, maybe. Unassuming. At five seven, he wasn't a big person. A little thick in the middle, but not so much that anyone would say he was fat. His long, dark hair hung limply past his shoulders, and oversized glasses pinched the narrow bridge of his nose. He kept his gaze fixed out the window, or downward when addressed directly. Even though he was as quiet as could be, folded tightly into his seat, as unobtrusive as the space would allow, he sensed dismissive glances in his direction.

What were they thinking?

For as long as he could remember, he'd felt judgments—scorn, really—hurled at him.

Weirdo.

Faggot.

Freak of nature.

Epithets, like those and others even viler, came not just from the mouths of strangers but his own family.

Sticks and stones will break my bones,

But names won't ever hurt me.

All of that was a lie.

His mother beat him when she caught him in her bedroom wearing her clothes when he was a little boy. He never did that again. Not around her anyway. His father and older brother did things to him that he could share only with a therapist. His entire life had been an exercise in unchecked violence, paralyzing fear, and severe trauma. When he finally gave in to his impulses and released his pent-up rage, he had myriad excuses.

She was gone.

They were bad.

It wasn't her.

It was him.

Yet on that long flight to Bangkok, maybe for the first time ever, none of that seemed to matter.

Going to make it all go away.

The silent passenger had made an appointment with a doctor he'd been told was one of the best in the world. The surgeon was going to undo a lifetime of confusion and shame that started the day he was born. There was always something different about him, down there. He had a penis and a scrotum, but they were small and underdeveloped. Functional, but not like his brother's or his dad's. Not like anyone's he'd ever seen. He didn't know it until deep into his adulthood, but he also had a vagina. His parents told him he was a "morphodite," a term replaced for a time by "hermaphrodite" to refer to an organism with both male and female reproductive organs. He loathed that word. Medical. Clinical. A cruel label. When the lexicon changed yet again to "intersex" some years later, it did little to make him feel like less of a joke.

God's cruel joke.

Whatever his situation, it rained down problems on everyone.

At birth, the family physician flipped a biological coin, sutured his vagina, and assigned male for gender.

With the swipe of a pen, he became his parents' second son.

A boy who would become a man.

No matter what it took.

Even if it had to be beaten into him.

At forty-eight, he had enough of thinking about himself in that derisive and unfair manner. He wanted to end the torture his biology, his family, and the world had visited on him. And so there he was on that Boeing jet en route to the other side of the world. Though the true and complete impetus might never be known with certainty, he was on a quest to make his body align with his identity. The operation would fix God's mistake. Gender-reassignment surgery was far from new, and it had been gaining traction. Christine Jorgensen in the 1950s and Renée Richards in the 1970s were two who became well known for transitioning from male to female. Famous or infamous? It depended on perspective, of course. While San Francisco's Board of Supervisors was about to approve up to $50,000 in lifetime benefits for city employees seeking to transition, the rest of the country didn't offer even the most basic legal protections for transgender people.

Not new, but also not easy.

Indeed, serious complications ensued on the operating table in Bangkok. Later, he told friends and some others who were paid to listen that he'd nearly bled out in the operation that commanded a grueling ten hours. Dying wouldn't have been the worst outcome. It certainly would have been better than living as he had.

When a soft-spoken woman wearing those same oversized glasses boarded the plane for the 7,500-mile flight back home to her growing herd of cats and guns, she left behind a bucket of blood and slivers of a discarded and incongruent anatomy in a medical waste container.

Right where, she'd insist, the SOB belonged.

She'd slayed the monster.

Put an end to a nightmare—hers and the other women who had passed through her former life.

At least that would be among her shifting stories.

Now, she'd be able to start anew. It was calculated, permanent, and risky, a reinvention that not only eradicated overlapping physiology but also could keep her safe from what lurked in her past.

All that thinking might have been true.

The operation was the proof Donna would offer to anyone who caught up with what Douglas had done.

She was not to blame.

PART ONE

Yolanda, Nickie, and Kathy

CHAPTER ONE

No one doing the work hunched over in a stranger's car, on the bed in a shithole motel, or crouched down low in some alleyway ever dreamed of being a street hooker. The vocation never found its way onto any girl's list randomly tucked somewhere between veterinarian, teacher, astronaut, or pop star.

Or even mother. Maybe mostly mother.

And if any had, they surely would have imagined plying the trade among the cloud-scratching towers of New York City or the adult fantasy land of Las Vegas—not a run-down stretch of blacktop along East Sprague Avenue that traverses the gritty edge of downtown Spokane, Washington.

And yet they were, all night. Every night. And, yes, more than twice on Sundays.

The women working on the east side of Spokane in 1990 were as much a part of the neighborhood as the boat marina, the post office, and the dank, sticky-floored taverns where 2:00 a.m. closing time came too soon for some. A few girls stayed with family or friends, while others rented rooms at fleabag motels like the Spokane Street, a faded relic of mid-century roadside architecture, its boxy two-story structure perched above a concrete retaining wall splattered with graffiti. The beat-up red-brown paint job of the Spokane Street Motel bore the marks of time, with streaks of rust and curly bits of peeling paint. And yet, its most prominent feature—its neon sign's dramatic arrow pointing toward the entrance—endured as a symbol of its once-ambitious effort to draw weary travelers off a thoroughfare that ran from Seattle to the Idaho Panhandle and points farther east.

By the 1990s, however, the weary had long been jettisoned and replaced by the broken down and lost.

Framed in white trim, the motel windows were streaked and foggy, offering only the slightest glimpse into dimly lit rooms of mismatched, threadbare furniture. Salvation Army rejects at best. The upper floor, accessible by an exterior staircase, had a long, shared balcony-style walk-way, where guests and stealth visitors smoked and looked out over the empty parking lot. Most who stayed at the Spokane Street didn't have a need for a car. Walking to work wasn't a big deal. Walking, of course, was an essential part of the job.

In a very real way, the Spokane Street Motel was a landing pad for survival, a home to those inhabiting the fringes of the Lilac City. Its rooms offered a certain permanence in the transient lives of those who slept there. Several women who lived there on the not-so down-low had formed an alliance, a kind of support group they called the Circle.

All members were acutely aware of the dangers of their profession. Not just from the ever-present threats of disease or pregnancy or the drug abuse and alcoholism that were commonplace, but also from the violence at the hands of their johns, boyfriends, or pimps. The women of the Circle were tough. They had to be. And resigned too. They were mired in a cycle that they all accepted likely had no happy ending. And when the ending came, most knew it wasn't going to be pretty. Pretty is never in the cards when days and nights are made up of transactions that are both very personal and not very personal at the same time.

When they weren't in the front seat of some guy's car or in some tucked-away space, offering up whatever freaky thing a trick desired, the women commiserated on what had brought each of them to that life. Drugs, bad choices. Mostly, the men in their lives. The reasons for that were the same old, same old. Abusive. Addicted. Forever out of work. They talked about how they missed their kids. How they were saving up for an ever-elusive second chance. And how dangerous things on the street really were. Women just like them were prey. Scores had been murdered by some psycho trick a half dozen years before in a string of unsolved cases in Seattle; Southern California; Vancouver, BC; and even Spokane.

And no one was doing a fucking thing about any of it.

It was all on them.

Like it always had been.

Cops were zero help. Obviously. Their men pled concern for their welfare whenever they were out working late at night, but what could they do? It wasn't as though their boyfriends, husbands, *protectors* could come on the job with them.

And really, it passed through their thoughts and seeped into conversations that maybe the men in their lives were more concerned about the money brought in than their welfare.

The women of the Circle lived with their fear and went to work, taking careful note of the vehicles the others slipped into. Some wrote down license plate numbers. They also made mental notes of the men who picked them up. Race. Hair color and style. Facial hair or clean-shaven? Big men. Small men. Smelly men. Professional men with clueless wives at home and pictures of kids on the dash. What they said during a transaction. Rough. Weird. Passive. Verbal. Apologetic.

Whatever.

Any little detail that could help in a search or investigation if one of their own didn't return from a date.

None knew if their efforts would really protect them. It simply was all they could think to do.

At sixty-seven, Catherine Crisler was fulfilling a promise she had made to herself long before the morning of February 22, 1990. Take a walk. Breathe in the fresh air. Enjoy the outdoors. Keep moving. While it was cold and foggy along the Spokane River Centennial Trail, it was an easy walk, mostly flat and paved. It wasn't hard. And nothing was ever remarkable about her routine, save for maybe catching a glimpse of some wildlife along the banks of the river or another walker with his dog or a jogger plugged into earphones and too preoccupied to wave hello or give a polite nod of the head.

This day, however, was remarkable for all the wrong reasons.

It was the morning Catherine found her.

At first, when she initially laid eyes on the scene, it appeared to be a floral-patterned blanket wadded up just off the shoulder of the road, near the embankment leading down to the riverbank.

What's that?

Catherine stepped a bit closer to get a better look. She scanned the area. Everything was quiet. The air was still with a veil of fog twisting its way over the landscape and down to the river. She looked down.

Again, what's that?

It can't be.

But it was.

She could see the figure of an African American by the river's edge.

Catherine drew a deep breath but somehow managed the resolve to stay calm. She knew that she'd stumbled onto something so sad, so tragic, and really, so terrible. She couldn't be sure if it was a man or a woman, but whoever it was hadn't gone down to the river naked and alone. Someone had put him or her there. Shaken, she returned home to her husband of forty-two years, called the Spokane Police Department, and waited for their arrival.

She told the responding officer that all the victim had on was a gold necklace.

And that she wouldn't have found it if not for the blankets by the road.

At thirty-nine, Detective Jim Lundgren was the kind of guy who lived and breathed law enforcement, right and wrong, and the search for justice, to such a degree that two of his three boys would eventually don the blue uniform too. It was a purpose-driven life. What else could they do?

Lundgren, who joined the force in 1973, was one of the first city police detectives to arrive on the scene of the murder. After completing his primary duties along the river, he returned to the police station at about 1:30 p.m. to find a message from the manager of the Spokane Street Motel. Linda Rose, forty-four, wanted to talk to the police about a missing girl. When Lundgren reached Rose, she asked, concerned, if any unidentified Black women had been admitted to a hospital. One of her motel guests, Yolanda Sapp, was missing. Linda told him that Yolanda worked the area around East Second Avenue and South Division Street near Perkins Restaurant as well as the nearby side streets. Yolanda, she said, occasionally worked on the section of East Sprague Avenue known by locals as the Stroll or the Track but had been avoiding that area because more cops had been patrolling there lately. Linda last saw Yolanda when she went to her room to give her a wake-up call at 6:30 p.m. on Tuesday.

A wake-up call? That kind of service seemed more high-end hotel than fleabag motel.

She mentioned that Yolanda's live-in boyfriend, Darrel Thomas, forty-one, had called her at the motel office early Wednesday morning to tell her Yolanda was missing. He was worried. Something wasn't right. Linda felt the same way. She didn't suspect a domestic dispute either. She added that Yolanda and Darrel, who went by "Doc," got along extremely well and had caused no problems while staying in unit 3 for almost three months.

Detective Lundgren made the obvious connection and checked police records to find a lengthy list of prostitution-related and other arrests for Yolanda Anastasia Sapp, twenty-six. She had eleven arrests over the last four years, including one just three weeks earlier on January

30 for loitering for the purpose of prostitution. He retrieved her fingerprint card from the file.

The pathologist from the coroner's office knew nothing about the Circle, but he knew that nothing had protected this victim from a brutal and degrading murder. While the fingerprint card confirmed who the victim was, the pathologist determined that Yolanda Sapp had died from three gunshots to the back with small-caliber bullets that damaged her heart and lungs before exiting from her upper chest. From the route of the wounds through the body, it appeared she had been lying face down when shot from above. The pathologist noted needle marks on both of the victim's legs that were evidence of a serious drug habit. He noted some small puncture wounds near her throat and another in her left breast that could have been one of the exit wounds by a bullet.

It was a merciless and violent end for a woman whom the evidence suggested was already struggling with a difficult life.

And her body was found some four miles from the areas where she normally worked—quite a distance for a woman who didn't own a car.

Detectives Nick Stanley, forty-one, and Bruce Nelson, forty-eight, were observing the autopsy at the hospital when Lundgren arrived. Lundgren told Stanley and Nelson that Yolanda had been living at the motel with Doc, who, like half the residents there, was on probation for one thing or another. His latest stretch in jail had been theft related. Still, Doc was a natural starting point for the investigation, not only as a source of information about his girlfriend, the people she had contact with, and her activities before she disappeared but also as the first potential suspect. Every homicide detective knew to investigate the in-laws before the outlaws.

Stanley had been with the police seventeen years, working almost every kind of criminal investigation there was. Nelson had more years on the force, having joined when he was just twenty-four in 1965 and starting as a motorcycle patrol cop. Both men looked like detectives, with dark hair and trim builds draped in unremarkable sport coats.

It was after 3:00 p.m. when they caught up with Doc in the motel office with manager Linda Rose. Doc didn't know Yolanda had been murdered, but he had his suspicions. Stanley took him back to his room to break the news and conduct the crucial first interview. Before Stanley could get a word out, Doc asked him straight up if the dead body by the river was Yolanda.

"Yes, sorry," the detective said.

Doc, a man who'd been through a lot in his life, slumped onto the bed. Between tears and rage, for more than fifteen minutes he rambled on about the unfairness of this happening now, when he and Yolanda were just starting to get things together.

When he settled down enough to be interviewed, Doc told the detective that he had last seen Yolanda at 11:00 p.m., Tuesday, February 20. She had begun her evening by hitting the streets at nine to look for customers about four blocks north of the motel. She came back to the motel a couple of hours later, complaining to Doc that the people she had encountered didn't want to do business and only seemed interested in "messing" with her. He urged her to stay home the rest of the night, but she left shortly after she'd arrived and walked down the dark street toward the boat sales lot called Trudeau's Marina, also about four blocks away on East Sprague Avenue where she sometimes met with customers in the boats on the lot. When she wasn't home by 2:00 a.m., Doc said he started to worry and began to look for her. He even called the city jail a couple of times to ask if she had been arrested; she hadn't. He reached out to several of her friends to learn they had not seen her since earlier that night. He went to the hospital to see if she was hurt. Finally, he alerted Linda Rose that something was up with Yolanda.

Something that, he was sure, was seriously bad.

Doc said Yolanda was no stranger to violence. She had come to Spokane from Seattle after the man she ran with there was murdered. Despite that in their background, Doc insisted neither he nor Yolanda owned a gun. He mentioned that Yolanda had left her two children, ages six and nine, who were living in the Seattle area with her mother. Yolanda, he said, was smart and careful. She insisted on condoms whenever she had sex with a customer and got them for free from a source in downtown Spokane or at an adult bookstore near the Covered Wagon on East Sprague.

Though obviously reeling from his loss, Doc appeared eager to cooperate. Without the hesitation of someone who had something to hide, he signed a form consenting to a search of their motel room. The detectives noticed some blood spatter on the headboard of the bed and on the wall near the bathroom door. But Nelson knew from his undercover days with the Narcotics Unit that spatter like that was often seen in drug houses and was caused by syringes plugging up while addicts shot up.

Doc provided Stanley with the names of Yolanda's friends he had enlisted to aid in his search for her, including a man he said was her "sugar daddy." Talking to him could be crucial. He might be able to help reconstruct Yolanda's last hours and fill out the list of the last people to see her alive, the places she had been just before she was murdered, and any incidents or conflicts that could have led to violence.

Doc also gave a detailed description of the clothes Yolanda was wearing when she left the motel that day.

The detective wrote: "*black, tight fitting pant jeans, a pair of black slip-on flat shoes, gray socks, and possibly some plastic type bags on her feet to keep them dry, a black T-shirt that may have been cut down the front to show the cleavage of her breasts [and] a rabbit fur coat with short waist length.*"

In addition, Yolanda wore a necklace, two rings, five loose bracelets on one wrist, and four on the other. She was carrying a small denim purse that looked like an old-style gym bag and should have contained the scissors she carried for protection and her cigarettes—Kool or Newport.

None of those items except for the necklace and other jewelry had been found at the scene.

Before the detectives left, they got permission to inspect some of the unoccupied rooms near Yolanda's for signs of violence that could indicate she was killed there before her body was dumped on the riverbank. The rooms were clean and orderly, and Linda told them she had found no evidence of any kind of incident in any of them in recent days. Linda also said Yolanda's room would have had two blankets—one in medium green and one in purple—but none were in a floral pattern like the one found near her body.

Yolanda Sapp's murder was known by the women of the streets before city papers printed a single word. News like that is water. It seeps everywhere—and quickly—starting as a trickle, then a deluge. Linda Rose felt it in her bones when Yolanda didn't come back to the motel that morning. Just *felt* it. She saw it on Doc's anguished face when the cops left. She heard it in the cries of another working girl.

Yolanda was gone.

While a few brushed off the icy chill of the news and ruminated how there was always a risk in a life like the one those women had been handed, for some, like Nickie Lowe, thirty-four, fear ratcheted itself up another notch. Not only had Nickie and Yolanda been in the Circle, for a time they had lived a couple of doors down from each other at the motel. Nickie was beside herself. How did this happen to someone as smart, as street-savvy, and really, as tough as Yolanda Sapp? Yolanda knew the score. She knew that there were freaks out there and that being careful was a billion times more important than earning an extra ten bucks.

And yet someone had killed her. Just like he'd done to all those girls found in clusters along the Green River south of Seattle.

Nickie was terrified. She needed a smoke. A fix. Something to take her out of the fear and paranoia that came for her.

"I'm going to be next," she told her longtime boyfriend, Gorden Lucas.

He pushed back right away. "Why would you say that?"

Nickie didn't know or couldn't think of an answer, but neither could she shake the feeling.

"I'm next," she repeated.

Nickie wasn't the first to have that sinking feeling that there was someone out there along the river who might ask for a date but want something more. Something darker. Something as final as murder. She wasn't the last either. A few months later, another prostitute, thirty-eight-year-old Kathy Brisbois, would find her way inside the Spokane County Sheriff's department D.A.R.E. van parked outside the Evergreen Club, a mental health center. The odor of booze wafted from her breath as she spoke. She was a mess, but she was sincere too. Sweet. Maybe a little sad. She wanted to let the officer know that she supported the efforts of the program to keep kids off drugs. She had three girls—all with a *K* for a first initial just like her—and she wanted them safe.

She wanted to be safe too.

She also wanted to get out of the life.

Before the officer could direct Kathy to a program and encourage her to take that first step back to her daughters, she was gone.

CHAPTER TWO

POLICE WILL RETRACE STEPS OF SLAIN SPOKANE WOMAN

The Spokesman-Review

February 23, 1990

Spokane detectives knew that it was patently unfair to reduce a person's life to the indifferent and harsh words of a criminal rap sheet. At the same time, Nick Stanley and Bruce Nelson also knew they had to dig into that slice of Yolanda Sapp's life to look for any possible clues into how she ended up dead on the banks of the Spokane River. They recognized that piecing together a portrait based on accounts of the worst things this young woman had been accused of doing was in no way a true picture of who she had been in life. And being dumped like trash along the river said nothing about her worth as a person but, in fact, spoke volumes about the perpetrator who'd left her there.

The police files on Yolanda Sapp presented to Stanley and Nelson were a history of a tough young woman who stood her ground—in a world that had been exceedingly unkind to her. She had been arrested for stealing at a variety of stores, sometimes after a scuffle with security guards or the police. She was picked up for fighting in the street with men or other prostitutes. One time Yolanda was cited after a man told cops she leaned into his car, flashed her breast, and put a hand on his leg while lifting his wallet from his back pocket with the other.

Her primary relationship was no bed of roses either. Yolanda once told police that Doc Thomas had struck her three or four times in the face. He was arrested for assault. A friend said she and Doc often fought, especially when one or both were under the influence of drugs or alcohol. The manager of another fleabag motel confirmed the nature of their drug-fueled relationship. She found syringes in their room after she gave the couple the boot following a row. Doc's probation officer said Yolanda was prone to violence and alluded to sketchy reports that she had stabbed Doc as well as one of her johns.

There was no victim blaming or shaming going on from those investigating her death, especially by Detective Lundgren, who adamantly insisted that what Yolanda did for a living, while illegal, wasn't an excuse to dismiss what happened to her as a cost of doing business. However, it was possible that Yolanda found herself going toe to toe with someone who ended up getting the better of her.

It was widely known that Yolanda sometimes stole from her clients to get money to feed her drug habit. A john reported that she and another woman tried to rob him after he got into their car, and when he fled, they ran over him. Yolanda herself reported to police that a student at nearby Gonzaga University held a sharp object to her back and raped her in his dorm room after they haggled over the fee for the encounter.

Tough, yes. Terrifying at times too.

Like those inside the Circle or those in its orbit, Yolanda had another side too. No one but those closest to her knew Yolanda was the mother of two girls, whom she loved very much. Or that her daughters' father had been murdered in Seattle. Few outside the environs of East Sprague Avenue understood that being a sex worker was merely a means to an end. It was a job. It wasn't all that the women were—or how they saw themselves.

The account of Yolanda's murder in *The Spokesman-Review* on Friday, February 23, led with the unvarnished facts:

"Detectives today will attempt to reconstruct the final hours of the life of a Spokane prostitute whose nude, bullet-riddled body was found . . . on an embankment above the Spokane River along Upriver Drive."

Only comments by Linda Rose kept the article from being as grim as Yolanda's life and history, which the detectives had gleaned from a sheet that included eleven arrests in the last four years. Describing herself as a friend, the motel owner said Yolanda and Doc had lived at her Spokane Street Motel for much of the last three years and had been trying to straighten out their lives by getting off drugs, keeping their commitments to the courts, and only occasionally going out "to whore every once in a while, to get money for food."

Linda said the couple had talked about changing their lives when Doc received an expected financial settlement for a neck injury.

"They always talked about how they were going to get a house and get off the streets. They would get so happy talking about it," she said in the piece that ran with a photo of Yolanda's body, covered in sheets, being carried on a stretcher up the north bank of the Spokane River.

For the cops looking for Yolanda Sapp's killer, the investigation seemed to be producing a fistful of pulled threads. Short ones at that. Leads emerged, each offering a glimpse of a possibility but nothing approximating a clear resolution. One came from a building maintenance guy heading to the midnight shift at Deaconess Hospital. Robert White said he stopped at Trudeau's Marina Tuesday night around 11:15 to admire the boats, and Yolanda waved from the corner she was working. White went over to her to talk and was hit hard by the smell of alcohol on her breath as they exchanged a few words. Yolanda soon returned to her corner, and he watched as a dark-colored, late-model station wagon drove up. Yolanda climbed into the passenger seat beside a man in his mid-thirties, dark-haired and dressed in a dark jacket. The car drove south and disappeared into the night.

Stanley added in his report a last observation that seemed to sum up all the leads so far: *He did not see the vehicle turn in any direction and no longer paid any attention to what was going on.*

The story gave Stanley and Nelson something to pursue.

Was the station wagon driver the killer?

Yolanda's mother, living on the other side of the state near Seattle, offered some family details and another chilling thread when the Spokane detectives caught up with her. She told them that Yolanda was the mother of two little girls, whom she had cared for on and off over the years while Yolanda tried to get things right so she could make a home for them. Like most of the women on the streets, Yolanda was doing her best—and that was that. She told them Yolanda had made a call to her six months earlier in which she was desperate, terrified. Yolanda told her that she owed money to a drug dealer named Chico and his partner, Mary. Chico had held a gun to her head during the call as he forced her to explain where the money had gone. Yolanda lied and claimed she spent some on gifts for her children and sent the rest to her mother. Like most mothers with children who'd used up a million chances at redemption, Yolanda's mother went along with the story. There was always something in which to contend.

Stanley wrote in his report: *[Her mother] said Yolanda never did pay these people to the best of her knowledge and Yolanda at one time told her that if anything ever happened to her to check out these two people.*

Was her murder tied to a drug deal? Drug dealing and prostitution had supply and demand complications inside their symbiotic relationship. For the most part, prostitution was transactional and brought immediate pay. Drug dealers didn't work on credit, but sometimes they accepted they'd have to wait to get paid.

Not long, however.

Each new lead was a pebble in a pool. Nothing more. A Spokane Valley man reportedly harassed prostitutes in a white Chevy sedan, posing as a police officer and flashing a badge. When detectives tracked down his car, the tires didn't match the treads in the mud found near Yolanda's body.

A rental car returned to the lot with a suspicious bloodstain in the trunk raised hopes, but that, too, fizzled out. It had been returned the day before Yolanda went missing.

An employee at a wood-molding plant reported hearing gunshots. He believed the sound came from a small-caliber handgun and traced the noise to an area two miles east of Trudeau's Marina, near where Yolanda was last seen. Concerned, he and a coworker drove to an abandoned lot frequented by prostitutes on the Stroll but found nothing.

And then there was Doc. Maybe this man who professed being so broken up over Yolanda's death had been her killer. Some things that he'd said didn't add up. Doc insisted he'd last seen Yolanda at 11:00 p.m. Tuesday night, but witnesses began to contradict him. John Graves, a bail bondsman, said he saw Yolanda and Thomas together the following afternoon, asking him for forty dollars to pay their motel rent and buy food. Graves's timeline checked out, making it clear Thomas had lied about the last time he'd seen her.

Another tip placed Yolanda and Doc together earlier Tuesday evening outside a bar, where Doc was inside making a purchase. Yolanda was described as wearing different clothes from the outfit Doc mentioned she had on later that night.

As the timeline unraveled, so did her boyfriend's credibility.

Most damning was the sighting of Doc at a drug house with three other men at 2:00 a.m. Wednesday—just hours after he claimed to be frantically searching for Yolanda. A witness noted Doc had a pistol tucked into his waistband, a stark contrast to his earlier insistence that he didn't own a gun.

Finally, after the give-and-take that comes with naming a person of interest and moving on to someone new, Doc found himself strapped in and wired up in a room at the Spokane Police Department, agreeing to a polygraph. As the examiner went through the list of yes or no queries to determine involvement in Yolanda's murder, his eyes on the unfurling graph paper of the polygraph, it was as conclusive as could be.

When Doc returned to the motel, he told Linda Rose the news she had hoped to hear.

"Passed it."

And just like that, as persons of interest went insofar as Yolanda Sapp's case, there were none.

CHAPTER THREE

The Greene Street Bridge juts over the Spokane River, connecting the industrial south with the placid, tree-lined neighborhoods to the north. Made of concrete in the 1950s, its trio of arch supports is a favorite of photographers looking to frame a shot. On Sunday morning, March 25, 1990, a credit reviewer for the local branch of Farm Credit Bank descended the path down the embankment and under the bridge. A recent transplant from Tulsa, Oklahoma, Ron Copeland had made running a loop around the river bridges a four- or five-times weekly routine. As his eyes adjusted to the dim morning light, something caught his attention. It was so out of place that it necessitated a double take.

It appeared to be a figure draped over the guardrail on the north side of the street, directly under the span.

Weird. A mannequin, maybe?

Ron drew closer, finally slowing to a complete stop.

He realized he was looking at the partially nude body of a woman, her legs bent over the railing as if she had been shoved backward. Red ran in rivulets down her bare skin.

"Lady!" He called to her and started moving yet closer.

Was that blood on her bare chest?

"Lady. Lady. Lady!" he called out, trying to rouse her.

There was no reply. She didn't move. He noticed what he thought was a bullet hole in her chest—and he suddenly knew she was dead. He ran to the first house with a light on and asked the startled homeowner who answered to call 911.

"I think I found a dead body," he said.

For the second time in a month, detectives found themselves once more examining the body of a young woman who had been murdered and dumped to be found by a random passerby.

The scene was grisly and haunting.

Nick Stanley thought the body slumped against the guardrail told another story of violence and humiliation. A single wound—likely a gunshot or stab—pierced the woman's chest, just to the left of center, and released blood streaking both sides of her torso. Her clothing, a blue-and-black pullover jacket and a white long-john shirt, had been shoved up high enough to expose the wound and her bare skin. Faded denim jeans and pink panties, along with long-john bottoms, were clumped down to her knees. Her belt was buckled, but the jeans' top button and zipper were undone. She wore white socks and no shoes.

As the detective stood at the murder scene, the detective's grim sense of déjà vu came swiftly. He quickly learned that a missing person's report for a woman named Nickie Inez Lowe, thirty-four, had been filed by her mother just hours earlier. Nickie was five foot nine, 145 pounds, with blue eyes and brown hair. When the detective reviewed the file, the pieces fell all too easily into place.

The photograph of Nickie Lowe matched the lifeless face at the scene.

Like Yolanda Sapp, Nickie had been shot, her body stripped naked or nearly so and then dumped in a public yet out-of-the-way location. The similarities were beyond dispute, but Stanley knew it was too early to draw conclusions or officially connect the cases. What he did know was that this was a killer with a message—a predator who viewed these women as disposable.

The investigation led Stanley and Detective Ron Graves six miles northwest of the crime scene to the modest red brick home of Nickie's mother, Diane Matney. Nickie and Gorden Lucas, her boyfriend of eleven years, lived inside this little brick-faced house on Stevens Street with Diane.

No cop likes the part of the job involving showing a loved one a morgue photograph to get an ID. Often it is cruelly necessary. Detective Stanley took no pleasure in showing the distraught mother a Polaroid taken by a coroner.

Diane hesitated a little, searching for some hope that there had been a terrible mistake. That somehow the police had come to the wrong house. That another mother of a troubled daughter should be shown the photograph.

She looked up after turning the Polaroid in her hand. "It looks like Nickie," Diane said, shaking her head, "but I don't think it's her."

Moments later, Gorden Lucas emerged from the basement, where he and Nickie had been living after the Spokane Street. His reaction was instant and absolute.

"That's Nickie," he said, a grim expression frozen on his face.

Detectives gently separated mother and boyfriend to gather details about Nickie and reconstruct her final hours.

Diane's description of Nickie's life revealed a mother's heartaches—a mother who'd endured massive troubles of her own. Diane had gone through a divorce, bankruptcy—more than once—and worked long shifts behind a bar where she'd been robbed at gunpoint. Even though she knew life wasn't fair or easy, she hoped for the best for her children. Hope, however, only went so far. Nickie had struggled as a kid, battling dyslexia and low self-esteem due, her mother believed, to a perceived weight problem. Nickie once dreamed of becoming a pet groomer but had dropped out of high school and eventually turned to prostitution as her best option for quick money to feed a drug habit. Diane had tried to dissuade her from hooking, but even a near-deadly strangulation by a client hadn't stopped her. She needed the money because she needed the drugs. After Yolanda's body was found along the river, Nickie told both Gorden and Diane that she was scared something might happen to her, but fear wasn't enough to keep her away from the streets.

"She thought she was too smart to get into trouble like that," Diane said.

Gorden "Luke" Lucas told detectives Nickie usually drove herself to meet clients. The night before her murder, however, she made an unusual request. He was to drop her off near the post office and the Covered Wagon Tavern on East Sprague around 10:30 p.m. She planned to meet a client named Al. She promised to return within an hour or two so Gorden could pick her up and bring her home, but she was a no-show.

Gorden stayed at the Wagon until 2:00 a.m., then spent the rest of the night in the parking lot, waiting. By 5:00 a.m., he went home to Nickie's mother's place, and they called the police.

The mention of "Al" grabbed the detectives' attention. Gorden explained that he had never actually met him but knew he was a married man who drove a white pickup truck and had a romantic crush on Nickie.

Gorden went back down to the basement and returned with a trio of heart-shaped balloons and a stack of letters from Al to Nickie, including one about a fight between them that remained unresolved. Despite their argument, they'd planned to meet on Friday night—the night before she vanished.

Nickie's mother added her own description of Al, whom she had briefly met. He was short and stocky, somewhere between thirty-five and forty years old, with dark hair and a complexion that suggested he might be Hispanic.

"There was something odd about his voice," Dianne added, though as hard as she tried, she couldn't explain further.

The investigation had its first real suspect—or at least a person of interest. Stanley and Graves knew they needed more than balloons and love letters to find the truth. The shadow of a killer loomed, one who was quickly making Spokane's grittiest streets his hunting ground.

Gorden Lucas returned from Vietnam a drug addict with post-traumatic stress disorder. The weight of his experiences in the army followed him into civilian life, where he drifted into a murky underworld. By the late 1970s, he had found work as the manager and bouncer at a massage parlor in State Line, Idaho—a border town where gambling, drugs, and sex were its currency and the massage parlor was its stock exchange.

It was there he met Nickie. Their connection was instant and intense, born from shared survival instincts and a keen awareness that the world could chew up and spit out anyone at any time. Before long, they were living together, and by 1990, he considered Nickie his common-law wife.

Gorden dabbled in small-time crime—burglaries, robberies, the occasional drug deal—while Nickie continued her work on the streets. They didn't dwell on each other's activities, but there was an unspoken agreement: He would look out for her. He wasn't her pimp, but he saw it as his duty to protect her.

Although Gorden told the police about dropping Nickie off at the Covered Wagon Tavern on East Sprague Avenue for a date, he didn't tell detectives what he'd done afterward. While Nickie waited for her customer, Gorden and an acquaintance attempted a burglary at a nearby shopping mall. He acted as the lookout, parked in the car while his partner tried to break into a store. But the man returned empty-handed, mumbling something about things going sideways. The whole episode left Gorden unsettled, and he drove back to the Covered Wagon to get Nickie.

She wasn't there.

That was strange. Something was off and he felt it right away. She'd been late in the past, but never like that. It crossed Gorden's mind that his common-law wife had been right when she said the members of the Circle were in danger. He had dismissed her worries then, but now he couldn't help wondering if she had been right all along.

JOGGER FINDS SLAIN WOMAN BY SPOKANE RIVER

The Spokesman-Review

March 26, 1990

The detectives wasted no time tracking down the man Nickie had planned to meet the night she disappeared. Using return addresses from the letters he had sent her, they found Al in Deer Park about nineteen miles from Nickie's home and twenty-three miles from where her body was discovered. Since Deer Park was outside their jurisdiction, they enlisted the assistance of a Spokane County sheriff's deputy to accompany them.

They caught up with Al outside his home and he readily agreed to talk. Inside his garage, he admitted knowing Nickie for about two months and claimed they'd last been together on Friday night—the evening before she vanished. According to Al, they grabbed a quick meal before heading to a shed at the lumberyard where he worked to have sex. He even told police where to find a used condom there as proof. His description of the clothes Nickie wore that night did not match what she was wearing when her body was found.

That there were two versions of what she was wearing when she disappeared was concerning. Gorden had one story. Al had another.

One or both were either lying or wrong.

Al insisted he'd stayed home all day Saturday, nursing a bad back, and went to bed early. His wife corroborated his alibi, saying he'd been home and asleep by 8:00 p.m. The detectives searched his house, garage, and white Isuzu pickup truck with his consent. While they logged several miscellaneous items, including a note reading *"I love pussy"* taped under the sun visor, there was no sign of blood or anything else tying Al to the crime.

A search of his locker at the lumberyard, followed by a trip to the shed where he said he and Nickie had sex, turned up nothing significant.

The shed did in fact contain a used condom but no evidence connecting him to Nickie's murder.

To close the loop and get the cops off his back, Al agreed to a polygraph. By 5:00 p.m. that same day, an examiner announced he had passed. None of his answers showed deception. While detectives worked to piece together Nickie's final days, a pathologist at Holy Family Hospital concluded her autopsy. The cause of death was a single bullet that had ripped through her pullover jacket and long-john shirt, entered her chest just left of center, severed her aorta, and lodged in her spine. Death had been instantaneous.

The bullet, appearing to be .22 caliber, was recovered and marked for evidence.

Abrasions, consistent with being dragged over the guardrail, ran in ghastly lines down her back. Samples of fibers, hairs, and fluids were collected from her body and clothing. Under the Luma-Lite forensic light, fibers glowed across her socks, clothing, and bare skin, but no foreign fingerprints were detected.

The pathologist concluded Nickie had ingested cocaine approximately an hour before her death.

That same day, the case caught a break when a man scavenging for aluminum cans behind the Royal Upholstery shop found Nickie's red wallet in a dumpster and alerted the police. Detective Bruce Nelson and others rushed to the scene, where the dumpster diver pointed them to the wallet and twenty-one other items scattered inside the otherwise empty container.

Among the contents were Nickie's blue-and-white athletic shoes, a syringe, a tube of lubricant, and a handful of welfare forms.

Some items had fibers appearing to match samples collected from Yolanda Sapp.

The dumpster's location added to its importance. It was not far from Trudeau's Marina and the Covered Wagon Tavern, and other places Nickie had frequented while on the job. Everything was bagged and tagged for the Washington State Patrol Crime Lab.

While detectives hoped the lab could provide a much-needed break, at that moment, they couldn't imagine how—or if ever—those pieces would come together.

CHAPTER FOUR

The news media were hot to connect the murders of Yolanda Sapp and Nickie Lowe, but the police weren't about to cross that line. Yes, Lieutenant Jim Hill, head of the Major Crimes Unit, agreed with reporters, there were obvious similarities between the murders. But he wasn't ready to discuss the possibility of a connection—a single killer, perhaps.

"That would be entirely conjecture. We're not far enough along in our investigation to speak to that," he told *The Spokesman-Review*. He was willing to offer a bleak assessment of the status of the investigation: "There are no leads and no suspects."

Lieutenant Hill didn't admit publicly that a host of facts associated with both murders went well beyond what could be considered coincidental. Both victims were prostitutes who worked without a pimp along East Sprague Avenue. They disappeared while believed to be on a date with a customer. Both were drug addicts. Both had been shot with a small-caliber gun. They were murdered somewhere else before they were dumped along the Spokane River within a few blocks of each other. They had been stripped or partially undressed in what could have been an attempt to degrade or demean or humiliate them—or to demonstrate their killer's utter contempt for them.

There was another common factor, too, that Nickie's mother pointed out to *The Spokesman-Review*: Nickie and Yolanda knew each other.

"I know Nickie knew her because Nickie talked about her after they found her body," Diane Matney explained. "They were just acquaintances . . . It just seems like these murders have to be related in some form. It's frustrating just thinking that they are."

Early Monday morning, March 26, Detective Stanley took steps to determine if there was another important connection between Yolanda and Nickie. He met with Bill Morig from the State Patrol Crime Lab and Spokane Identification Officer Sergeant Dick Gasper to use the Luma-Lite to examine fibers from Nickie's body and clothing as well as the floral blanket found near Yolanda's body.

Morig found that the fibers on Nickie's body were like those on the blanket found near Yolanda, but he couldn't establish a definitive connection. He took the fibers back to the lab for more analysis and comparison.

Cruising East Sprague looking for hookers was never a difficult endeavor. Those working didn't carry signs or stand in front of a reader board with services displayed for all to see. Sure, they wore the fur-trimmed this and that, the short shorts, or a top cut down to *there*. All of that was window dressing. What got attention—and customers—was the power of their gaze. Street hookers knew that eye contact was the most effective way to telegraph what they offered and the interest of the men looking back.

The gaze was a barbed hook on both ends.

When Detectives Stanley and Graves descended on East Sprague to look for prostitutes who might have information about Nickie Lowe's activities or suspicious johns, there were plenty to ask.

First up was Baby Doll, a twenty-four-year-old prostitute who told Graves then that she had been raped at gunpoint by a man who picked her up along East Sprague Avenue in his gray Toyota pickup truck about midnight on Christmas Eve three months prior. The man was abusive, angry, and profane, slapping and hitting her while he stripped her, holding a small handgun to her head, and then calling her a whore and a slut while raping her. He had done the same thing to other women in the east end. Baby Doll described him as in his late thirties, hair just below his ears, mustache, clean-cut, might have worn eyeglasses.

Another prostitute was convinced her ex-brother-in-law had taken six or seven prostitutes to his apartment and all had wound up dead. She also said she had seen Nickie Lowe Saturday night before she disappeared. Graves ultimately rejected her story, especially after he intentionally misstated what Nickie had been wearing, and the supposed witness readily adopted the false details. She was only trying to get her ex-brother-in-law in trouble.

Stanley and Graves also tracked down a man Nickie's mother had identified as leaving phone messages for her daughter. Although he had left his name as Jim, the phone number came back to a man named Patrick. Patrick denied knowing Nickie or anyone named Jim and said he had not heard about a prostitute being killed. He admitted picking up prostitutes on East Sprague but said he didn't have sex with them because he was afraid a condom could break. He said he had been a cop for two months in 1973 but was fired for backing his car into a telephone pole. He would take a polygraph, he said, if it was solely related to whether he had killed a prostitute. While discussing a polygraph, the man confessed to using the name Jim because he didn't want prostitutes to know who he really was.

Stanley and Graves visited him at his home a day later, and as expected, he began to alter his statement. He now said he had met a woman named Nickie a year ago at church but things didn't work out between them.

Church?

He didn't know how he would have gotten Nickie Lowe's number and didn't recognize her from her mug shot. Finally, he said he might have met her at a place where he goes dancing, but he didn't really remember her.

Asked about his activities the previous Saturday, Patrick said he picked up his boat from Trudeau's Marina around 4:10 p.m. He agreed to let the detectives search the boat, and they used tape to take some swatches from the upholstery and carpet. They also searched his car and took more swatches from cushions on the back seat. They noted that he stored an unloaded .38-caliber pistol in a holster under the driver's seat—and there was one .38-caliber bullet sitting on the console. An interesting insight into Patrick, but not the caliber of the firearm used to kill Nickie or Yolanda.

Graves asked again if Patrick remembered phoning Nickie on Saturday, and this time, he said he had called her then to see if she would come to his house about 11:00 p.m. and stay overnight. She didn't show up and called him Sunday afternoon—which would have been at least six hours after her body was found—to acknowledge she didn't keep their date.

Patrick's changing story troubled the detective, and it was clear the man was obsessed with his social life—or as Graves believed, his lack of a social life. He said he had moved into his apartment complex to meet a single woman and that hadn't happened. He had joined numerous organizations for the same purpose with the same lack of results. And he insisted that, although he frequented prostitutes on East Sprague Avenue, he did not have sex with them.

Graves later exposed the samples from Patrick's boat and car under a Luma-Lite, and nothing lit up like the samples from Nickie's and Yolanda's bodies, Nickie's clothes, and Yolanda's wig and blanket. Graves booked the samples from Patrick into evidence anyway but was fairly convinced he had spent a lot of time investigating another convoluted and ultimately dead end.

The next day—Tuesday, March 27—Stanley got a call from Deer Park Al wanting to meet at a restaurant on East Sprague. Al, it turned out, was concerned because he thought some of the information in that morning's *Spokesman-Review* story about Nickie's murder was wrong. Stanley agreed that some of the details were inaccurate. But he steered the conversation back to Al's relationship with Nickie, asking if they always went to the shed at Al's lumberyard to have sex. Al said yes, except for the first two times, when Nickie directed him to other locations. Al took Stanley to the first, a spot west of the restaurant on Riverside Avenue, and then to a second location in a parking area for a business that apparently worked on or manufactured boats and boat trailers that were scattered around the lot.

When Stanley returned to Major Crimes, department identification officers told him some of the fibers found on Nickie's body had indeed matched some recovered from evidence in Yolanda's murder. With that strong link between the two killings, Stanley decided a new investigative focus was needed on the area that seemed central to both cases—the locations around East Sprague Avenue, Trudeau's Marina, and Royal Upholstery. Both victims frequented that area and had been there just before they disappeared, and the dumpster containing some of Nickie's personal property was located near the upholstery shop.

And while the police were examining the evidence from Nickie's murder, they noticed a distinct odor from her clothes—solvent or gasoline?

Stanley remembered seeing what he thought were oil drums in the parking lot by Trudeau's. He returned to the location and, in another dumpster there, found a piece of carpet that looked to be similar in color, fabric, and construction to a small piece found on Yolanda's body. Stanley sent the carpet to the State Patrol Crime Lab for review by Bill Morig, whose verdict was that the fibers from the piece in the dumpster and the one from Yolanda's body were "quite similar" and should be tested further. The entire dumpster was taken to the Spokane Police Academy for a more detailed search—yielding more carpet samples, fibers, and different kinds of solvent containers.

One of the first goals in the East Sprague review was to see if boats at Trudeau's were carpeted or upholstered with anything that resembled fibers that had been recovered from the victims' bodies and other evidence. A detective went to the marina pretending to be a customer interested in buying a boat. A sales rep showed him several boats, but none had anything that resembled the suspect carpet or was in any shade of green.

Over the next week, testing and analysis of the fiber and carpet evidence continued to build the connection between the Sapp and Lowe murders. Technicians at the State Patrol Crime Lab updated their test results regularly for the detectives, expanding their conclusion that the carpet sample from the dumpster at Trudeau's could be from the same source as the samples from the Yolanda Sapp investigation to an 85 to 90 percent likelihood that they were from the same source. And the tests also indicated an 85 percent likelihood that the fibers found in the Sapp and Lowe cases were the same fiber.

While all of that was welcome news, it didn't go far enough. Testing was hampered by the failure of some of the carpet fibers to dissolve in the chemical solution needed for the tests. It wasn't over, of course, and the detectives on the case were assured testing would continue. Barring an unexpected confession coming from God knew where, it was pretty much their only hope.

The Trudeau family's boat business had been a fixture on East Sprague for decades. Bill Trudeau's father had run various enterprises in the area long before the freeway altered the neighborhood. Bill Trudeau, balding and normally a smiley guy from ubiquitous commercials on Spokane TV, wasn't exactly thrilled when Stanley and Graves arrived at Trudeau's Marina on April 20 to confront him about potential links between him and his business and the murders of Yolanda Sapp and Nickie Lowe. They told Bill that, while they did not consider him a suspect, he was a person of interest. First, they said, they had information that he had engaged in sex with Nickie Lowe. The owner denied that and said it was unlikely he had even met her. He didn't recognize her name or photograph he saw in the newspaper. He admitted he had frequented prostitutes between 1970 and 1981 when he was drinking heavily and doing drugs. Those days were long gone. He'd been clean and sober since the '80s.

The detectives showed Bill the green carpet sample from the dumpster and said it was the same as the fibers found on Yolanda Sapp's body. Bill wasn't sure. It didn't look like carpeting used in the Sea Ray brand of boats he sold, but it could be a new color. He added that all the work on carpets, curtains, canvas, or other fabrics on boats for Trudeau's was done by Royal Upholstery across the street.

Later that same day, detectives and identification officers met with the boat dealership owner and used the Luma-Lite to inspect carpets. Several pieces appeared to match fibers found on Yolanda's and Nickie's bodies. Bill identified the fibers as a 1990 Sea Ray carpet color simply called "green," which was being used in new boats up to twenty feet long.

The police now faced a new and direct link between the murders and Trudeau's. The first look into Trudeau's didn't provide anything useful when background checks on all of Trudeau's employees produced no records that would indicate any involvement by them with prostitutes.

On April 26, Nick Stanley got a call alerting him that a woman was waiting down at the station who wanted to talk to a detective about Nickie Lowe's murder. Her name was Kathy Brisbois. Kathy said that she was a prostitute who worked the East Sprague Avenue area and knew Nickie. She recently had two experiences with customers she wanted the police to know about.

She was scared.

CHAPTER FIVE

Kathy Ann Brisbois had never been one to hide who she was, even when life made her a little rough around the edges. She had a wild streak, a quick smile, and a knack for making people feel like they'd known her forever. Her personality and good looks might have played a role in her work in the sex industry, but it was never what she was all about. Those who loved Kathy knew that behind all her bravado was a woman searching for a way out of the mess she had made of her life.

The previous year, around Christmas, Kathy wrote a letter to her eldest daughter, Kaishea, who had just given birth to a baby in Oregon, where she'd been living for years.

God had answered Kathy's prayers.

"My higher peace has brought me home and I am happy! I am having my emotion at life and dreams. But with a lot of prayer, I am feeling pretty good about myself. Wednesday, I attended a 2 ½ hr. drug dependency class that will be every week for 4 months."

She'd been working hard to get clean and looking for the best way to reconnect with her two littlest daughters—with whom she'd been estranged.

"I also have an appt. Monday to obtain a public defender to help represent me. I want to do this right! I don't want to make any trouble. I want what is good for the girls. I am afraid, as well as excited about my new life. Fear of failure as well as fear of success!"

While Kathy had not been the mother her daughter needed or wanted, she still had some motherly advice.

> *I know things get hard sometimes for young families.*
> *I pray for all of you! Be patient with one another and*
> *always count your blessings! I do, Kaishea. I took so much*
> *for granted, you included, and I hope you will be patient*
> *with your mom. Thank you for loving me! I love you too!*
> *Give our baby a kiss & hug from Grandma, Mom.*

It was a letter never sent.

A bomb of sorts that started ticking when Yolanda was found had detonated. Kathy knew it. Nickie had known it too.

Kathy took a seat in an interview room at the Spokane Police Department and spilled her guts to Detective Stanley. She didn't know who it was, but she knew without a shred of doubt that someone was stalking the girls on their turf along East Sprague Avenue.

She recounted how a week earlier, she got into a big maroon '70s car with a man in his late forties who said he was a police officer but refused to show her any identification. He told her if she didn't do as he said, she would end up like the other two prostitutes.

Kathy knew exactly whom he meant and what he was threatening, and she was scared. Being scared sometimes came with the job. It was, she knew, a job after all. She gave him the sex he wanted without any further threats or issues.

Two weeks prior, Kathy had what she told the detective was a "weird" experience when she got into a small nondescript car with a big man approximately fifty years old with gray hair. "The man wore gloves the entire time," she said.

The whole time.

She had not seen either man or their cars since then. The detective asked Kathy to get license numbers if she came across them again.

She promised she would.

About a week later, Kathy arrived at her sister's door, unannounced, looking worn but still flashing a familiar smile. Still hopeful. They sat and talked, the kind of conversation sisters have when one knows the other is hurting. Kathy admitted things weren't exactly going as planned but didn't offer much detail. She wasn't after pity. She only wanted to feel normal for a little while.

Maybe now, her sister hoped, Kathy would figure things out. She had every reason to—her three daughters.

A close friend named Tabitha Mora caught up with Kathy.

"She was bragging about how beautiful the kids were and how she wanted to change her life. She was the most beautiful woman, kind-hearted. She'd do anything for anyone."

Around that same time, Kathy reached out to her older brother Dick Brisbois. It wasn't like her to ask for help, but this time, it seemed like she really needed it.

"I need to get out of here," she said, her voice low and full of urgency.

The streets of Spokane weren't kind to anyone, least of all Kathy. She'd been staying under the radar, trying to make it through another day, but even that wasn't enough to keep the fear at bay. Dick would later say she'd been afraid for weeks. She didn't say why, not directly, but he knew something was wrong.

Dick didn't hesitate to help. He loved his sister. Everyone in the family did. He grabbed his keys and drove to get her, hoping, as he had before, that this would be the start of something better. Another second chance. Kathy climbed into his pickup truck, her small bag of belongings tucked under her arm, and they pulled away from the city streets that had held her captive.

For the first time in eons, Kathy seemed like she might be ready to leave it all behind. Dick could feel it, sensing a quiet resolve as his sister peered out the window as they drove away. They didn't talk much, but they didn't need to. Kathy was going to stay at his home in Fruitland, an hour and a half north of Spokane, to a less chaotic, less dangerous life.

It wasn't a perfect situation, but fresh starts seldom are.

And then out of nowhere, red and blue lights filled the rearview mirror. A routine traffic stop—expired plates. Dick grumbled about his luck, but otherwise took it all in stride. When the officer approached, Dick stepped out to explain the situation. It should have been a minor inconvenience, a ten-minute delay in Kathy's escape from Spokane.

When Dick returned his attention toward the truck cab, the passenger seat was empty.

Kathy had slipped out quietly, vanishing into the night like a ghost. Dick called her name and scanned the roadside, but she was nowhere to be found. He got back in the truck and drove aimlessly through the streets, hoping to catch sight of his wayward sister. But she was gone.

That was the last time he saw Kathy, and the moment would play in his mind countless times in subsequent years. If he'd only updated his plates, if he'd only been quicker to get back in the truck, if he'd only . . . The truth was, Kathy's world had always been like quicksand, pulling her back even as she tried to claw her way out.

Something was coming.

Time was running out.

Kathy knew it too.

When she showed up at the D.A.R.E. van on May 14 to ask for help, she was unraveling.

CHAPTER SIX

On a spring evening, May 15, 1990, the Spokane River glimmered with the last rays of daylight as a pair of East Valley High School students set out on what was meant to be a routine botany class assignment to collect and identify local plants. Mattias Grenback, an eighteen-year-old exchange student from Sweden, and Amy Kirby, a sixteen-year-old Spokane native, pedaled their bikes along Trent Avenue, searching for plants to collect. They parked alongside the west bank of the river, between the Trent Avenue Bridge and the Burlington Northern Railroad trestle. The road's rough edges disappeared into the shadows of the trees.

The students wandered down the path, scanning for flora among the brush and leaves, when Amy suddenly froze.

"Mattias," she called, her voice tight. "I think I see . . . a leg."

He turned sharply toward her and traced her gaze. At first, it was difficult to make out in the dimming light—something pale against the darker earth. Mattias stepped cautiously closer, the realization hitting him like a cold gust of wind.

A human leg.

A few more steps, and the rest of the terrible truth came into view—a nude woman, face down in the brush, her body entangled in the undergrowth. Blood streaked the soil beneath her head.

Mattias stumbled back, his breath catching.

"She's dead," he managed to say. Without another word, the teens bolted back to their bicycles, adrenaline pushing them toward the Blue Keg Tavern at the corner of East Trent Avenue and North Pines Road.

They needed help.

Inside the tavern, the students explained what they'd found, their words tumbling over each other in their urgency. At 7:53 p.m., a bartender called the Spokane County Sheriff's department.

Sheriff's Deputy James Speaks caught the call.

A body near the river.

It wasn't a phrase he ever wanted to hear, but he knew what it meant. Speaks, along with two other deputies, met Mattias and Amy at the tavern and listened as they recounted what they'd seen. Then, with the teenagers leading the way, the officers walked to the riverbank.

Deputy Speaks aimed the beam of his flashlight through the darkness.

The shaken kids were right. The body of a woman, face down. Her head was turned slightly to the left, and blood trailed from her left ear and nose.

No question—she was dead.

The deputies secured the scene, their radios crackling as they called for detectives. As Speaks worked, Mattias described a vehicle he had noticed earlier—a primer-painted or rust-colored Ford pickup truck parked facing the river on the upper bank north of Trent Avenue. He had seen it both before discovering the body and again on his way to the tavern. Now, as he looked around, the truck was gone.

Amy, shaken but composed enough to help, pointed out a multicolored striped shirt caught in the bushes a short distance from the body. Speaks made a mental note to make sure it was collected. Moments later, a passerby found a black coat lying farther up the riverbank, just above the dirt road.

The area just up the riverbank showed indications of a life-or-death struggle: disturbed brush and soil, scattered items of clothing such as a blue denim skirt and a multicolored scarf, clumps of hair, and bloodstains across the area and on some items. Police also recovered green fibers—reminiscent of those found in the first two murders—in multiple locations not far from the body.

The autopsy early the next day would prove just how hard she had battled her killer. She suffered multiple blows to the head that fractured her skull, and she had three broken ribs. And she had been shot three times—in the head, chest, and right arm—wounds inflicted almost in contact with the barrel of a .22-caliber handgun. The lack of fabric remnants in the bullet wounds told the pathologist that the woman had been nude when she was shot. She had been dead for just an hour or so when her body was found shortly before 8:00 p.m.

Sheriff's Detective Jim Hansen had talked to city detectives regularly over coffee or a beer to keep up with the investigations into the murders of Yolanda Sapp and Nickie Lowe. A tall man with broad shoulders, a salt-and-pepper mustache of the style cops had clung to since the 1980s, and sharp eyes framed by wire-rimmed glasses, his calm demeanor and no-nonsense presence hinted at years of hard-earned experience. Hansen exuded confidence. He was the kind of cop who didn't need to raise his voice to command respect.

Detective Hansen had heard that his city colleagues had been called out to a murder along the river not far from the city-county line. In fact, he'd already taken a drive to check out the crime scene; he called it professional curiosity. And it gave him the chance to invoke the long-standing if morbid joke that detectives for the city and the county always checked for marks on a victim's back to determine if a body had been dragged across the line from one jurisdiction into the next to hand off a murder case.

He didn't consider himself fully informed on either murder investigation, but he knew the basics and, out of professional curiosity by an experienced homicide detective, had followed developments on the two similar homicides that happened so close to his jurisdiction.

But now, called to the riverbank near the Trent Avenue Bridge at 11:00 p.m. on May 15, 1990, he found himself assigned to work the third murder of a prostitute in twelve weeks, the first found across the city-county line in Spokane County. Even though he knew there were many unsolved murders of prostitutes in the area, Hansen hadn't been involved in those homicide cases during his twenty years with the sheriff's department. Over the years, however, he had on occasion talked to some of the women who worked in the strip clubs, massage parlors, and even in prostitution in nearby State Line. He learned that prostitutes and other women in the sex industry might be willing to pass on useful information if you treated them with respect and convinced them you had zero interest in interfering with their livelihood. If approached honestly and without intimidation or threats, the women might be willing to tell you what they had seen or heard about the crime you were investigating.

After he graduated with a degree in criminal justice, then known as police science and administration, from Washington State University in 1970, Hansen worked briefly at a Sears warehouse, but then started on a temporary basis as a patrol officer with the Spokane County Sheriff's department.

Years later he would chuckle when he'd tell people about that first year.

"They gave me a gun and a belt and said, 'Now you're a cop.' No training. Hadn't even shot the gun. Just thrown into it."

At least he *looked* like a cop—like he had just walked out of an interview with Keith Morrison on NBC's *Dateline*: trim and clean-shaven with close-cropped brown hair.

After patrolling the streets for a while, Hansen did an undercover stint with the Narcotics Unit before landing the job he wanted as a detective in Robbery/Homicide, which later became Major Crimes.

Over the years, Hansen had developed good relationships with detectives from the Spokane city police that were about to deliver benefits during the upcoming investigation. He noted that the sheriff and the police chief didn't get along well—some kind of territorial friction, he thought—but the detectives from the two departments had learned to work well together. "We had to work together. It was us against the cases," he said.

Hansen also hoped he could apply his experience and perhaps tap into friendships and resources he had developed when he spent a year as a member of the Green River Task Force, which investigated the famous and still unsolved serial killer case involving forty-nine victims—many of them prostitutes—in Seattle in the 1980s. Hansen had once thought they had located a good suspect for those murders in Spokane, but he wasn't the guy.

Jim Hansen's boss, Sheriff Larry Erickson, was at the scene where the third victim was found that night to address the first question raised by the media and the same question being asked by Spokane residents who were paying any attention at all.

Did the glaring similarities in the murders of Yolanda Sapp, Nickie Lowe, and now this unidentified woman mean they were killed by the same person?

Were they victims of a new serial killer preying on women in Spokane?

Erickson told reporters no such conclusion had been made officially yet, but he had asked the detectives from the Spokane city police who worked the first two murders to come to the scene and consult with his detectives.

"Obviously, there are similarities," the sheriff said. "It's a young female, she's nude, and she's by the river. We've asked the city detectives to come down here, but I can't tell you that it is connected."

The public information officer for the department offered the newspaper a slightly more direct assessment: "Obviously, if this person had the same lifestyle as the first two, there could be a real connection. But until we know who she is, that would be speculation."

After the city detectives arrived, Lieutenant Jim Hill of Major Crimes told the media that detectives had not had a chance to make comparisons between all three cases. And then he offered a frank, realistic, and perhaps pessimistic assessment of the status of the Sapp and Lowe investigations: The police had no suspects in either murder.

CHAPTER SEVEN

SERIAL KILLINGS SUSPECTED

Kitsap Sun

May 17, 1990

While Spokane law enforcement officials didn't want to say it out loud—until they were nearly certain—three women over three months murdered and dumped by the river made it tragically apparent they were chasing a serial killer. The media pounced on it right away, and Spokane County Sheriff Larry Erickson and Police Chief Terry Mangan knew at the start that their departments couldn't tackle another serial without some help. Not enough resources and, to be fair, not enough experience despite dealing with the waves of murders of similar MO over the past dozen years. The day after Kathy Brisbois was found, they announced the formation of a joint task force to handle the case—a concentrated effort involving up to ten of their most experienced detectives.

Lieutenant Hill was named to lead the team, while Detective Hansen of the sheriff's department would play a central role. Chief Mangan, who had cut his teeth on LA's Hillside Strangler case when serial killer Kenneth Bianchi committed two murders in Bellingham, Washington, where he was chief of police at the time, emphasized urgency. While there was no evidence linking these murders to the unsolved Green River Killer cases in Seattle, the similarities were unsettling enough to warrant reaching out to the Green River Task Force for support.

As the task force was introduced to the public, the identity of the third victim was finally revealed: Kathleen Ann Brisbois, age thirty-eight. Forensics confirmed what detectives feared—it was Kathy, the same woman who had visited the police station, trembling with fear, after the murders of Yolanda Sapp and Nickie Lowe.

Kathy's connection to the other two victims also deepened the sense of urgency. She had stayed at the Spokane Street Motel, like Yolanda, and was close friends with Nickie. Her murder carried the same grim hallmarks: Her body was discarded like refuse near the riverbank, just as her friends had been.

Chief Mangan admitted investigators had suspected the same killer was behind Yolanda and Nickie's deaths, and Kathy's murder fit the pattern too neatly to dismiss.

"There's good reason to think that these three women were all victims of the same killer. That's the way we're conducting our investigation," he told the press.

The immediate focus became the victims' lives—uncovering every detail of their routines, connections, and the men they interacted with. Investigators scoured their backgrounds, piecing together where they worked and lived and the circumstances surrounding their final days.

The FBI's Violent Criminal Apprehension Program, ViCAP, was brought in to analyze the case for links to other murders nationwide. Chief Mangan warned that the Pacific Northwest had become a breeding ground for serial killers.

"We seem to have more serial killers running about—highly motivated killers—than we thought we did," he said.

Fear became palpable on East Sprague Avenue. Traffic from prostitutes slowed as women began taking extra precautions—refusing unfamiliar customers, avoiding car dates, and sticking to motels and bars.

Still, many refused to believe they, too, could end up like Kathy, Nickie, or Yolanda.

Tips started trickling in, some more unusual than others. Just eighteen hours after Kathy Brisbois's body was found, Sheriff's Deputy Paula Schwerin answered a call that set her on edge. Identifying herself only as Gloria, the caller sounded jittery and possibly drunk. Gloria claimed she'd seen Kathy the night before her disappearance getting into a tan-and-brown station wagon.

"And now she's dead, and the guy keeps driving around down here."

As she listened, Gloria's rambling tone seemed familiar to the deputy.

Her words spilled out in a chaotic rush. She was calling from the Covered Wagon and said she had seen the station wagon circling the area.

"First Yolanda, then Nickie, now this girl," she muttered. "And the guy is just driving around."

Then her thoughts took a darker turn.

"I could hitchhike and try to get a description of him," she said, her voice suddenly resolute. "If I had a knife or gun, I'd go out there and take him on. No one else knows who he is."

Deputy Schwerin began to suspect the caller was a woman named Gloria Harris, whom she had encountered at the jail reception desk when Gloria was there to visit her husband. When she asked Gloria if her husband was still incarcerated, she confirmed her suspicions and unwittingly gave away her identity.

Deputy Schwerin tried to calm Gloria and discourage her from any attempts to confront the driver. After several minutes, Gloria agreed to wait at the tavern for deputies to arrive and interview her.

For the families of the murdered women, the police efforts brought hope that their loved ones wouldn't be reduced to mere statistics.

Kathy's death wasn't just a headline; it was a devastating blow to those who knew her as more than just another victim.

Diane Matney told *The Spokesman-Review* she wanted people to remember that her daughter Nickie lived a real life. "Nickie was with the same man for eleven years. She cleaned her home and cooked meals and went to the store just like anyone else. I don't think people realize that."

Kathy's family echoed the sentiment, reminding everyone that the woman they lovingly nicknamed "Wiggy" was more than her struggles. Her life was a mix of resilience and heartbreak, shaped by choices and circumstances that could be both relatable and unimaginable. One-quarter Spokane Indian, Kathy often spoke about wanting to embrace her heritage and live on the reservation with her girls—if she could manage to get her youngest two out of foster care. She'd spent the last several years determined to make one of her second chances work.

Kaishea Rain Kegley wasn't surprised when the authorities contacted her at her dad's house in Eugene, Oregon, to inform her of her mother's murder. She'd grown up with that strange and sad "push me, pull you" life of having a mother who made a living hooking—and there was never a shred of doubt that it was a dangerous life. As the cops told her what they knew, she seized on a peculiar and tragic irony as to where her mom's body had been found. Her mom loved the Spokane River, maybe more than any other place in the world. Having been dumped there by some creep seemed especially cruel. After Kaishea gathered herself together and made calls to her sisters, aunts, and uncles, she was left to revisit the what-ifs that eluded her throughout her young life.

If drugs had not been involved?

If she'd really quit once and for all?

A mother herself now, she wondered if her mom knew how much her girls had wished things had been different.

Although she didn't speak much of the things that her mom did or allowed, they were there. All locked up. Those memories started at the Spokane Indian Reservation, where Kathy and Dale worked driving trucks at a uranium mine in Ford, about forty miles northwest of Spokane. Her parents would collect their paychecks and spend every dime on getting high—first alcohol, then pills, and finally, heroin. Kaishea, whose middle name was Rain because her mom said it was rainy on the day she was born, had the weight of being the eldest sibling. Their parents would leave them for days, only returning to get something to keep the party going. Not really to check on the kids. Often there was nothing to eat. They didn't have money for diapers, so Kaishea improvised by using towels for her baby sister. Home was a place of fear too. Kathy and Dale brawled all the time. The knock-down-drag-outs that ensued over nothing half the time left both battered and bruised. As Kaishea saw it, Kathy was usually the instigator. It almost seemed as if she wanted to fight.

Once, Kaishea was at an apartment belonging to one of her mom's friends when some creep sidled up to her and offered her money to take off her clothes.

Not doing that. No thank you.

Kaishea talked to God a lot when she was a girl.

This isn't how I'm going to live. When I grow up, I'm going to make sure my kids don't go through this shit.

While her relationship with her mom was complicated, there was one thing that stood steadfast: Kaishea loved her. It was true that Kathy was a terrible mother and the worst possible role model.

None of that really mattered.

When the cops told her that her mom had been murdered, it not only hurt like hell, but also put a stop to the hope that had lingered, often deep below the surface, that maybe she'd get better.

And they'd all be together.

Kaishea knew her mother's life in Spokane had been a grueling cycle of addiction and recovery. She heard from her family that some had seen glimpses of the Kathy they loved and prayed would come back to them. Five months before her murder, she surprised everyone by showing up clean and sober to celebrate Christmas with the family. She had emerged from a halfway house optimistic and determined to rebuild her life. That holiday was filled with laughter and hope—and talk about seeing her children and her new grandchild.

By spring, however, Kathy had returned to the dangerous world that eventually led to a pair of high school students' discovery along the Spokane River.

CHAPTER EIGHT

FBI ENTERS SPOKANE PROBE OF MURDERS

The Columbian

May 22, 1990

Six hundred potential suspects.

That's right. *Six hundred.*

Within a month of the launch of the city-county task force to investigate the three murders, detectives had assembled more than six hundred "clue sheets" that each contained the name of at least one potential suspect and the supporting information gathered during interviews with prostitutes or others who provided tips that could be useful.

Detectives had some of those listed on the sheets submit to lie detector tests after they offered suspicious or even incriminating accounts of their dealings with prostitutes. One man admitted he had been living a double life—happily married for seven or eight years, but still bringing prostitutes home when his wife was at work. He said he often used nitrite products such as Rush to make himself more sexually aggressive with them. He said he could get verbally abusive with the women but never got physically violent or displayed a weapon and would back off if they looked like they were going to cry. He said he planned to seek professional help to deal with his infatuation with prostitutes.

Another said he had dated prostitutes for three or four years. He knew but had not dated Yolanda Sapp, although he had taken her and a man he thought was her brother to buy drugs. He did not know Nickie or Kathy but recognized them on sight. He said a friend had dated Yolanda. And he named a man he thought might be involved in all three killings because he was always saying someone should kill the hookers on East Sprague. He had no proof of the man's involvement and didn't want him to know he had given his name to the police.

Despite statements such as those, the detectives watched as the polygraph examiner administered the tests and concluded all the men were being truthful when one after another after another denied killing any of the women or knowing who did.

For Jim Hansen, the seven or eight other detectives on the task force, and the group's director, Lieutenant Jim Hill, all the work and running down leads and conducting interviews was producing little more than frustration. As Lieutenant Hill announced on June 22, the police were no closer to solving the murders than they had been when the task force was formed the day after Kathy Brisbois was murdered more than five weeks earlier.

"We started out with little evidence, and we've got little evidence now," Hill said. "We've had people we've paid a lot of attention to, but we wouldn't call any of them a suspect."

How could that be? cops wondered. *Out of six hundred leads investigated so thoroughly, not one single solid suspect?* And Hansen and his colleagues were worried that the killer could strike again while they were chasing leads that turned out to be dead ends. A month after Kathy was murdered and as the summer weather warmed up, prostitution in the East Sprague area seemed to be returning to the level it had been before the murders.

Hansen often drove down East Sprague and through the Stroll, pondering how three women could disappear off busy streets without a single viable witness.

How could they go to their deaths and then to the riverbank in the middle of the city without anyone seeing anything?

Every bit of evidence was being examined and analyzed by the State Patrol Crime Lab. The review of two bullet fragments recovered from Kathy's body confirmed that they were .22 caliber but concluded that their characteristics suggested they had been fired through two different gun barrels. The examiner said that could mean the firearm had been a two-shot derringer that fires bullets through separate barrels, which create different class characteristics. One of the bullets, marked Item #13, probably could be linked to the specific gun that fired it if the gun were recovered and tested, but the other fragment, marked Item #11, might not have sufficient markings for a conclusive identification.

The police also had the fragments analyzed by an independent forensic laboratory in Newport, Washington. That review concluded that a third bullet fragment recovered from Kathy, marked Item #21, might have been fired through the same barrel as Item #11. It found differences between fragments #11 and #13 that also supported the conclusion they were fired through different barrels. The powder-burn patterns on Kathy's skin suggested to this examiner that the use of a *"multi-barreled firearm"*—such as a derringer—was more probable than the use of two separate weapons.

The Behavioral Science Unit at the FBI Academy was about to become world famous when the film *The Silence of the Lambs* was released a few months down the road in early 1991. The chief of the unit, Special Agent John Douglas, had essentially invented the science of creating psychological profiles of people who commit violent crimes and serial murders, based on his interviews and studies of serial killers imprisoned across the country. The profiles set out the mentalities, characteristics, personalities, motivations, habits, appearances, professions, and sometimes even the kind of car the killer might drive, which could help police zero in on the most likely suspects and, in some cases, draw suspects into the open with tactics that created irresistible and incriminating responses from even the most intelligent or clever killers.

It wasn't Jim Hansen's first visit there—in fact, over the years, the bureau and Spokane law enforcement had partnered multiple times. Even so, there was something special about presenting your credentials at the reception desk in the huge entry area, where a receptionist called for an escort down halls, into the lower level, and past more offices where agents were hard at work sorting through cases. In this case, however, the anticipation of the meeting between the Spokane detective and the FBI's experts just a week after the Brisbois murder didn't lead to new insight. The FBI couldn't provide much assistance to smoke out the killer now haunting Spokane.

Special Agent Douglas, however, opened a case on the three murders in the FBI's National Center for the Analysis of Violent Crime so that any similarities with other cases across the country would automatically be noted, providing another opportunity to link the murders to other cases and perhaps even identify the killer.

For family members and the public who wondered if the case of three prostitute murders was getting the right kind of attention, it was proof that those working the case were very serious about stopping the killer of three women.

No matter what they did to survive.

Almost six weeks into the work by the task force, Lieutenant Hill noted on June 22 that detectives had sought assistance not only from the FBI, but also from Washington State law enforcement agencies to try to link the Spokane murders to others elsewhere in the state. But he told *The Spokesman-Review*, "We haven't gotten anything either from the state or the FBI. He appears to be unique to this area."

Hill also defended the police decision not to conduct "john sweeps" using undercover decoys to lure prospective prostitution customers who could be interrogated. Although the task force knew that tactic had appeared to stop the murders by the Green River Killer in Seattle some six years prior, the many differences between the murders by the Spokane and Green River killers convinced the police that focusing on customers in Spokane would not be productive. Hill went so far as to admit to a reporter the harsh lesson every detective who ever chased a serial killer had learned: The only way to stop a serial killer is to arrest him.

After months of almost frenzied activity by the task force, urgency faded as other investigations and activities demanded attention. It was natural, but not intentional. Many of the officers working the murders were needed to set up and conduct security for the Goodwill Games, a kind of apolitical Olympics held in Seattle that summer. That assignment not only drew a lot of man-hours from other police work, but seemed to suck a lot of the drive out of the serial killer investigation, even for the members of the task force.

When the games and the hoopla surrounding the elite athletes from all over the world were finished that August, there was noticeably less intensity in the search for the killer of Yolanda, Nickie, and Kathy. And by the time the last calendar page for the ugly year of 1990 was turned, the task-force investigation was essentially over. Two of the members, Sheriff's Detective Jim Hansen and city police Detective Jim Peterson, however, couldn't let it go. They continued chewing on the cases in regular conversations with each other. They realized there still were some loose ends—leads that weren't followed, tips that weren't checked out, people who weren't interviewed, theories that weren't tested. There had been so much information coming in and being handled by so many detectives that no one knew everything the other detectives knew.

In January 1991, Hansen and Peterson sought approval to work together on the three murders in something of a rejuvenated joint investigation. They met with Sheriff Erickson and Chief Mangan, who agreed to give the pair thirty days to start, with extensions of thirty days at a time if they made progress.

The new team of two didn't know if the killer was still in Spokane, if he was in prison, or even if he was still alive. They were confident, however, that the killer could be found if they could harness good police work with some solid information and some lucky breaks.

Hansen and Peterson began by taking almost a month to go through the more than six hundred clue sheets from the task force and consolidate them into one system, giving each tip a number and documenting the information on three-by-five index cards. The system was like the one that Hansen had used as a member of the Green River Task Force. He and Peterson worked out of an office at city police headquarters and were given essential and expert help by assistant Suzette Charbonneau. She eventually got a word processor—this was before the advent of computers—that she used partly to compile a list of suspects who were mentioned in multiple tips. Hansen and Peterson were amazed at how much new information they assembled from their review of the clue sheets.

A theory that had not been given much consideration before was put through its paces. What if Yolanda, Nickie, and Kathy weren't killed because they were prostitutes but because they were drug addicts who got too deeply in debt to dealers? All three had high-dollar habits. Kathy spent $300 a day. Nickie's boyfriend put her heroin addiction at $60 a day. Yolanda's mother recalled a phone call with her daughter, who told her she was being held at gunpoint at that moment over a debt she owed to drug dealers named Chico and Mary that she apparently never paid. Yolanda and Kathy had reputations for stealing from customers and possibly others to support their habits. The women knew each other, traveled in the same circles, and likely used the same drug dealers.

Could that be the key to their murders?

The new team also had the time and resources to identify and investigate details and clues that had been overlooked or dismissed too quickly before. That included the odd markings in the abrasions or possibly burns on Kathy Brisbois's back. As they studied photographs of the marks, Hansen and Peterson wondered if some of the images in the marks could be numbers. Had Kathy been lying on something like the hot engine located between the front seats in some vans and been burned by the engine's serial number? They sent the images to the FBI for analysis, and the expert opinion was that the marks did not include numbers and the object that made the marks could not be identified. A worthy effort but no useful result.

Detective Hansen wanted to take another run at applying a psychological profile of their killer. He requested one from Ronald M. Holmes, a professor at the University of Louisville's Department of Justice Administration and prolific author of books and professional articles on serial killers. Using his studies of serial killers and information from Hansen on the Spokane case, Holmes concluded in March 1991 that the killer was likely a white man with a high school education and normal behavior in school. He might travel long distances to select his victims, so police should not assume he was a resident of Spokane or the immediate area where the bodies were found. The killer was probably of at least average intelligence and capable of making and executing elaborate plans with attention to detail, which would make him difficult to apprehend.

"Remember," Holmes cautioned, "this killer is not psychotic. His mental facilities are usually sharp and lucid. He will not hear voices or see visions demanding that he kill. He is not mentally ill in the traditional sense."

Holmes said the killer might live with his own family in a tidy home like others in his neighborhood. But since the victims were prostitutes, there was a chance the killer was single, still lived with his parents, and was often considered by acquaintances to be "a nice young man." Holmes noted that two notorious serial murderers—Son of Sam Killer David Berkowitz, who killed six people in a year between 1976 and 1977 in New York City, and Wayne Williams, thought to be responsible for at least twenty-four of the thirty Atlanta Child Murders in 1979 to 1981—were single.

It wasn't lost on Hansen that the serial killer expert's choice of Berkowitz and Williams as examples of serial killers who were single demonstrated some of the difficulties with psychological profiling. Each of them differed from some of the general assumptions about serial killers already set by Holmes. Berkowitz claimed he was driven to kill by demons, and Williams was a Black man.

Serial killers are often involved in productive occupations, Holmes said, and sometimes that brings them into direct contact with others, such as a "*talent agent, social worker, postal worker, etc.*" And Holmes concluded that the Spokane killer probably did not have a lengthy criminal record.

"*Do not look for a person with a criminal record in your files,*" he wrote. "*He may have a good reputation in the community.*"

Hansen and others underscored a portion of the profile:

> *The reasons for his killings lie not in any particular sexual area. He kills because of reasons that are of importance to him, getting rid of a certain group of "undesirable" people. Therefore, sexual problems are normally not of any consequence in his determinations to kill.*

And then another.

> *This killer will continue to murder until he is caught, dies, moves to another area, etc. There is no particular cycle in his killings but there may be a decrease in the times between the killings. For example, the time between the second and third killing will usually be greater than the time between, say, the fifth and sixth killing. There will usually be no increase in the amount of violence which is used. The violence is not the important issue; violence has not been eroticized. He is killing because of a self-imposed mandate to rid the world of a group of "bad" people.*

Holmes suggested the killer might change the way he disposed of the bodies, depositing them in *"far-flung areas"* rather than leaving them where they were killed. He considered the car he used to transport the victims from the abduction site to the murder site *"an integral part of his mission to kill,"* and it would likely be neat, clean, and mechanically sound. The killer's personality would be reflected in his car, which often would be a sporty model and in good cosmetic and operating condition. The actual murders would continue to be similar with little or no torture or mutilation. He would continue to choose victims from a targeted group and stalk them. He might, however, widen the area from which he would choose victims, not only to stalk them but to confuse the police.

"His intelligence gains for him some advantage in this matter," he wrote.

Holmes recommended a police investigator try to build a personal relationship with the killer based on sympathy rather than authority. He reminded the police that the killer was not psychotic or responding to voices or visions and warned them not to lie to the killer, which would risk destroying any cooperation that may have been built between him and the police.

"This killer will respect a professional in every sense of the word."

POLICE NO CLOSER TO SOLVING RIVERBANK KILLINGS

The Spokesman-Review

June 22, 1990

Detectives Hansen and Peterson also chased several new potential suspects. They learned that five or six tips suggested the killer could be

Michael Lee Haney, whom Hansen already knew from earlier investigations into robberies and burglaries. The new tips suggested Haney had told some prostitutes who owed him money that he killed Yolanda, Nickie, and Kathy, and would kill them if they didn't pay him. When Hansen and Peterson tracked him down, he said he had simply been lying to the prostitutes to intimidate them and ensure prompt payment for drugs he sold them.

"If they thought I was the killer, I thought they'd pay me," he explained.

A cynical and despicable debt-collection tactic for sure, but there was no evidence he was a serial killer. Haney had taken two polygraph tests the previous year. The first, in August 1990, asked him if he shot or caused the death of any of the three women whose bodies were found along the Spokane River, or if he knew who did. The second zeroed in on Nickie Lowe, asking if he was the one who shot her, if he knew whether he ever touched the gun that shot her, and if he participated in any way in her death.

He answered "no" to all six questions and was judged to be truthful. And his fingerprints didn't match those collected at the crime scenes.

Next, the detectives tracked a potential suspect known to have killed his own mother in a nearby county. When they drove there to try to interview the suspect, the local sheriff ordered them out of his county unless they got a search warrant from a local judge.

So much for professional courtesy and cooperation.

Later they learned that the suspect had gone to Washington, DC, where he was arrested for carrying a gun near the White House.

A truck driver connected to the murders of two prostitutes in Portland, Oregon, also drew some attention from the Spokane cops. He was suspected of killing one of the women the day before Yolanda Sapp's body was found. Police were trying to connect him to murders in states including Oregon, California, Ohio, Indiana, and Illinois. There was a brief spark of interest in him in Spokane, but Hansen and Peterson soon ruled him out because of substantial differences in his MO and that of their serial killer.

The women this man was suspected of killing were stabbed, strangled, or suffocated. None had been shot.

After a year of intense activities like those, the detectives had exhausted all the leads and clues they had generated or encountered. In 1992, the second dedicated search for the serial killer who murdered three Spokane prostitutes faded into what had to be considered a cold case. Hansen and Peterson still believed the murders could be solved and the serial killer apprehended, perhaps with an unexpected tip or a lucky break a year or two down the road. And while they had to move on to other cases, they kept the cases of 1990 open and agreed to follow up on any clues or tips that popped up in the future. They took advantage of advancements in investigative tools, especially DNA analysis, which was becoming more and more sensitive and conclusive. They submitted every DNA sample collected during the three investigations to the FBI's National Center for the Analysis of Violent Crime, which was rapidly expanding its ability to match unidentified DNA samples to those from suspects and killers in other cases across the country whose DNA was now on file in the FBI database. The system continuously cross-checked samples to search for matches—with some jurisdictions closing out cases that had been considered unsolvable.

But nothing came for Spokane.

POLICE DEPEND ON TIPS WHEN TRAIL GROWS COLD

The Spokesman-Review

November 13, 1993

Jim Hansen retired in January 1996 at forty-seven years old. The unsolved murders of the Circle hung over his head as he packed up his office and took copies of some of the files, which he wanted to keep within reach even after he left. The dozens of big cases he had solved, the bad guys he helped put behind bars, the crime survivors he had given some measure of justice—those successes were hard to balance against the open murders of Sapp, Lowe, and Brisbois. He moved far away from all of that by taking a great job as head of security for Spokane's Rosauers grocery chain.

And yet even when Hansen was working for the grocery, he stayed up to date on new prostitute murders by meeting for coffee or lunch with detectives working the cases. There were many too. Each new death stung him and deepened his frustration at retiring while the murders of Yolanda, Nickie, and Kathy were unsolved. Even as the investigations indicated their murders were unrelated to the new ones, Hansen still chafed at knowing those cases—his cases—remained unsolved.

Three years into his so-called retirement, one of his former police colleagues asked if he was interested in joining the Washington State Attorney General's HITS team, the Homicide Investigation Tracking System made up of retired detectives from across the state focused on unsolved prostitute murders. Hansen snapped up the chance and soon found himself back on the hunt for the killers using the streets of Washington State for their hunting ground.

Hansen needed to know what happened to Yolanda, Nickie, and Kathy's killer.

The young women deserved better. Their families deserved answers too. When he finally handed off the cases to HITS colleagues for a real retirement, Hansen couldn't have conceived what was going to happen on the Spokane streets in the last years of the twentieth century.

CHAPTER NINE

It had been seven years since Yolanda Sapp was found near the river, leading off a string of murders that included Nickie Lowe and Kathy Brisbois.

And Spokane investigators still couldn't catch a break.

And then in August 1997, it happened again.

Jennifer A. Joseph, age sixteen, was last seen on East Sprague getting into a late '70s model white Corvette driven by a man described as thirty to forty years old. Her decomposing body was found August 26 by two farmers at the edge of a farm field near the intersection of Judkins and Forker Roads in northeastern Spokane County. She had been shot multiple times. A history of running away from her family's home in Tacoma was punctuated with arrests for prostitution in San Francisco and Salem, Oregon, in the year before she was murdered.

The same day her body was discovered, a man collecting aluminum cans in an overgrown lot behind a business on East Springfield Avenue in Spokane found the body of Heather Hernandez, age twenty, who also had been shot. Police believed she was killed five days before, only a month after she arrived in Spokane, most likely from Arizona, California, or Idaho. In those few weeks, the homeless woman had been arrested twice for prostitution.

The curse on the women of the streets in Spokane continued to be relentless and merciless. Through 1996 and 1997, police found themselves investigating the murders of twelve new victims, and by 2000, the number of women's bodies dumped in and around the city had reached the astounding count of eighteen. Eighteen unsolved prostitute murders in the sixteen years since 1984. City police and the county sheriff's department reactivated their task force in 1997 after twelve victims were found that year and the year before. As many as twenty detectives from the city and county reexamined evidence and took new looks at old leads and suspects. The police thought as many as ten were victims of a single serial killer. The killer had adopted a startling signature—leaving many of the victims with a plastic grocery bag over their heads. Jennifer Joseph had been shot, as had Yolanda, Nickie, and Kathy seven years earlier. Although the first three had not been subjected to grocery bags on their heads, the police were still looking for any evidence that they were victims of the same killer as Joseph, Hernandez, and the others. One officer went so far as to tell the media that police had concluded they were. There seemed to be hope that investigators now had a real direction to pursue in the Sapp, Lowe, and Brisbois cases.

POLICE SEEK LINK IN PROSTITUTE MURDERS

The Spokesman-Review

September 3, 1997

A man driving the Corvette connected to Jennifer Joseph's murder was stopped in the East Sprague Avenue area by police twice in the fall of 1997, the first time on September 24 for an unspecified traffic violation five weeks after Joseph was murdered and the second two months later on November 28 for speeding. The driver, Robert Lee Yates Jr., lived in the city's South Hill area five miles or so from the Stroll on East Sprague. A married father of five whom everyone called "Bobby," Yates was an army pilot and native Washingtonian. Almost a year later, on

November 10, 1998, police stopped Yates again, driving a different car, after they saw him pick up a prostitute. He told the officer he was giving her a ride home. The cops weren't buying that from the man known to have driven a white Corvette at the time Jennifer Joseph was murdered after she was seen getting into one. And under questioning by police, Yates appeared nervous and refused to provide a DNA sample—all adding to suspicion about this man.

It turned out that Yates had sold the Corvette in May 1998, but police tracked down the new owner and searched the car. They recovered blood with DNA linked to Joseph, a mother-of-pearl button that matched those on her jacket and could have been the one missing from the left cuff, and fibers matching those recovered in the investigation into her murder.

The evidence linking Yates to Joseph's murder made him the prime suspect as the serial killer responsible for at least a dozen prostitute murders over the last two years—and possibly the murders of Yolanda, Nickie, and Kathy in 1990 and two others before them. Prosecutors charged Yates with suspicion of murder in Joseph's death, and police nabbed him driving from home to Army National Guard duty in Yakima on April 18, 2000. The new face of a likely serial killer was bland and unremarkable. He was a laborer at an aluminum smelter, and a helicopter pilot during his eighteen years in the regular army before he resigned and then joined the National Guard. His in-laws described him as a loner they never got to know very well. Neighbors recalled watching him play catch with his son and tinkering with old cars in the driveway. An East Sprague motel manager said he was a regular guest about three times a month, who always paid the $28.95 bill in cash. He was the last man she would have suspected of being a serial killer. A prostitute interviewed on the street said she and a friend had been with Yates on several occasions and insisted he was never violent.

"He was just a cheap date . . . a regular cheap date," she said.

With Yates now sitting in the Spokane County Jail, police got a search warrant to take DNA samples. The results of the tests stunned the community. Sheriff Mark Sterk soon announced the DNA linked Yates to the murders of at least twelve of the serial killer's victims and as many as eighteen. Prosecutors were able to upgrade the charge against Yates to first-degree murder in Joseph's death, and he was held pending payment of a $1.5 million cash bond.

That was just the beginning, however. The evidence continued to link Yates to more and more violence and depravity against women. Prosecutors charged him with first-degree murder in seven more of the prostitutes' deaths and attempted murder in one case where he shot a woman in the head, but she survived. With the evidence piling up and a lethal injection looking more and more likely, Yates agreed in October 2000 to plead guilty to thirteen murders in Spokane County between 1975 and 1998 if prosecutors took the death penalty off the table. He even drew a map for police to find the body of a woman he buried in the flower bed outside of his bedroom. He also confessed to killing a fourteenth victim, but prosecutors decided to hold that case in reserve in the event something went wrong with the other cases.

The judge levied a prison sentence of 408 years against the Spokane serial killer. At the sentencing hearing, Yates offered an apology to the family of each victim as he recited their names, one by one. But he found no forgiveness as many of the relatives angrily and bitterly tore into him in statements at the hearing, which a reporter described as "a cross between a church memorial and a vigilante meeting."

The roll of Yates's victims covered by his guilty plea: Susan Savage and Patrick Oliver, a young couple shot to death in 1975 while on a picnic; Stacy Hawn in 1978; Shannon Zielinski in 1996; Jennifer Johnson, Heather Hernandez, Darla Scott, Shawn Johnson, and Laurie Wason in 1997; and in 1998, Sunny Oster, Linda Maybin, Michelyn Derning, and Melody Murfin, the woman Yates buried in his yard. The fourteenth victim not named in a charge was Shawn McClenahan.

The list did not include Sherry Palmer, whose body was found in a wooded area near Mount Spokane Park Drive in May 1992. The nineteen-year-old had been shot, and like many of Yates's victims, her head was covered by a plastic bag. But police had been unable to find the evidence needed to charge Yates in that case.

And quite noticeably, the final list of Yates's victims compiled in 2000 did not include Yolanda Sapp, Nickie Lowe, or Kathy Brisbois. The evidence clearly showed they had been the prey of a separate if equally evil serial killer, but not Bobby Yates. He killed his victims with a .25-caliber pistol and wrapped their heads in plastic bags. The members of the Circle were shot with a .22-caliber handgun, and no plastic bags were involved. Further, army records showed that Yates was on active duty in Germany and on the East Coast when the three women were killed, and there was no evidence he had traveled to Spokane at those times. In a polygraph arranged by his attorneys, the examiner concluded Yates was truthful when he denied killing them. The women's families were disappointed that their murders remained unsolved, as were the serial-killer task force investigators who had been working on those cases for nearly a decade.

THREE 1990 KILLINGS BAFFLED DETECTIVES

The Spokesman-Review

January 11, 1998

CHAPTER TEN

By 2009, nineteen years had passed, and the dead women of Spokane had long ceased being fodder for media coverage and conversation. No one outside their families or the cops who worked the cases gave Yolanda, Nickie, and Kathy the slightest thought as their cases grew colder and colder. No caring souls fashioned any makeshift memorials along the riverbank at the spots where an elderly woman, two high school students, and a transplant from Oklahoma had stumbled onto their remains.

For much of the world, they were largely overlooked, both in life and in remembrance.

But not by Spokane Detective Jim Dresback.

And not by a young forensic scientist named Mariah Low.

Mariah worked for the Washington State Patrol Crime Laboratory in Marysville, north of Seattle. In January 2009, nearly nineteen years after the murders, she began testing and analyzing evidence from the murders of Yolanda Sapp, Nickie Lowe, and Kathy Brisbois. That wasn't the only case the twenty-nine-year-old worked, of course, but there almost always seemed to be something to be done in hopes of developing forensic evidence that could help identify the serial killer who left three bodies along the Spokane River, particularly as her specialty—DNA analysis—continued to mount increasingly consequential advancements.

Despite her youth, Mariah was the head of a lab that employed seven forensic scientists in the DNA unit there. The work was important, and sometimes very routine. Always exact. And sometimes dull. The office and lab were made up of a warren of cubicles, a lab bench, and an array of equipment needed for the testing and analysis of evidence from across the state. It wasn't fancy. And though it was rewarding work, it wasn't glamorous like the TV crime shows that inspired Mariah—and so many others at that time—to embark on careers in forensic science.

It was, decidedly, not CSI.

Mariah was looking for DNA on pieces of evidence from which she could develop a profile of the unknown donor that, in the best of all worlds, would be matched to a known DNA profile from the person who could be the serial killer of these three women.

She performed her first tests on requests for analysis by the detectives from the Spokane police and the county sheriff's department who had been working together on the case for years. They hoped the lab could find incriminating forensic evidence on five items or groups of items collected from Kathy Brisbois's body: ten fingernail clippings; swabs and lab slides with smears from Kathy's oral, vaginal, and anal cavities; tubes of whole blood; and a card with a dried bloodstain from an unknown donor that had been prepared years earlier by another of the lab's scientists.

Mariah started with the whole blood samples, which had degraded substantially since their collection. Even so, she was able to locate enough DNA in the blood to match the DNA on the dried bloodstain on the card.

Big sigh of relief.

With that, she was able to create a complete profile for Kathy's DNA that could be used for comparison when testing other samples.

She was only too happy to make the call to Spokane investigators about the important development.

She knew it was only a start. A start, however, was sorely needed. The cases were spinning wheels and going nowhere, and Mariah didn't want Kathy or the others to be one of those cases that just stays stuck forever.

Mariah pulled her hair back into a ponytail, put on her gloves and mask, and turned her attention to Kathy's fingernail clippings. There, she found the presence of blood on the clippings from the left little finger and the right middle finger and ring finger. Other clippings tested negative.

DNA results on the clippings were even better. Mariah recorded a mixture of two profiles on the nail from Kathy's left middle finger. One was female and one was male, and they were in approximately equal portions. Mariah removed the female DNA and was thrilled when she was able to recover enough male DNA to create a full profile well above the lab's detection threshold—which meant it was a very strong one.

That was a surprise—and a welcome one.

DNA testing on fingernail clippings was not one of the lab's more productive tests. They always found DNA from the person on the nails at levels that overwhelmed any foreign DNA. In this case, however, Mariah thought the male DNA would very well represent that person's profile for comparisons. She submitted that profile for a search for a match in the FBI's database called CODIS, for the Combined DNA Index System.

Six months after she'd turned her attention to these cases, in June 2009, Mariah made another call to Spokane to announce the advancement in DNA profiling of the likely killer from Kathy's fingernails.

After that, she began working on the swabs and smears on microscope slides and was able to make another leap forward. She matched the male DNA profile from Kathy's fingernail to the profile of an unidentified man whose DNA was found on a slide with a vaginal smear from Yolanda. That meant the same man had likely killed Yolanda and Kathy, and his DNA profile was already filed in the FBI's database, where it was constantly being compared to other profiles by CODIS.

She notified the police with that good news in July 2009.

And then the promising advancements made by the crime lab stopped.

Mariah Low had worked hundreds of cases, and she knew that the hopes and desires of those trying to solve a homicide needed to be tempered with patience.

Lots of it.

On September 14, 2012, while hunkered down in the always-busy lab doing routine tests for another case, Mariah Low received an alert from CODIS on her computer.

A cold hit on the male DNA profile for the Spokane case.

That meant it had been matched to a known profile for another man. Both profiles were identified only by a sequence of numbers assigned to them by CODIS.

The message indicated to contact the source that had submitted the identified profile—the FBI—for details.

A beat later, the FBI sent the name and birth date of a man.

Getting a cold hit on a DNA profile from CODIS was not that rare for the Washington State Patrol Crime Lab or for Mariah Low. Even so, this one stood out in the way only cold cases can.

This DNA hit had likely identified the serial killer who murdered Yolanda Sapp, Nickie Lowe, and Kathy Brisbois twenty-two years ago.

A man the dozens of police detectives had been hunting for more than two decades.

A man the women's families had been waiting to find through long, slow, and painful years.

Mariah reached for her phone and dialed.

Jim Dresback could have been mistaken for a college professor rather than a hard-nosed, pragmatic police detective: balding with a mustache and goatee. While he could be intense, he also had a ready sense of humor and a quick smile. He was born in Montana in 1955, and his family moved to Spokane in 1970 when his father, a preacher, took a position there. Dresback attended the private Northwest Christian High School because tuition was free to a pastor's kids. He married in 1979 and had three children in rapid succession. He was working in a warehouse and going to school to get a certification as an aviation mechanic—one of his two longtime interests, the other being law enforcement—when his wife saw an ad for an employment test as a jail guard with the Sheriff's department. He needed a more stable income—"The kids wanted to eat. Pesky that way." So he thought, *Why not?*

He was hired in 1985 and served as a guard for the Spokane County Jail before his contact with patrol deputies convinced him to seek that role. After stints on patrol and undercover with Narcotics, he became a sheriff's detective in 1996.

"I didn't start out as a cop for noble reasons," he said later. "I just needed a steady paycheck. But after a while, I realized I'd do it for free. It's that interesting."

Returning to the streets after working undercover brought an unpleasant revelation. There seemed to be guns everywhere. He half joked that he wanted to return to undercover drug investigations because it was safer. One of the things he noticed was that the public was more skeptical of the police and their court testimony—a shift he attributed to Mark Fuhrman's debacle in the O. J. Simpson case.

Dresback became known for engendering trust and confidence with victims and witnesses during investigations, especially in cases involving high-risk activities and complex psychological dynamics. By the time he was assigned the prostitute murder cases, he knew how to treat the women in that occupation with respect and dignity, and how to convince them to help by talking to him. "Police work isn't about driving fast and shooting guns," he said. "It's about information . . . People ask why these things happen. Sometimes, the 'why' is the one answer we never find. But that's never stopped me from looking."

Dresback, a respected veteran detective in the mold of the retired Jim Hansen and Jim Peterson, had been assigned to the Kathy Brisbois case more than seven years earlier, in January 2005. He knew Kathy's murder was connected to Yolanda's and Nickie's, and that if he solved one, he would solve them all.

Among the detective's first steps on the Spokane prostitute murders was to check in with Lynn Everson, coordinator of a needle-exchange program for the county health district, who also worked to keep prostitutes safe from threats not directly related to health issues—as in serial killers. In addition to providing free clean needles and condoms, Everson counseled the women to stay safe by working in pairs and groups and checking out customers before they got into their cars. Everson kept a list of dangerous johns and their vehicle descriptions, which the prostitutes helped her assemble. The vast majority of those on the list were white guys in pickup trucks, Everson once said. And eventually, her list reached 140 men named below the headline "Bad Tricks List."

Dresback asked Everson to urge sex workers who had survived a dangerous date to report it to police. She agreed but took a verbal swipe at the detective for referring to the "girls" on the streets. Those women deserve more respect than to be called "girls," Everson insisted. They were wives and mothers and daughters and sisters trying to make a living the only way they knew how, and that was complicated these days by trying to avoid being murdered. Dresback got the point, and he was more careful when talking about Everson's acquaintances in the future.

Another of Dresback's first efforts was to painstakingly and methodically ensure that all the items collected from the cases that might contain blood, DNA, fingerprints, hairs, fibers, or any other trace evidence had been submitted to the state crime lab and tested. In several instances, he employed a belt-and-suspenders approach and resubmitted items he thought could point to the killer, such as Kathy Brisbois's fingernails. There was a chance, he thought, Kathy had scratched her killer during her epic battle to stay alive in the mud and underbrush on that riverbank. He hoped he could get the lab to take a fresh and expedited look at the evidence. He knew there was a lengthy delay in analysis by the lab because of the increasing amounts of materials being submitted by law enforcement.

Indeed, DNA was all the rage among both the public and law enforcement. Old cases. New cases. Whenever there was a question that couldn't be answered by the men and women working the case in the field or the office, samples were dispatched. The seventh annual DNA Day was looming later in the same month—April 2009—that Dresback learned that the state crime lab had sent some of the DNA testing to the independent Orchid Cellmark lab to get around its backlog. It seemed to the cops that the lab's normal backlog in processing DNA samples had worsened dramatically under a new supervisor—so much so that the detectives nicknamed him Backlog Bill. When he was transferred to a different department, the workflow on DNA tests resumed at its normal pace.

Not fast, but much improved.

The technology was getting better and better. Mariah Low was convinced answers would come all in good time.

She was right too.

The call from the Washington State Patrol Crime Lab to the Spokane County Sheriff's department came on September 14, 2012. Jim Dresback had received periodic updates from Mariah Low three years prior and was disappointed that there had not been more good news after that. He was glad to hear from her again, of course, hoping she had made another advancement with the evidence.

As it turned out, he wasn't prepared for what he would hear.

"Are you sitting down?" she asked.

Dresback took a breath. That was a good sign. That question usually preceded good news—a significant development.

And then the forensic scientist on the phone proved his instincts right. Mariah said the male DNA profile from Kathy's fingernail matched a profile for a sixty-year-old man identified through CODIS.

"His name is Douglas Robert Perry."

That was great news, and it got even better.

Mariah said the Spokane man was already in custody in the US Marshals Service's SeaTac facility, a center for temporarily holding federal prisoners near the Seattle-Tacoma airport.

Dresback almost leaped off his chair. He was ecstatic. There it was. After all these years and all the work, frustrations, and disappointments, there was a name—maybe even *the* name.

Douglas Perry was almost certainly Yolanda, Nickie, and Kathy's killer. Modern forensic science—specifically the analysis of DNA, the genetic blueprint known formally as deoxyribonucleic acid, which forms the basis of human life—had identified the serial killer that a cadre of Spokane detectives had chased for more than two decades.

Now, Dresback thought, *we'll complete a new investigation into Douglas Perry, charge him with three murders he no doubt has thought he got away with, convict him in court, and perhaps even send him to death row.*

Dresback assigned Detective Lyle Johnston—who had just that day joined the investigative team—to contact the SeaTac facility for information about the potential suspect's incarceration there. Only moments later Johnston returned with some incredible information that no one could have seen coming.

Douglas Perry had been moved to a medical facility for federal inmates in Carswell, Texas.

But there was more.

A lot more.

"It's a women's prison."

"What the . . . ?"

"Right."

"His name now is Donna Rebecca Perry."

Murdered and unsolved.

That was about all Kathy's daughter Kaishea Rain Kegley knew as the years flew by. No one from the police or sheriff's department reached out with even the smallest tidbit of news. She figured maybe no one would ever know who took her mom to the banks of the river, did what they did, and left her there. Not surprisingly, unanswered questions did little to bring together a family as fractured as they were. One of the last times they were all together was at her burial in Fruitland on the reservation, a sacred place to all of them.

Kathy wore pajamas to meet her maker because she'd once told the family that's what she wanted.

"If anything happens to me."

Something *happening* had always been a real possibility. Two other members of Kathy's family also worked the Stroll, and they had talked about the fear that hung over working girls when the Green River Killer was busy killing in the Seattle area. Kathy and another family member had been attacked and brutalized by a john around that time.

The possibility was always there that something—something bad—would happen.

Kaishea was working at a law office in California when she got a call that they'd identified a suspect in her mother's murder. If she could scarcely believe her ears that someone had been named, the next bit of news was beyond comprehension.

The suspect in her mother's murder was a woman.

PART TWO

Douglas

CHAPTER ELEVEN

The investigation into the murders of a trio of sex workers in Spokane in 1990 had always been a whodunit. A classic whodunit at that. The evidence developed by a long line of detectives all pointed to one perp—an elusive serial killer whose identity had remained hidden for twenty-two years. It wasn't Spokane's Robert Lee Yates. It wasn't Green River Killer Gary Ridgway. So, who was this serial killer? Just whodunit?

And how was it that Douglas Robert Perry's DNA profile was a match to a profile of a woman named Donna Rebecca Perry—a female in a federal prison health facility?

The "who" in "whodunit" had just become an entirely different kind of mystery. How could the most basic evidence linked directly to Douglas Perry lead to Donna Perry? Who was Donna Perry?

The basics of Douglas Perry's identity and history were easy enough to trace. There were reams of records floating around the legal system from one jurisdiction to the other.

Douglas Perry, Dresback learned through a records search, was born on February 26, 1952, in Pogue Flat near Omak, Washington, the third of four children of Bruce and Ruth Perry. The Perrys owned and operated an apple orchard in the mostly farming region in the foothills of the Okanogan Highlands in Okanogan County—less than an hour's drive from the Canadian border. The detective's interest jumped over the basic facts in Perry's biography and went directly to a decades-long record of losing encounters with law enforcement that started when he was twenty-two.

A mug shot from an early arrest showed a slender young man of five foot seven, approximately 160 or so pounds, with shoulder-length brown hair, black-rimmed eyeglasses, and a navy-blue pullover with sleeves pushed up to his elbows. He had an average-looking face with something of a square jaw. He presented an emotionless gaze into the camera.

As Dresback discovered, Douglas Perry's arrest record was anything but average.

August 1974: a second-degree assault charge.

March 1979: illegal possession of firearms/dangerous weapons with a guilty judgment.

March 1986: another charge of second-degree assault and malicious mischief with no disposition listed.

October 1986: a confrontation with a neighbor that ended with Perry shooting their dog.

May 1987: reckless endangerment and aiming/discharging a firearm.

On April 26, 1988, he was arrested for simple assault in a domestic violence incident against his mother. As part of the arrest, agents of the US Bureau of Alcohol, Tobacco, Firearms, and Explosives searched his home and seized five pipe bombs, twenty-two handguns, twenty-seven rifles, four shotguns, and twenty thousand rounds of ammunition. He was charged with possession of a pipe bomb, adjudged guilty, and sentenced to five years' probation. It was the first of what would be tons of evidence that Douglas Perry was obsessed with firearms and explosive weapons—a genuine gun nut.

Later that same year, police went to the Perry residence yet again to investigate an allegation by Douglas Perry's mother, Ruth, that her son assaulted her. Police records noted several instances of what they called domestic violence by the son against his mother.

And then, on August 13, 1989, Spokane police arrested him for patronizing a prostitute. There it was: the first official connection between sex workers and the man now suspected of being the serial killer who murdered at least three of them.

In early 1994, police learned Douglas had returned to the East Sprague Avenue Stroll, but this time dressed as a woman and working as a prostitute to make money to buy more guns. What a strange intersection between what was surfacing as two primary factors in Perry's life—guns and prostitutes.

June 30, 1994: Douglas Perry was arrested on a charge of being a felon in possession of a firearm. The following day, he was charged with being a felon in possession of ammunition. But his arrest was not a simple matter. When ATF and Spokane police arrived at his house on East Dalton Avenue to arrest him and search for firearms they believed he was illegally accumulating, he refused to come out of the house or let them into the house, creating a standoff that led police to evacuate the neighbors while a police negotiator talked to Perry. He eventually surrendered peacefully.

December 23, 1994: Douglas drew prison sentences on those charges—forty-one to fifty-one months for possession of a firearm and forty-six months to be served concurrently for possession of ammunition. He was paroled in late 1997 after serving forty months in a state prison.

On January 6, February 3, and March 3, 1998, he was accused of violating his parole.

On July 22, 1998, Spokane police stopped him at East Sprague Avenue and Helena Street after watching him circling the Stroll. He denied he was there to engage in activities with prostitutes. Even though the police officer described him as hostile and armed with a knife and a stun gun, he was not arrested.

On December 31, 1998, Douglas picked up Valerie Katrell, age twenty-three, at Pacific Avenue and Cowley Street, just a few blocks south of East Sprague, and drove her to his home at 2006 East Empire

Avenue. They had sex and he told her not to worry, that he would not hurt her because he liked her. She said she saw quite a collection of guns and knives at his house, and it scared her. Right after Douglas returned to the Stroll, Valerie made a beeline for a police officer to tell him about her unsettling date. Amid telling him, she stopped abruptly and pointed to a blue Chevy Geo prowling the street.

"That's him!" she said.

The officer who stopped Douglas quickly discovered he was carrying two knives and a stun gun, which Douglas indicated he brought along because he wanted to help the prostitutes get off the streets. The police report noted his car contained *"attorney papers which said that Douglas Perry has a gender psychosis disorder where he does not like females."*

After that, nothing for four years. Until March 14, 2012, when he was picked up on federal charges of being a felon in possession of numerous rounds of .22-caliber and 9-millimeter ammunition—but was identified in charging papers as a woman named Donna Perry.

How could the person identified as a man named Douglas in all those previous charges over the past thirty-eight years now be identified as a woman named Donna?

Detective Johnston found the answer when he contacted prison officials in Texas and learned that Douglas had undergone gender-reassignment surgery in Thailand in 2000. According to the records relayed by the prison, Perry had his penis and testicles removed and replaced with a surgically constructed vagina. When he returned to Spokane, he had renamed himself Donna Rebecca Perry.

As he pondered all the questions about this unique development, Jim Dresback wondered how a man with such limited resources could afford what had to be a relatively expensive gender-reassignment surgery.

Dresback pored over the records a second time and got another shock. Perry was on federal parole from his release from prison in 1997 when he underwent the surgery. And if he was still on parole, he had to get approval not only to travel out of the country but probably to undergo the surgery.

And if all that was true, Dresback thought, did that mean the surgery was financed by the US Parole Commission, the section of the Department of Justice that supervises parolees? Did taxpayers' dollars go to turning Douglas into Donna, a drastic step that might have helped a suspected killer escape detection for so many years?

In all his cases in all his years as a cop, Dresback had never encountered anything like that. Not even close. Sitting at his desk, he wondered why Perry had taken this extreme action to alter his sex. It made no sense to Dresback, who readily admitted the concept of gender identity/confusion/reassignment was difficult for him to accept or understand. Beyond that, he had to wonder what Douglas becoming Donna meant for the case against a serial murderer who took the lives of Yolanda, Nickie, and Kathy.

Did the sex change mean that Douglas didn't exist anymore? Could the recently created woman named Donna be criminally liable for murders committed by a man she used to be but no longer was? Were Douglas and Donna separate and distinct people under the law?

CHAPTER TWELVE

As it turned out, Donna Rebecca Perry was not unknown to Spokane cops. In fact, she was well known. She complained to Spokane police in late May 2010 that she was on her motorcycle, stopped at a red light, when a man she didn't recognize pulled up next to her and said, "Welcome to Spokane. You can't change it here"—possibly a reference to her sex change, which he guessed or somehow knew about.

Donna said she felt threatened by the stranger's conduct because she already had been having problems in her neighborhood. She had recently reported that someone tried to start a fire on her property.

Police records also contained a report showing Donna was arrested for an unspecified "animal offense" in 2011, and as part of the investigation, she was involuntarily committed for psychiatric treatment.

Donna's most crucial arrest, insofar as Spokane cases were shaping up, came in the spring of 2012. Those charges were based on Douglas Perry's record of felony convictions in 1988 for possession of a pipe bomb and 1994 for being a felon in possession of firearms and ammunition.

Donna was picked up after a retired police detective secretly photographed her as she bought ammunition and a magazine for a semi-automatic pistol at a military surplus store called the White Elephant on East Sprague Avenue. The detective sent the photographs to the

Bureau of Alcohol, Tobacco, Firearms, and Explosives, knowing it was a federal crime for a felon convicted of a crime punishable by more than a year in prison to be in possession of firearms or ammunition. Perry's convictions in 1994 for being a felon in possession of firearms and ammunition made her eligible for new federal charges.

Jim Dresback recognized charging Donna for that violation meant federal prosecutors had already decided that Donna was legally liable for Douglas's previous crimes and that Douglas and Donna officially and in the criminal courts remained the same person. He took that as a good omen for the task force's pursuit of Donna as the serial killer who was identified by the DNA evidence left behind by Douglas.

The investigation by ATF agents had been completed in short order.

The manager at the White Elephant informed federal agents that Donna had been coming into the East Sprague location for years and usually made one or two purchases a month. She also frequented another White Elephant location on North Division Street.

Federal agents arrested her at her place on East Empire Avenue in Spokane on March 14, 2012. She was rough-looking, wore no makeup, and had dull, graying brown hair that fell below her shoulders. She looked very much, cops noted, like a sixty-year-old man trying to pass as a woman.

ATF Special Agent Todd Smith executed a search warrant on her house, which he described in reports as filthy, in shambles, and reeking of cat urine. He recovered twelve guns and a staggering 12,499 rounds of ammunition. The guns reflected an eclectic taste in firearms. There were four handguns: two Czechoslovakian CZ 52 7.62-caliber pistols, a Beretta Centurion 9-millimeter pistol, and a Colt Army Special .38-caliber revolver. Rifles included a Russian Mosin Nagant 7.62 caliber, a Russian M44 7.62 caliber, a Mossberg 100 ATR 30-06 caliber, and an Izhmash Saiga .223 caliber. There was one shotgun—a Chinese Model 87 12-gauge.

Although police had always thought Yolanda, Nickie, and Kathy had been shot with a .22-caliber handgun, ATF noted that they seized three .22-caliber rifles from Perry's house: a Remington Arms 597, a Marlin Firearms 925, and a Ruger 10/22.

During the search, Special Agent Smith pried open a bedroom closet door that had been painted shut. Inside, he found some bras and a couple pairs of women's panties he thought would fit Donna Perry. He also recovered a pair of fancy pink panties he judged too old and too small to fit her. He did muse, however, that they certainly could have been the kind of item some killers kept as trophies from their kills. He also found what he called "old sex toys" and catalogs offering transgender products. He didn't take any of the items from the closet since the search warrant authorized only firearms and ammunition.

Smith told Dresback that during the search, two brothers named Mark and Bruce Massengale showed up and said they had been friends with Perry for twenty years. They said Perry had a key to their place in Spokane Valley, and they discovered some guns were missing from their gun safe. They suspected Perry had taken them, but they didn't call the police about it. And the Massengale brothers indicated their friend had told them she had done some bad things, but they didn't have details about that.

In addition, Special Agent Smith told the Spokane detective that ATF agents had run traces on the handguns seized at Perry's house, and about a third of them had been procured by buddy Mark Massengale. When ATF traced the guns seized in 1994, all but two had been bought originally by Bruce or eldest brother, Glen Massengale.

A week after her arrest, a federal grand jury indicted Donna Rebecca Perry on a charge of being a felon in possession of firearms and ammunition. She pled not guilty, and a judge ordered a review of her mental condition and current medications. While that was in the works and Perry's court-appointed lawyer sought routine delays in hearings and trial dates, Donna decided to plead guilty, and a judge sentenced her to twenty-seven months—with a recommendation that she be assigned to a facility that could provide mental health treatment.

She was held in the SeaTac facility until June 2012, when she was transferred to the Federal Medical Center in Carswell, Texas.

While Dresback's team was trying to build a life story for Douglas/Donna Perry and secure evidence to strengthen the link to the murdered prostitutes, he got another important report from the Spokane city police's forensic investigation. Almost a month after DNA evidence first tied Perry to the murder of Kathy Brisbois, the crime lab reported matching fingerprints on the tube of lubricating jelly found among Nickie Lowe's possessions to Perry's index and middle fingers.

That was another huge leap in the evidence against Donna Perry. Now the police could connect Donna directly to Nickie's murder through fingerprints and to Kathy's murder through DNA. The evidence came from the time the suspect was Douglas Perry in 1990, but it clearly applied to Donna Perry as the case against her was being built in 2012.

And Dresback learned that same day that Donna Perry was being returned to the city of her crimes. He contacted the Federal Medical Center at Carswell, Texas, to find out if Perry had any visitors or mail and found out that she had been transferred on October 5 to return to Spokane for a federal trial on the weapons charges filed against her by ATF in March.

The official at Carswell said she had no visitors on her list, nor had she been the recipient of any correspondence.

Although Donna Perry had been in jail since March and the house at 2006 East Empire Avenue had been vacant since then, Jim Dresback decided the evidence that ATF Agent Todd Smith remembered leaving there was worth another look.

On October 17, he led a team of detectives with him to execute a search of the small house. Spokane police had assigned veteran Detective Mark Burbridge to the case, and he brought along another detective and a Forensic Unit specialist. The team went through the back door, which was standing open, and passed through a small porch and a small room that led to another open door into the rest of the house. The latch on the door was damaged from what Dresback assumed was a forced entry by vandals sometime after Perry was arrested. The door led into a small and extremely filthy kitchen. A door into the only bedroom opened on the north kitchen wall, and the doorway to the living room was on the kitchen's east wall. Burbridge found a quart-sized plastic container in a coffee can on a kitchen shelf that contained an old Washington State driver's license in Douglas Perry's name.

The odor of cat urine and feces was overwhelming.

Donna was a cat lover, or to be more exact, a cat hoarder.

The detectives moved into the living room, where cloth ropes had been strung between the south and east walls as makeshift clotheslines, a few articles of clothing still draped over the ropes. A dirty and rusted video cassette recorder was on the floor under an old dresser, from which all the drawers had been removed. The cops moved into the bedroom and began to shift piles of clothing there into the living room to enable a search of the bedroom.

The bed had been overturned and was atop layers of clothes, papers, documents, and mail, some of which bore Douglas Perry's name. A second mattress stood on its side in the bathroom that adjoined the bedroom and where the bathtub contained more clothing. Everything was covered in dust and dirt.

Dresback went to the bedroom closet, where he saw the marks on the doorjamb left by ATF Agent Smith when he had pried open the door during his search in March. The door had been removed and still leaned against the wall. And as Smith had reported, there were boxes in the closet that contained an assortment of women's underwear. Burbridge collected four bras in sizes 34A and 36B and a white string bikini that bore no labels or size. One of the 34A bras had a tag that bore the name of Ruth Perry.

Weird. His mother. What's that about?

Dresback photographed but didn't collect several more pairs of women's panties. But just inside the doorway to the closet, he found the light-pink, lacy, size 5 bikini panties the ATF's Agent Smith had recalled.

Way too small for Donna Perry, their existence led Special Agent Smith to speculate they were "trophies" taken from Perry's victims.

Dresback bagged them as evidence.

In the junk pile in the bedroom, Dresback had some syringes and wigs photographed but not collected. Before the cops left, Burbridge cut a piece of fabric from the box springs on the bed, which bore what he described as a "brownish red stain."

Burbridge even checked the tight, fetid crawl space under the house. *Nothing.*

The next day, Dresback confirmed that Donna Perry had been booked into the Spokane County Jail and was under a hold order by the US Marshals Service so she could attend her federal trial on ATF charges in March.

Dresback and Burbridge made plans to conduct the potentially significant interview with Donna Perry as soon as possible. There was a lot at stake and both men knew it. It would mark the first time she would be confronted by an official accusation that she murdered Yolanda, Nickie, and Kathy twenty-two years ago when she was Douglas Perry.

Detective Mark Burbridge had a reputation as a tough cop experienced in cases from the city's gritty underworld, but still bringing a deep empathy for victims and witnesses to his work. His early life had been marked by family instability, but that had made him resilient as well as driven to find justice for people who had suffered from the criminal acts of others. He had learned how to read people and avoid attempts to manipulate him. His good looks with brown hair and dark eyes seemed to mask a tendency toward unvarnished candor.

He was born in Great Falls, Montana, in 1962. He and his three younger brothers seemed to be constantly adjusting to their mother's several marriages and constant moves. Adopted by one of her husbands, Burbridge moved with the family when his father, an employee of the phone company who sometimes had to relocate twice a year, moved to Wenatchee, Washington. He met the girl who would become his wife in high school, and they maintained a long-distance relationship for a year while he was working in Alaska for a company that prepared and shipped materials for fishing boats out of Dutch Harbor. It was during that time that he helped foil a burglary at a store and had some interaction with the police. He enjoyed that and began to think it was something he might like to do. He studied criminal justice in college, marrying after his wife graduated from college and he had a year left.

After college, he worked for a security company until he was hired by the Spokane city police as a patrol officer. He learned how to handle a variety of cases during a time he remembers Spokane grappling with drug problems with crack and cocaine and with prostitution that, before the internet, was conducted visibly on the streets in the Stroll in east Spokane. His breakthrough case as a detective was busting a major pot operation after a bank teller reported a customer depositing money that smelled like marijuana. The investigation revealed two women who owned multiple grow properties while conducting a rivalry over who could collect the most luxury items, such as a lynx fur coat for one and a Russian chinchilla coat for the other. Police seized nearly $2 million in assets from the dealers. Burbridge developed an appreciation for long-term investigations into complex cases, all while focusing on "taking down the bad guys."

Burbridge was still on patrol and serving on the SWAT team when the murders of three prostitutes he was now investigating happened in 1990. That was the year he and his wife's first daughter was born. A second arrived in 1992, and a son was born in 1994. The Burbridge family lived on the side of a mountain, a location so remote that if someone ended up on their driveway, they were meant to be there.

Or they were lost beyond all measure.

Burbridge sought a way to ease the burden of representing the many crime victims whose cases he investigated. He developed a sacred ritual, a special way of communicating with them. He often would end his day by stopping on a hill on the edge of Spokane to offer a special and heartfelt goodbye to each of the victims, especially the children. He stacked up twenty-four stones at the spot as the memorial where he could speak to the souls lost to violence and then say goodbye as he walked away. "You can't carry that, but you always do."

While detectives searched Perry's house and dug into his arrest records, others working the case interviewed the Massengale brothers—Glen, Bruce, and Mark. The trio offered police an interesting perspective on the man they said they had known for many years before and after he became a woman. The Massengales said Douglas suffered from severe mental illness and paranoia and was unable to resist acquiring guns even after he had been prohibited by law from possessing firearms or ammunition because of the related convictions. The brothers denied having bought guns for Perry to help him get around that prohibition, but they said they knew he had been involved in buying, selling, and trading guns for years.

Bruce Massengale, however, admitted to transporting some guns for Perry and said he feared he would get in trouble. The detectives assured him they weren't interested in that.

The brothers said they had been concerned about Perry associating with questionable people, and Glen said he had warned him against doing "bad things" because he could get into trouble. He said Perry wouldn't listen to him. They said they didn't know anything about any of the people with whom Perry associated. They were all but certain Perry was never involved with illegal drugs.

"He never told me what he was dealing in and whatever he did do," Bruce Massengale said. "He didn't tell me what was going on. I don't know what was wrong with him. He needed . . . he needed help. I tried."

Bruce met Douglas while they were both getting treatment at the Spokane Mental Health Center and spending time at the Evergreen Club, a center that provided counseling and activities for people with long-term mental illness. Mark and Bruce said their gun-obsessed friend had stayed with each of them separately in the months right after he got out of prison on the 1994 weapons charges. Bruce, who said he had some difficulty recalling dates, times, and events and could be somewhat difficult to understand due to a stroke, said Perry was going to stay with him for only a few days because he had nowhere else to go, but ended up staying for three months.

The brothers also remembered Perry living with a prostitute named Clairann Gallaway for some time, perhaps between 1990 and 1994. They didn't know much about her, except that she had several children and a willful streak. Although they said they had met her only once, they described her as severely mentally ill. They said she eventually disappeared, and they heard she had taken a bus to Seattle. They never saw or heard of her again.

Bruce added he didn't know one way or another if Perry had been involved with any other prostitutes.

The brothers recalled Perry owning a 1969 International Scout, a 1970 Pontiac LeMans, and a 1970 Pontiac Catalina. The detectives now had three vehicles they had to find and search on the assumption that Yolanda and Nickie were killed somewhere else and their bodies taken by car, where they were dumped along the Spokane River. Kathy was probably killed on the riverbank itself, but she had to have been delivered there somehow.

Even after all these years, it was possible there could still be trace evidence in the killer's vehicle.

Prior to an expected interview with Donna Perry, Jim Dresback asked the forensic team to assemble a group of photographs of prostitutes from the 1990s, including the three victims and Clairann Gallaway, the prostitute with whom Perry purportedly lived at the time of the murders. Dresback hoped putting those faces in front of her—along with the other forensic interview techniques they would apply—would draw some level of a confession or other incriminating statements from the woman they were sure had been a man who killed at least three prostitutes.

Dresback also got a search warrant signed by a judge to authorize the collection of a new DNA sample.

On October 24, Dresback and Burbridge contacted the US Attorney's Office to arrange to see Perry and were unapologetically rebuffed by federal prosecutors and the US Marshals Service. No interview whatsoever until *after* the disposition of pending federal charges. An assistant US attorney told the cops that they believed she would enter a guilty plea in their case on November 13—some three weeks later, and they could interview her after that.

"The feds won't let us talk to her even though she's sitting in our jail," Dresback grumbled. "We can't talk to her until the feds are done with her silly little probation violation before we can talk to her about three murders."

WOMAN LINKED TO PROSTITUTE KILLINGS

The Spokesman-Review

November 21, 2012

The next few weeks—after Donna Perry was identified as the likely serial killer and before police could interview her while she was in federal custody—were filled with new efforts to link her to the murders and fill in the background of the man who grew up in Omak, lived in Spokane, and became a woman in Bangkok.

Detective Michael Drapeau called the Okanogan County Sheriff's department and asked Deputy Kreg Sloan to send any reports he had on criminal conduct or other background on the suspect's years in Omak. Sloan made serious efforts to put together that information, although he learned some of the documentation—such as the papers from when the suspect was booked into the Okanogan County Jail—had been destroyed in a routine purge of old paperwork. He was able to send two of the mug shots taken when Perry was booked into the county jail back in 1988—one in color and one in black and white.

Deputy Sloan contacted Tommye Robbins, the records clerk for the Omak Police Department, to request any reports the city cops still had on Perry. She agreed to send along whatever she could find. Then she added that she had grown up next door to the Perrys and would be willing to talk to the Spokane police about Douglas Perry. She surprised Sloan with an odd question: Did he know about the deer the Perrys had hanging in their basement? Sloan chuckled and said he did not. He assumed that was a strange tidbit from her inside knowledge of the family next door.

The deputy also found reports on the disposition of the Perrys' property after Ruth Perry died in 2001 at the age of seventy-two. All three parcels owned by the family on the north side of Vic Smith Road had been sold by Ruth's estate in June 2003.

Deputy Sloan did a drive-by and noticed a new house had been built, and it appeared that only one of the buildings from the Perrys' time was still standing. He couldn't tell if it was the old house or one of their outbuildings. It was modest and in rough shape.

On November 13, Dresback and Johnston made what they considered the boring 140-mile drive northwest from Spokane to Omak to retrieve the background information and criminal records Kreg Sloan had collected when he started poking through the latest chapter in the Perry saga, one that had been part of local lore and gossip for decades. As the detectives got closer, the landscape of the Okanogan Valley shifted from the gray green of sagebrush and Old West tumbleweeds to the emerald of apple and cherry orchards.

The wonders of irrigation brought prosperity to the desert.

Most in the region knew Omak for one thing—an annual event that transforms the town of five thousand to a raucous thirty thousand every August for the Omak Stampede and "World-Famous Suicide Race," in which horses and riders race down Suicide Hill—a sixty-two-degree slope that runs for 225 feet to the Okanogan River.

After Sloan handed over all he'd learned about Perry, the pair went to speak to the records clerk at the Omak Police Department. Tommye Robbins had first-person knowledge of the suspect. They'd been neighbors. When they got there, the police chief quickly ushered them into his office and shut the door.

"I don't want you talking to her without my permission," he said.

Seriously?

Dresback was mystified.

"Why not?" he asked. "You're in law enforcement. I'm in law enforcement. This is a major case here. What am I missing?"

The chief offered no explanation or justification, and the Spokane detectives never managed to speak to the suddenly reluctant clerk. The chief's resistance made Dresback wonder if he knew something he didn't want them to know or if he merely lacked the professional courtesy common among police agencies.

Regardless, it was peculiar, in a case that was already next-level weird.

Dresback spoke about the encounter later.

"The chief wouldn't let us talk to her. That is so freaking weird. It made it seem to draw attention where attention wasn't necessary. The chief says she doesn't really want to talk to you. Well, she's probably forty or fifty. She's probably old enough to decide for herself whether she wants to talk to us. 'Well, I don't want her to talk to you.' I never heard from her. She was somehow involved with Perry or why would he care?"

CHAPTER THIRTEEN

Weird.

That was the word applied repeatedly when friends, neighbors, and associates tried to describe what Douglas Perry was like when he was growing up and as a young man living on an apple orchard in Pogue Flat.

In fact, "weird" was also applied liberally to the other members of the Perry family. Not so much to Douglas Perry's three siblings—Lawrence, Katherine, and Karen—but certainly to his father, Bruce, and especially his mother, Ruth. Bruce Perry was born into the apple business by way of family who had homesteaded in the area and helped lead the way for increased irrigation in the Okanogan to further agricultural interests there. He was active in the local grange, even taking on a leadership role as a master. Outside of that, there was nothing remarkable about Bruce, except for maybe his hair. He wore it shoulder-length—long before the 1960s, when long hair was fashionable for some younger men. It was so dark that most believed he'd used black hair dye, which was considered unusual at the time. He also rode a bicycle to and from town—also considered peculiar in the farming community when most drove a pickup.

Ruth, five years younger than her husband, was another matter, however. She inspired fear in local children. That had a lot to do with her strange behavior, of course, but her appearance was also a factor. To be fair, no one running a farm, ranch, or orchard in Omak was a fashion plate. Ruth cut an unkempt figure, be it on the farm or in town. She had Bell's palsy, which froze half her face and made her gaze seemingly unable to track another person's own. Her dark hair hung long and stringy over the knobs of her shoulders. When a stray lock fell forward and obscured her eyes, Ruth didn't sweep it away.

She didn't even seem to notice.

When Ruth rode a bike around town, muttering to herself, she reminded some kids of the Wicked Witch of the West from *The Wizard of Oz*.

It was a strange family, but also a sad one.

The Perrys were dealt a double blow in less than a two-year period. First, Katherine Perry, then seventeen, died in a car crash on the highway to Twisp in April 1968. If it seemed that Ruth's mental state was a mess before that April, some thought she grew worse and had a severe psychological break with the death of her eldest daughter.

The other shoe dropped in November of the next year.

Ruth said she found Bruce Perry dead on the kitchen floor. The coroner's report determined Bruce had succumbed to a coronary embolism, fell, and hit his head.

Some who knew the family weren't quite so sure about the coroner's conclusion.

A neighbor who knew the Perrys later spoke to an investigator of the incident: "My dad told me that Ruth inflicted fatal injuries on Bruce by shoving him down a flight of stairs."

That gossip might have been rooted somewhere between truth and innuendo. The idea of being thrown down the stairs at the Perry household came up repeatedly in conversations with those who knew the family.

And from Douglas too.

In the halls of Omak High School, Douglas Robert Perry was a kind of quiet wallflower that other kids teased and bullied but mostly avoided.

A classmate told another investigator years later: "He was super shy and never looked up from his large black glasses that he was always pushing up on his nose. In school he didn't have any friends that I remember and always was a loner. Often muttering to himself almost like he was carrying on a conversation with an invisible person! I think he was intelligent, but he never participated in class and usually kept his head down in a book. He carried a Bible with him in high school. I always felt sorry for him because he was teased a lot and probably bullied."

Douglas didn't play sports and was considered at best an average student—though he'd later brag of having an IQ of 180. His only extra-curricular activity was his membership in the Omak Chapter of the Future Farmers of America. His 1970 senior portrait depicts a spectacled young man wearing a paisley button-down shirt with a wide collar. His hair is neatly parted on the side.

He might have looked benign, but he wasn't.

Not by any real stretch.

After graduating, Douglas—who was a proficient mechanic—enrolled in vocational classes. If he planned a career fixing things, however, he never managed to get there. Instead, he continued to live at home with his widowed mother and work the family's orchard. He was still working in the orchard in 1988 when he injured himself in an equipment mishap seriously enough to qualify for monthly Social Security disability payments of $766. Some later contended those payments were based on Douglas's mental illness, but no one knew for sure.

A perpetual loner, Douglas spent his free time in the hills around the orchard, wandering around with a fishing pole or a gun. Mostly guns. He not only loved to target practice and hunt but also loved the feeling of a gun in his hands.

Almost nothing felt better.

Debra Fecht was five when her family moved from Nebraska to pick apples and start a new life in the Okanogan in 1958. For many, Omak could be a stand-in for TV's fictional Mayberry—a small town, lots of churches, sports activities, and, of course, the orchards that ran the valley with spring clouds of blossoms and the glistening red of the fruit that followed. All of that was lovely, but from where Debra sat, none of it matched reality. Orchard life was hard. Her family worked sunup to sundown at one orchard or another. It was subsistence living at best. Picking fruit in the summer, collecting a paycheck, and supplementing that with growing their own food. The winter? Running out of money, chopping wood, and trying not to freeze so they could do it all over the next season.

The people living in town worked hard, too, Debra would later concede, but they didn't—couldn't—possibly have had it as bad as the orchard kids out in the country. They could see it in their clothes, the way they cut their hair, all the markers that divide the adolescent haves from those without.

In high school in the late 1960s and early 1970s, Debra knew she wasn't like other girls—and it wasn't because she came from a poor family. She didn't hang around the lunchroom talking about some cute guy. Boys didn't do it for her. She wasn't sure if she was gay back then, mostly because it wasn't an option, or even something that could be a concrete thought.

She didn't know what to do with her life, but she had to do something.

In the spring of 1973 when she was twenty, Debra said yes to twenty-four-year-old orchardist's son Lawrence Perry when he proposed marriage.

Maybe, she thought, being married was her lot in life as it had seemed to be for most of the other girls around the valley.

Debra knew the Perrys owned a sizable orchard off Vic Smith Road out on Pogue Flat. So, when she accepted the proposal, it mostly was because she didn't know what else was possible. Lawrence was nice enough. Not exactly handsome, but not homely either. He was quiet, unassuming. He made no real demands on her.

Later, when she thought about it, Debra wondered if Lawrence was also unsure of what he was supposed to do. That he wasn't in love with her either. That maybe he was looking for more of a companion than really anything else.

No one from either the bride's or the groom's family attended the courthouse wedding. In fact, the witnesses were two people who happened to be there on other business. That afternoon, the new couple moved into a small house on the property—with Uncle Dick, Bruce's brother.

Lawrence never mentioned he had a younger brother named Douglas.

Not even once.

Or that he had a little sister, Karen.

And as far as his mother was concerned, Lawrence didn't seem too fond of her. Ruth wasn't really a part of her son's life.

In fact, Debra only met her mother-in-law one time, at the low-slung white house she lived in on the other side of the orchard. The meeting was stilted, awkward. Ruth sat in the kitchen off to the side and barely uttered a word. No meal was served. Very little was said between the three—at least nothing Debra could ever recall. It was a strange encounter, but then again, their marriage was strange. For one thing, Lawrence didn't shower his bride with affection or try to romance her. He gave her one gift. When a Great Dane needed a new home, he asked if she wanted it. Debra said yes, and she got the dog she named Blue.

Debra tried, albeit halfheartedly, to make a go of things. She worked alongside Lawrence and Uncle Dick in the orchard. When the alarms sounded that spring to warn that the temperature had dropped low and posed a threat to the budding fruit, she helped scatter smudge pots throughout the orchard to fend off a possible freeze.

It passed through Debra's mind that maybe that's all Lawrence wanted—a helper. Not a wife. Just someone to run the orchard with him when Ruth met her maker.

"When Mom dies," Lawrence told her, "all of this will be ours. We'll move into the house."

That didn't seem like a winning proposition to Debra.

Less than a month after their courthouse nuptials, Debra made a crucial decision. She didn't say anything to Lawrence. There was no row. This wasn't it for her, and she was sure that he felt the same way.

Which was nothing.

She quietly slipped out the front door in the middle of the night. And that was that.

Debra saw Lawrence only one other time when she returned to get Blue and ask him to pay for the annulment or divorce—whatever it was called. She only wanted her dog and her name back. He agreed without a trace or hint of emotion.

A year later, Debra did just what her two older brothers had done. She enlisted in the military. She had a path and a plan. A life away from the valley where she could be herself.

She never saw any of the Perrys again.

Ruth Perry, who told Douglas she wanted to be a Jehovah's Witness but didn't like the proselytizing that came with the sect, was by all accounts very troubled. Neighbors had heard that she had been committed to a state mental hospital for treatment. It wasn't idle whispers either. Ruth had been a patient at Eastern State Hospital, a psychiatric hospital southwest of Spokane.

Town talk also had it that Ruth had been battered by her husband. While Detective Dresback was unable to scare up a single arrest record for Bruce Perry, the Okanogan County Sheriff's department handed over cryptic reports indicating it was Ruth who had been booked into the Okanogan County Jail four times for unspecified incidents between April 1988 and January 1990.

Jim Dresback quickly learned that police clerk Tommye Robbins wasn't the only one who didn't want to talk about the Perrys.

As it turned out, almost no one did.

Certainly no one related to Douglas would speak up. His sole surviving sibling, little sister Karen, never returned any of the investigating officer's calls.

And if Douglas had felt that he was alone growing up in isolation in Omak, abandoned by everyone, it was a situation that tracked the orchard kid into adulthood.

It followed Donna too.

Douglas Perry was always lurking around and watching.

Kris Lingle, who grew up across the road from the old Perry place, suspected Douglas had been watching from the orchard when she held outside slumber parties for her girlfriends. The girls, about ten years old at the time, played hide-and-seek late one summer night. Kris found the perfect hiding spot in the limbs of a cherry tree. From her vantage point, she caught a glimpse of Douglas, then about twenty, walking silently among the trees in the orchard.

What was he doing?

It came to her later that he was peeping on the girls at the party.

What kind of a person does that?

She also recalled an incident when Douglas got angry with his mother and drove a tractor to chase her around the yard as she was driving a pickup truck.

"It was like they were the crazy people across the street," Kris explained years later. "It was the kind of family that you steered clear from, that I'm sure everybody in the neighborhood or on the street over there said, 'Hey, don't go to the Perry house.'"

Amy Charles not only knew Douglas from school, but her parents also owned orchards on two sides of the Perry property. She always thought he was "a little strange . . . a little odd . . . just his mannerisms."

She often would see him changing the sprinklers in the orchard with his long hair covered by a knit stocking cap—when the temperatures were more than one hundred degrees. She thought his mother had mental issues but seemed "good when she took her medicine."

Amy's family began to have trouble with the Perrys after they purchased a section of land from Douglas's uncle, Dick Perry. Almost right away, Ruth and Douglas disputed the property lines. When the Charles family held firm, odd things began to happen. One time someone vandalized the Charles family's smudge pots that burned diesel fuel to ward off cold temperatures threatening the apple crop. Amy's family always suspected Douglas.

Bonnie Worley not only grew up near the Perry orchard but also had unique insights into the family because her uncle Walter Bissell took up with Ruth Perry for a while.

Walter Bissell, then in his fifties, rented a house next door to Ruth and started to help out by picking apples for her. Ruth was widowed by then—and alone. Her oldest son and youngest daughter had moved far away. Douglas, then in his late teens, however, was a constant, lurking presence.

Walter and Ruth dated for a couple of years—and he considered that one of the biggest mistakes he'd ever made. According to Walter, Ruth was volatile and unpredictable. She'd talk to herself too. She'd fly off the handle at a moment's notice.

The next minute?

As sweet as apple pie.

Douglas's omnipresence hadn't made things smoother for Ruth either. Indeed, it was the opposite. It was true that he worked hard—when he worked as a mechanic or around the orchard. He seemed so enmeshed with his mother that it was disturbing.

Mother and son had started to look alike—the same long hair, the mannerisms. Bonnie noticed it. So did her uncle.

They could be twins, Bonnie thought.

It had always been odd over there, but it was decidedly moving toward next-level freak show. That realization came to Bonnie when her beloved Labrador, Bree, didn't make it home. She and her husband conducted a thorough search but came up empty-handed.

Where was Bree?

The next day they made a chilling discovery and put two and two together when they came across two dead dogs not far from the Perry orchard.

The dogs had been shot.

What in God's name is going on over here?

And when his .22 went missing, Walter Bissell suspected Douglas had taken it. He was always messing with guns. He never went anywhere without carrying one. Not only that, when Walter was away, Douglas, uninvited, had been letting himself inside a rental house where he'd fire up the woodstove to melt down the weights used to balance wheels on cars when working as a mechanic.

Walter couldn't figure out what Douglas was doing until he found casings scattered about his kitchen. Douglas, he was convinced, was making his own ammunition.

Walter made mention to Ruth that he thought it was time for him to pack up and go, but she wouldn't hear of it.

Ruth begged him to stay. It wasn't because she loved Walter. She wanted him to know that she didn't know how Douglas would react if Walter left the orchard.

Left her.

Hurt her.

How would Douglas react? It didn't make sense, but Walter had seen enough to take those concerns to heart. He wanted out of there, but he thought there was a very real possibility that Douglas might do something to him. What's more, Walter also couldn't trust Ruth not to throw fuel on the fire. She was unstable and dangerous. Ruth lived in that space that kept her on the verge of a court-ordered intervention by mental health professionals or the police.

Walter called the Okanogan Sheriff's department and asked if someone could come when he packed up.

He was afraid Douglas might kill him.

"He's crazy," Walter said flatly.

More than familiar with the Perry family history of mental illness and domestic violence, the sheriff's deputies drove out to the orchard right away. Being there was always like defusing a bomb. Figuratively, of course, but given Douglas's escalating behavior, there was always the chance that maybe such a thing was possible.

Later, when Douglas was picked up for possessing illegal weapons, Walter Bissell wasn't surprised in the least to learn he'd amassed an arsenal. What did raise his eyebrows was that it wasn't garden-variety gear—the cache included military weaponry too.

Ruth knew firearms were a huge problem, and she confronted Douglas more than once that guns would be his demise.

"If you leave the damn guns alone," she insisted, "you'd be in a hell of a lot less trouble."

Her words were both hollow and true at the same time. It was Ruth who got her son deeper and deeper into the shadowy world of weaponry—her own paranoia playing on his. She was convinced that some unknown person was plotting to steal the orchard away from her after Bruce died.

And that was never, ever going to happen.

"She used me as her private army to keep people away from her," Donna Perry explained later when she was fishing for a reason why she'd done the things she did. "And I took the fall for it."

Ruth had made her son into her private army.

Another neighbor recalled seeing Douglas with a rifle, lying on his belly in the orchard like a sniper. He was screaming that somebody drove on the road toward Conconully, and they have to come back.

"And I'll get them."

Jim Williams installed and serviced telephones around Omak from 1976 until he retired in 1999, and he remembered at least five or six odd calls from Ruth Perry, who feared her telephone was tapped. Jim considered Ruth paranoid, and she never would allow him into her house or the basement to check the lines and equipment inside. She always said it was too messy. He never found any evidence on the outside lines indicating any tampering.

While there had been missing cats in the vicinity of the Perry orchard, a greater number of incidents involving other people's pets concerned dogs.

Douglas even shot his brother Lawrence's dog. Later, he recalled the incident.

"I shot my brother's dog because he sicced the dog on me . . . He had a pit bull and then he had some kind of great big Saint Bernard–type dog. They tore my pant leg. They chased me home through the orchard."

He was in his early teens at the time.

In October 1986, Douglas and a neighbor from across Vic Smith Road became embroiled in a confrontation over the neighbor's dog. Decades later, no one could recall exactly what the dispute was about; all they remembered was that Douglas fired his rifle, killing the dog.

Right there in front of everyone. As though it was justified. Like it was nothing.

"Our neighbor was out working in his orchard one day and Douglas was across the road, and he shot the dog. And our neighbor started over there and Douglas said, 'You get back over there where you belong or I'll shoot you too.'"

One local viewed the incident as a harbinger of the brutal crimes against the Circle that would surface nearly three decades later.

Detective Burbridge knew sociopathic personalities often take their first steps toward serial killing at a young age by torturing or killing small animals. Ted Bundy, Jeffrey Dahmer, Richard Ramirez, and others were among those cataloged with that history by behavioral scientists at the FBI.

Douglas Robert Perry, it seemed, was another name to be added to that list.

CHAPTER FOURTEEN

Ruth Perry called police on multiple occasions to report being abused by her youngest son, when he was still living at home. Douglas, then thirty-six, was arrested for simple assault against his mother on April 26, 1988. The police classified the incident as domestic violence.

It occurred just two years before the murders of Yolanda, Nickie, and Kathy.

Ruth reported that Douglas had struck her in the ribs three times and had threatened to get a gun. She feared what he might do next. When police arrived, he had locked himself in the basement. He threatened to shoot or blow up with a bomb any police officer who came down the stairs. Okanogan County Sheriff's Chief Criminal Deputy Toney Fitzhugh had dealt with the orchardist's son several times and considered him and most of his family to be "crazy nutcases."

Fitzhugh didn't take Douglas's threats seriously and wasn't intimidated.

"I didn't believe half of what he had to say," he told investigators later. "All these allegations and threats. And I didn't believe anything he said . . . I just identified myself and yelled down in the basement. Told him to get his ass up there or I was going to come down after him and he was going to be sorry. It was a bit of an argument back and forth . . . And he finally just gave up . . . and he came up."

Douglas was charged with simple assault and domestic violence. The next day, police got a search warrant for the basement, where they and ATF agents seized five black-powder pipe bombs, twenty-two handguns, twenty-seven rifles, four shotguns, and twenty thousand rounds of ammunition. ATF Agent Lance Hart noted that half of the firearms were loaded. Experts from the Washington State Patrol later defused the bombs.

Douglas Robert Perry pled guilty to a domestic-violence charge of third-degree assault for striking his mother. An Okanogan County judge ordered him to undergo psychiatric treatment at the Sacred Heart Medical Center.

But that wasn't the end of it.

Douglas was indicted on federal firearms charges too. He pled guilty four months later to one count of possessing a firearm not identified by a serial number. US Magistrate Judge James Hovis sentenced him to a five-year suspended sentence with five years' probation. The judge ordered Douglas to surrender his federal firearms license, which authorized Douglas to buy and sell firearms from other dealers and manufacturers in other states, and to forfeit all his firearms. Judge Hovis called it absurd that an individual with a documented history of mental problems could qualify for any such license.

Douglas was ordered to continue psychiatric treatment at Sacred Heart, and Judge Hovis said he would be arrested if he left the hospital before completing treatment or caused problems in the psychiatric unit. In addition, the judge also ordered Douglas not to return to the Omak area without permission from his probation officer, which led to Douglas's relocation to Spokane.

That same year, Douglas continued to grapple with an awareness that he had inherited the mental illness that afflicted his mother. In fact, he'd already been diagnosed with paranoid personality disorder while being treated at Eastern State Hospital.

The director of the hospital's legal offender Competency Evaluation and Treatment Program wrote in a letter that Douglas's paranoid personality was not a thought disorder that could be treated with psychotropic drugs. The disorder was defined as meaning Douglas lacked the ability to be sensitive to the feelings and thoughts of others whom he committed offenses against or placed in danger.

Later, Donna would say her family, particularly her parents, dealt with her mental illness while she was still living as a young boy in less than compassionate or appropriate ways.

"What they did with mental illness back in the day, they left you at home and then went out for dinner or out to a horticultural meeting or something like that. Basically, I was left home with a babysitter until I got old enough to just sit there myself . . . I was the kid that didn't exist."

Donna considered the lack of treatment or understanding for her mental illness as a different kind of pain from what was generated by the physical, psychological, and sexual abuse Douglas suffered from birth.

When Douglas was born on February 26, 1952, he presented with both male and female genitalia. His parents decided the baby should be raised as a male because they already had two daughters and only one son. A surgical procedure sealed the infant's vagina—leaving scar tissue where the vagina would have been. It was a decision, an "either-or" one at best, that took the entire family into a downward spiral of epic proportions.

Bruce Perry was deeply disappointed over what God had foisted on him, and his bitterness quickly grew into violence and abuse. Called Douglas names. Locked him in the basement. Bruce pitched him down the basement stairs for not being the boy he was supposed to be. At one point, Bruce smacked Douglas with such force that it cracked the boy's head open. That wasn't presented as an act of abuse, however. It was an attempt to stop the auditory and visual hallucinations that made Douglas so peculiar. So weird. Such an aberration.

At least that's how Donna later saw it.

And, as Donna would later insist, the abuse was even darker. Both father and older brother, Lawrence, sexually abused Douglas.

For her part, Ruth Perry wavered between joining in the physical and verbal abuse and comforting Douglas as the pair forged a disastrous and parasitic relationship that was singular in each other's lives. On some occasions Douglas would present his mom as his protector. That she alone had been his lifeline through the nightmare of his childhood. Sure, she had mental health issues—that was obvious to everyone who encountered her at the orchard or in town. At a young age, people saw Douglas talking to himself or to people who weren't there.

Just like Ruth.

Douglas later recalled times when his mother tried to keep him safe at great risk to her own safety.

"My mother took terrible beatings from my father and stuff for sticking up for . . . trying to protect me. My mother got between my older brother and me."

At the same time, Ruth could give as good as she got. Donna told people that Ruth could be abusive too. Name calling, mostly. But also physically. Ruth once pushed Douglas through a window, injuring the toddler so severely, Donna would wonder years later if her mother had meant to kill Douglas.

"They had to pull and stretch the skin on my face to stitch me up," she said.

The cumulative effect of such trauma lay dormant for a while, ticking like the pipe bombs that would hold great fascination throughout Perry's life. It was always there, nipping away. The steady stream of brutality growing up left Douglas perplexed, agitated, and unable to process the difference between right and wrong—which included all the things done to him by those who should have loved him.

"You don't know what morals are," Donna said later. "You think that what they're doing to you is OK. Then later, when you find out it wasn't OK, you're kind of thinking, 'Why did I put up with that?'"

Despite all the stories of a demented and destructive relationship between mother and son, there is at least one document that presents a boringly normal moment between them. Ruth wrote to Douglas while he was in prison on a federal weapons charge. Its banal contents betray the insanity or acrimony that seemed to be the basis for the relationship between mother and son.

> *Dear Douglas,*
> *Just a short note to let you know I'm thinking about you. The weather here has been cold. I have to wear my sweater around in the house. We had some pizza for supper, I don't like pizza . . . My hair is long & straight it needs cutting haven't gotten around to do it yet. I haven't been doing very much. I still get up at 12: o'clock each day . . . I haven't heard anything from Lawrence [Douglas's brother] I guess he is just fine . . . I can't think of anything more to write about so will close for now as ever.*
> *Love,*
> *Mother*

CHAPTER FIFTEEN

Mark Burbridge wasn't a psychologist, but detective work had schooled him on the preoccupations that put some people behind bars. Pedophiles were at the top of the list. Something deep inside couldn't be undone to stop them from reoffending. Serial rapists and peepers were similar in their inability to thwart a compulsion. Stalkers and the men who routinely battered their partners were another on the list of those for whom "No" meant, well, nothing at all.

There was something else, a complication, to Douglas Perry's pathology.

Before he found himself on the banks of the Spokane with a dead body to display, the Omak orchardist's fixation, his *obsession*, with firearms of all sizes and shapes and calibers—rifles, shotguns, and handguns—was pathologic.

Douglas and guns.

Peanut butter and jelly.

Tom and Jerry.

As Burbridge sifted through Perry's considerable rap sheet, it seemed as though there was never a time when the pairing of Douglas and various weaponry wasn't the source of a run-in with the law. Report after report documented Perry's collections of dangerous, almost obscene numbers of firearms and amounts of ammunition beginning at an early age and evolving into something more troubling while he lived in the Lilac City.

The reports jogged Burbridge's memory of a notorious case that made national headlines back in June 1994—a spree killing and stand-off at Fairchild Air Force Base hospital.

Dean Mellberg, age twenty, had been discharged from the air force on diagnoses of personality disorders when he returned to the base hospital armed with a semiautomatic rifle with a seventy-round magazine and killed a psychiatrist, a psychologist, and two others, including an eight-year-old girl. He wounded twenty-three more before a military police officer fatally shot him in the head. It was then, and likely will always be, one of the darkest days in Spokane's history.

Apparently, Douglas, mad about his care, his benefits, just maybe mad at the world, didn't catch the significance of the event when he invoked Mellberg's name in a threat to counselors at the nearby Okanogan community health center.

James Blue and other counselors notified the authorities that Perry had threatened their lives in a series of phone calls.

"Mister Blue has screwed up my life since 1988 and I'm going to take care of Mister Blue the same way Mellberg took care of Fairchild."

When the threats made their way to the feds, ATF Agent Lance Hart immediately knew whom the police were dealing with. He had participated in the investigation into the standoff at Perry's childhood home in Omak in 1988, where a mountain of ammo, guns, and pipe bombs were seized. Hart saw the Perry case all the way through the guilty plea and the sentencing to five years on federal probation.

Ten days after Mellberg went on his rampage, Hart once more found himself leading a raid with federal, county, and city officers on Perry's house—this time the little yellow house on East Dalton Avenue—to seize what was expected to be another arsenal of firearms and ammunition.

When Perry, obviously armed, refused to allow the authorities to enter his residence, Hart and the team of ATF agents and local police evacuated the neighbors, who for the most part saw the standoff as confirmation that there was something off about the guy who kept to himself. They told investigators at the time that he was creepy, loony, weird.

The standoff lasted for more than five hours.

When Douglas Perry finally emerged with his hands up and head down, he told Agent Hart he had thirty to forty firearms and a cache of ammunition in the house. He waived his rights and admitted he bought the firearms for cash from people on the street since his previous firearms conviction made it illegal for him to possess guns or ammunition. He also admitted he had invoked shooter Dean Mellberg's name in his threat to the counselors.

Inside, police recovered a new arsenal of twenty-seven rifles and shotguns—some of them loaded—along with eleven handguns and thousands of rounds of ammunition that weighed three hundred pounds, including tracer, hollow-point, and armor-piercing rounds. Two of the rifles were the same kind of Chinese-made assault rifle used by spree killer Mellberg. In addition to the firearms, police recovered collections of blowguns, crossbows, and knives. And they found a life-sized man's silhouette—the kind sometimes used for target practice—on Perry's bedroom wall. They also found a collection of wigs and women's under- and outerwear.

In a jailhouse interview with *The Spokesman-Review* the day after he was arrested, Perry made surprising admissions about his gender identification some six years before Douglas became Donna. When asked about the women's clothing, Perry described himself as a mentally disabled transsexual diagnosed with a paranoid personality.

"I like to wear women's panties and bras—that's part of who I am. I'm a woman in a man's body . . . I'm a disabled adult with a psychiatric illness, but I'm not violent. People probably think I'm crazy, but I just wanted to fit in and be left alone with my own family."

Burbridge was surprised to see that Perry had made such revelations about his sexuality so long before his gender-reassignment surgery in 2000. And his reference to his "own family" probably referred to Clairann Gallaway or possibly the dozen or more cats that lived in the house.

Well before Doug Perry mentioned being transgender, he denied that his references to Dean Mellberg were threats that he could become a copycat mass murderer. The comments were, he insisted, an effort to call attention to the mistreatment of mentally ill people.

"Mellberg got dumped on by his psychologists and psychiatrists who told him he was disabled and crazy," Perry said later. "That's similar to the way they've treated me."

He went on to say what the counselors interpreted as threats were really just complaints that he had been forced out of the mental health center when he was seeking assistance and treatment and was left without medication or counseling for at least three years. "The psychologists and psychiatrists make a diagnosis, and then they abandon people. You either live with it, or you rebel. Mellberg picked up a gun. I didn't do anything," Perry said.

He said he had been seeking help from the mental health workers to find a job. He said he had worked as a welder, pesticide applicator, and truck driver. "I just wanted to be part of society, but they would never do that for me . . . Yes, we may be mentally ill, but we still have wants and needs. There are just pieces missing in our personalities."

Burbridge read how Perry also seemed to confirm an obsession with firearms, which the detective thought should have set off warning bells with mental health workers that Perry had a need for treatment. "The guns to me were like my family and my children," Perry said. "I wouldn't do anything violent with them or hurt my children . . . I like the damn guns, and I wasn't doing anything violent. I'm a historian and a collector."

The newspaper noted that ATF agents had remarked on how clean Perry kept the barrels and stocks of the weapons he owned. One officer said Perry referred to himself as a "barrel sucker" in describing his love affair with his guns.

"Everybody needs a purpose in life and mine is guns. I'd sit up nights, take my guns apart and clean them, and read books about them . . . I bet I know more about these guns than the ATF guys do . . . All I wanted to be was one of the guys, you know, go out to the shooting range with soldiers or the police," he said.

Burbridge and others on the case read other comments by Perry that shed light on his obsession with guns. Perry said his father had been a military weapons instructor. Although his parents would fight and cause tension in the household, everything seemed okay when his father would take him and his older brother out for target practice. "All the family fighting would end as long as we were out there shooting our guns. But then we'd come back home, put the guns away, and the fighting would start again," Perry said.

The detective considered it very telling about Perry's state of mind when he said that, of all the things that had happened to him, he was most saddened by the loss of his gun collection, which was then in a police evidence vault and slated to be destroyed. In fact, Perry revealed a key element of his mental health and personality when he explained, "I picked up dog dung, mowed lawns, and even pulled tricks on East Sprague as a male prostitute for extra money to buy my guns."

That had been another telling reference to Perry's connection with prostitutes on the Spokane Stroll, Burbridge thought. Why hadn't that made the police look at the gun-obsessed, mentally ill transsexual and male prostitute as a potential suspect in the three murders in 1990? And would that possible miss by police in 1994 have any effect on the case against Donna Perry?

Despite all of Perry's explanations about Mellberg and his life as a mentally ill transsexual, he apparently recognized he had no legal defense against the charges that he was a felon in possession of firearms and ammunition. That was an uncontradicted fact. On September 9, 1994, he pled guilty and was sentenced to forty-six months in federal prison by Chief US District Judge Justin L. Quackenbush of the Eastern District of Washington. He served thirty-seven months and was released on October 31, 1997, to begin three years of what essentially was parole but was called supervised release in the federal system.

Records showed he was arrested five months later, on March 28, 1998, on allegations by his probation officer that he had violated the terms of supervised release "by submitting untruthful written monthly reports" in January, February, and March. He was released from jail on March 31 to await a hearing on June 9, 1998, for the judge to decide whether to revoke his supervised release and send him back to prison to serve the remaining nine months of his sentence. There was no record of the hearing, but afterward the judge ordered Perry released to continue on supervised release as before. Perry's probation officer filed a statement saying Perry admitted failing to meet certain requirements but was once again in compliance. The judge's order said Perry "acknowledged his obligation to comply with the terms and conditions of his supervised release."

Looking back at all the elements of Donna Perry's life and that of Douglas Perry before 2000, Detective Burbridge wondered how prosecutors would build their case against such a troubled and complex defendant. An abusive childhood. Mental illness. A paranoid transsexual. A male prostitute posing as a woman while living with a mentally ill female prostitute. Gender-reassignment surgery. A new life as a woman.

Everyone working the case wondered how that history and those bizarre factors fit together to tell the story of a serial killer with at least three victims snatched off the streets in Spokane.

CHAPTER SIXTEEN

The official battle for Douglas to become Donna began in earnest the week before Christmas, 1998.

One of Douglas Perry's federal public defenders, Gerald Smith, brought up the idea of the US Probation Office paying for "the gender/ sex reassignment change the defendant seeks" during a telephone conference call with the judge and federal prosecutors. Smith and cocounsel, Public Defender Judy Clarke, then filed a motion on January 19, 1999, asking Judge Quackenbush to order the US Probation Office to pay for more extensive mental health services for the troubled man, including continuing sessions with his therapist, Helen Bonser, appointments with a physician/counselor experienced in gender dysphoria and one licensed to prescribe treatment for gender dysphoria, and any additional treatment prescribed by such a physician.

The motion did not specifically seek funds for gender-reassignment surgery, but the implications were more than clear and obvious.

The motion quoted Ron Dyson, a program services probation administrator at the federal corrections and supervision division of the Administrative Office of the US Courts, who said no public funds were available for the medical expenses for "gender-reassignment change." But Dyson told Perry's attorneys that the funding would be made available if the court ordered it.

In support of the motion for the government to pay for Perry's mental health and by implication, physical treatment related to his gender issues, the defense attorneys said Perry had recently been diagnosed with "gender dysphoria," which they defined as a psychological condition resulting from the "dysfunction between sexual identity and sexual organs." They said Perry had participated in therapy meant to treat the condition that was paid for by the Probation Office. Helen Bonser had recommended getting him treated by a "physician/counselor" experienced in gender dysphoria and able to prescribe treatment. Bonser suggested Perry's condition would improve with "hormonal therapy," in which the motion said he was eager to participate.

The motion said the Probation Office had been "reluctant" to provide money for such treatment because it had never been done before and such funds were reserved for treating defendants with "serious psychoses." Apparently, the motion argued, the Probation Office did not consider gender dysphoria a "serious medical problem." The motion argued, however, that other courts had recognized gender dysphoria as a serious psychosis and the Probation Office had made money available for treating other people with the condition. The motion also noted that Minnesota made public funds available through Medicaid for people seeking sex-change operations.

"Several courts have held that prisoners cannot be denied treatment for gender dysphoria when in the custody of the Bureau of Prisons," the motion said.

Defense attorneys said Perry had been ordered to undergo mental health treatment as a condition of supervised release.

"It would be unjust to deny payment for Mr. Perry's treatment based solely on the unusual nature of his affliction. Therefore, Mr. Perry asks the court to use its discretion and order the Probation Office to provide payment for Mr. Perry's treatment," the motion said.

The Probation Office argued in a court memorandum that there simply was not enough money to pay for Douglas Perry's treatment for gender dysphoria, including hormonal treatment or surgery. Scott M. Morse, the deputy chief probation officer in Spokane, said just $10,000 was available for mental health treatment for all the people on supervised release throughout the Eastern District of Washington, a district including more than one million residents and covering nearly forty-two thousand square miles.

In a ruling on February 26, 1999, Judge Quackenbush cited Morse's statements in denying almost all of Perry's request for the Probation Office to pay for more mental health treatment. "The court finds that there is no funding available through the court or the Probation Office to fund any hormonal treatment or surgery for Mr. Perry," the judge said. He ruled, however, that the Probation Office would pay for Perry's continued treatment by counselor Helen Bonser.

Twenty-two months after the government denied funding for gender reassignment, Douglas Robert Perry boarded a jet in Seattle and flew to Bangkok, Thailand, to undergo the complex surgery that allowed *him* to return to Spokane as *her*—Donna Rebecca Perry.

Detectives looking into the matter could find no records establishing just how Donna Perry financed her surgery or whether she was ultimately able to get the federal government, perhaps through the US Probation Office, to provide the funds since she was still serving three years of supervised release after her stretch in prison from 1994 to 1997.

It was unlikely the patient paid for the operation herself, given a lifetime of dependence on Social Security Disability Insurance. Cost estimates for such surgery ranged from $5,500 to as much as $40,000.

As far as anyone working the case could tell, there were limited funding options in 2000 for a sex-change patient in Washington seeking government funding as a felon on SSDI. State and federal policies on transgender health care were much more restrictive then, making it uncommon and difficult, but not impossible, for public funding.

CHAPTER SEVENTEEN

If there was any hope for Douglas Robert Perry to find love, or even a place in the world, it came in the form of Clairann Elizabeth Gallaway. At least that's how he saw her, nearly from the instant they met on the streets—first as a client and customer, then something more. Just what that was wasn't entirely clear. Were they a couple? Or was she like a gun or a bomb? Something he was obsessed with.

And for her part, Clairann never talked about Douglas and what role he had in her life.

Not a single mention to anyone.

Ever.

And yet for Douglas, she was the only woman, *only person*, he ever loved. She was hope, love, and compassion. She was also completely, unabashedly a mess. At the same time, she was 100 percent lovely.

No one, except maybe Clairann's older sister, could have foreseen the trajectory of her sad life.

Viola Eberle and her sister grew up on a dairy farm that their parents owned and operated, near Port Angeles on Washington's Olympic Peninsula.

Detectives who sought clues in her background that might have led her to a relationship with someone like Douglas Perry would find nothing in her early years.

Indeed, the pages of the Port Angeles newspaper would portray Clairann as a golden girl. Miss American Dream. Clairann modeled clothes for a mother and daughter tea. She was pictured with her doll-house to celebrate a Christmas event. Dairy princess, of course. Top magazine salesperson in her middle school. She was an excellent student, with a GPA between 3.4 and 3.8. As a teenager, she vied for the coveted title of Miss Irrigation in the annual Sequim festival pageant. And the piano? She played with enviable skill, giving her first public recital at age ten.

Clairann was all of that, and more.

How she ended up with the likes of Douglas Perry was a head-scratcher for the ages.

Spokane detectives were all but convinced that the murders involving Yolanda, Nickie, and Kathy were connected in some fashion to Clairann—not as an accomplice, but as a trigger that led Douglas to troll East Sprague Avenue with the intent to kill women.

There were no accounts of how Douglas and Clairann met or how quickly afterward she moved into 544 East Dalton Avenue. Detectives knew that this prostitute, who had eight children, was in the area as early as 1990 and that the suspected serial killer would say years later Clairann was the only person he ever truly loved, and he'd asked her to marry him several times.

She always said no.

Douglas even suggested that he could come up with the money to buy a bigger house and allow her children, all of whom were living with other relatives or were in state custody, to live with them.

Clairann immediately put the kibosh on that offer too.

The blond, blue-eyed woman described as beautiful by those who knew her continued to work as a prostitute despite Douglas's adamant opposition. He said there were times in the early '90s when she would disappear for days, and he would find her on the Stroll making money to pay for a coke addiction, where he'd "manhandle" her into his car so he could take her home.

To keep her safe.

Or possibly to control her.

And over and over, Douglas insisted he could help her qualify for disability benefits like the ones he received so she wouldn't have to work as a hooker.

Again, no thanks.

On the occasions when she was arrested for prostitution, Douglas would hang out at the jail to visit her until he could come up with the cash to bail her out. But before long, she would return to the streets.

Rinse and repeat.

Untreated mental illness can be that way.

Clairann might not have understood that, but some family members did.

Viola was certain that Clairann inherited the schizophrenia that afflicted their father and others on his side of the family. And their mother was eventually diagnosed as a borderline personality, who seemed to her children to be two distinctly different people. So, the schizophrenic young Clairann was also burdened with a dysfunctional family in which her father—who often seemed to Viola to be in his own world far away from the family dairy—often beat his wife, who seemed to work hard at pushing his buttons. She might then inflict a beating on Viola.

"I have horrific childhood memories of the beatings and trying to get between my parents," Viola recalled many years later. "Then, the other side of it is, my mother was vicious. She had two personalities. She beat the shit out of me, and she was verbally abusive . . . I don't think she beat my sister.

"What I remember of the sick family dynamic . . . my mother was . . . she was the control figure. And she tried to pit my sister and I against each other."

Viola left home shortly after graduating from high school in 1970. Clairann was left behind with her parents, but she soon took up with the young farmhand who worked for the family. Handsome and kind,

Dan Gallaway was fifteen—three months older than Clairann. Over time, the two fell in love. They left for Minnesota where they married in 1974, and eventually moved to tiny Cavalier, North Dakota, to start a family that would grow to six children—four boys and two girls.

Viola would always wonder if the rapid succession of so many babies escalated Clairann's mental problems.

"The more kids she had," she said, "the harder it was for her to function."

Dan began to notice odd behavior right away when a second child, a daughter they named Carolyn, was born. He couldn't find a way to reconcile what was happening when the nurse brought in the newborn. There was no snuggle or cuddle between mother and daughter. No counting of the little toes or fingers. None of that.

Instead of reaching for her daughter, Clairann held her arms tight against her torso.

She didn't want a thing to do with her baby.

Dan stood there in shock.

Something was wrong. Really wrong.

Beside himself, Dan tried to make things right. Better. Normal. Putting it off to being nervous about having a second baby. Maybe Clairann was in some kind of depression. Some moms, he'd heard, experienced that. Or maybe just overwhelmed with the responsibility?

It turned out to be something else. Clairann said she didn't like little girls. She didn't want daughters. She loved their firstborn, a son. Not her daughter.

Dan didn't know what to do with that. He wondered if having a daughter instead of a son had maybe triggered something deep inside of his wife. Maybe something had happened to her when she was younger?

When Viola heard what was going on, she asked her sister about it.

The explanation made zero sense.

"God is punishing me," Clairann said. "I wanted a second son. I was wishing for a boy."

Viola insisted that couldn't be the case, but Clairann stayed firm. She wasn't being scary or mean. Just kind of resigned.

Oh, God, Viola thought at the time, *she's mentally in bad shape.*

When the Gallaways returned to Washington, they settled in Snohomish, just north of Seattle, where Dan got a job at a dairy. Clairann had wanted to live in Seattle, but Dan was a country boy at heart, and there was no way he'd live in the big city.

Almost right away, he began noticing Clairann's car seemed to be low on gas more often than reasonable, given that all the necessities to run a household full of kids weren't far from where they lived. He found out why when Clairann was involved in an accident in Seattle. She told him that she'd been driving into Seattle regularly, though she didn't really say why.

It might have been boredom with farm life.

Maybe a way to get a break from the kids.

Some excitement.

Or something else.

Dan never asked for specifics. He didn't know how. He just patched together ideas of what might have been making her unhappy.

Clairann's odd behavior escalated around that time.

Sometimes when making dinner, she would stop what she was doing and just stand there, not moving. Not saying a word. She'd hold a blank expression on her face until Dan or one of the kids could get her to snap out of it.

Sometimes nothing worked.

Dan wondered if his wife was using drugs. He half hoped that had been the reason because he knew there were issues of mental illness in the family, and he wasn't sure if something like that could be fixed.

He talked with his sister-in-law and told her about the strange, almost fugue-like state Clairann seemed to inhabit.

All of this greatly alarmed Viola. She remembered a time when Clairann froze in front of an adoring audience. She couldn't talk. Her eyes didn't track. She just stood there and had to be escorted off stage.

Whatever that had been, it scared Viola and made her worry more about how she was treating little Carolyn.

Something was up. Something no one seemed to be able to address.

Clairann took their two-year-old son and infant daughter and disappeared shortly after Carolyn was born. Dan told friends he spent two months of hell not knowing where his wife and children were, but assuming they were homeless somewhere. When she finally returned, Dan never sought out the details of what had gone on while she was away. Part of him just didn't want to know. For a time, things improved, and they had four more children. Things appeared to stabilize a little—but the improvement was nothing more than a mirage.

The Gallaways divorced after ten chaotic years of marriage. Clairann was a shell of her former self by then. Drugs, her declining mental health, and the rigors and reality of sex work all played a part. She had trouble maintaining a normal life with the children. She often received mental health treatment while state and local social services agencies monitored her care of the children and sometimes even took custody when they determined she was unable to care for them. By then Dan had remarried a woman who agreed to help him take custody of their four boys while the two girls were put in custody of Clairann's mother. Clairann once took the kids who were in Dan's care to Seattle, and he had to go retrieve them from a women's shelter with their mother.

It was the last time he saw her.

Dan heard his ex-wife had two more children after they separated and that she was supporting herself as a prostitute to pay for the drugs on which she'd become increasingly dependent. He heard she was sinking lower and lower, and there seemed to be nothing anyone could do about it. It crushed him because he never stopped loving her. He just couldn't. The Clairann he knew was a good person, both beautiful and kind.

After being shuttled from one foster home to another until she was three, Carolyn Gallaway moved in with her grandparents on the Olympic Peninsula. Her little sister didn't have to go through the foster system to find her way there—Clairann handed her over right after she was born.

Our mother doesn't like girls.

While that sentiment was debasingly hurtful, Carolyn, like her dad, didn't stop loving her mother. In some ways she was in awe of her too. Her mother was a woman of impressive talents, from playing the piano to drawing to writing stories—all abilities Carolyn shared too. She listened intently to family stories about her mom being so much fun, such as her ability to perfectly mimic a horse's neigh.

Clairann had two more boys after separating from Dan. The first was born while she was living in San Diego, and the authorities there took him away from her despite her efforts to keep him. Clairann's mother flew to Southern California and got custody of her grandson and later adopted him.

When Carolyn was six, her grandmother hosted a birthday party at which her mom made a surprise appearance, albeit in a fog.

It was as if she was in the throes of some kind of bizarre and unshakable trance. Clairann didn't speak. Not a single word. All she did was stare.

Right above her head where she sat was a string of balloons that suddenly, and inexplicably, began to pop. One by one. No one touched them. They just popped.

Carolyn's eyes widened to take in the scene.

Is Mom doing that somehow?

There were other visits too, though not many. Each time her mom returned, hope and excitement filled the air. Maybe she'd stay and play the piano? Maybe she would color with the girls or take them on a walk in the woods.

Hope and excitement.

Every year Clairann would send a Christmas card, no personal note. No letter about how much she missed the kids or promises to see them in the new year. She only wrote "*Merry Christmas*" and listed each of her children's names.

All the kids' names stayed on the card, even her son Greg after the boy died in a bicycle accident in 1986.

Carolyn later wondered if her mom had known about the accident.

Or if she somehow had put it out of her mind.

Other times Carolyn considered that the Christmas cards or occasional birthday cards were really coming from her grandmother to ease the pain she and her little sister felt over being abandoned by their mom.

Grandma made attempts at sweeping any unpleasantness under the rug.

She said one time the reason for all the drama and arrests concerning Clairann was that she'd been panhandling. She needed money to take care of the kids—and herself.

Later, Carolyn brought up the subject of the arrests to her aunt Viola.

"Well, you know, your mom is a prostitute."

Carolyn refused to accept that. Wouldn't. Not at all. Her mom most definitely was not a hooker. The idea shocked her to the core.

She told her little sister what their aunt had said.

"Well, duh, Carolyn."

The last time Carolyn saw her mother was in 1987, when she accompanied her grandparents to Seattle to bail her mom out of King County Jail.

"Panhandling, again," her grandmother insisted.

Of course, it wasn't anything like that at all. Indeed, the summer and fall of 1987 had been a banner year for Clairann insofar as her growing arrest record in Seattle. In August she was booked into King County Jail for prostitution and false reporting when she gave her name as Joan Rae Nelson.

The reporting officer wrote:

> *I made eye contact with her and pulled to the curb. She opened the passenger door and asked if she could have a ride. I said sure, and she got in. She asked me if "I would spend $60.00." I said that was pretty expensive, because all I wanted was a blow job. I then asked her if she would do more than just a blow job for $60.00. She said that she would. I then asked her if we could have "sex" also, she said yes. I then drove to a lot in the 11700 block of Aurora. There I asked her if she wanted the money first. She said that it did not matter and started to take off her clothes. At this time, I pull out my police I.D., and placed her under arrest.*

Clairann was booked, appeared in court, and agreed to the terms of probation—stay away from known areas of prostitution.

She managed to keep the promise for two weeks before another officer recognized her as a frequent flyer.

> *I pulled up by her and she got into my car and asked me if I wanted to date, I said yes and we talked sex and she reached over and touch my penis in my groin area, (outside of my pants). We talked for a few min, and then she got out of my car and started to walk away. I drove over to her and showed her my police badge and told her she was under arrest for SOAP, probation violation and lewd conduct. After we got to the N. Station, she told me*

*her name was Jonn Wilson. I asked her to spell her first
name and she spelled it Jonn.*

She was arrested, booked, and, once more, was back in court.
The next month Clairann was picked up again.

*She made eye contact with me, and I pulled over. She
asked if I was dating, and I said yes. She said it was going
to cost me $60 and I said that I had that much. She got
in and asked where I lived. I told her in the North end,
but I didn't want to go out that far. I asked her if we
could have a car date and she said yes. She directed me to
a parking lot. I told her that I didn't want to screw in the
car but would like a blow job and asked her how much
that would be. She said $40 and asked if that would be
all right. I told her that I never paid more than $25 for
a blow job before. She said how about $30, and I said
that would be fine. She asked for the money, and I showed
her my police badge and placed her under arrest. She gave
the name of Rene Johnson which is not her true name.*

After Clairann was processed and released from jail, the family
got a place in the ferry line to make the return home to the dairy
farm. Carolyn was overjoyed. Hopeful even. She was finally getting her
mother back. It felt so good sitting next to her.

At one point, Clairann, who had been mostly silent, announced
that she needed to use the bathroom. Saying she would be right back,
she got out of the car.

The family waited for what seemed like forever, even missing the
first boat. They made several trips to the terminal to look for Clairann,
but the search was futile.

No one had seen her.

Clairann Elizabeth Gallaway had vanished.

"That was terrifying," Carolyn recalled later. "I was like, 'Where is she? Why wouldn't she want to be with me?'"

She wasn't really gone, of course. Clairann just didn't want to be found. In 1988, she was arrested a few more times in the Seattle area. In February a vice officer wrote out an arrest:

> *She came up to my car, opened the door, and asked me if I could get her a room.*
>
> *"I'd be willing to get you a room, but I was looking for a girl to have sex with."*
>
> *"Yeah, that's fine, but I need to have a room tonight."*
>
> *She got into my car, and I drove off. She told me that there was a motel down by the Seattle Center that we could go to.*
>
> *"Now wait a minute, I'm willing to get a room, but are we going to have sex? I mean are you willing to suck and fuck me for the price of a room?"*
>
> *"Well," she said, "I was hoping that you could give me a little extra too. Could you do another twenty?"*
>
> *"Ok," I said, "For the price of a room and another twenty you are going to suck and fuck me real good right?"*
>
> *She said, "Yes."*

In May, Clairann asked another cop if he'd get her a room, plus forty dollars.

> *I recognized her as a prostitute I had arrested before. I said yeah, I'm sure we can work something out. She smiled and got into my car. I asked her if she was sure she was clean, and she told me she was. I then told her that I guessed I could pay for the room and give her twenty bucks for the blow job. I asked her if that was a good enough deal for her, and she told me it was. I signaled*

*another vice officer, and he assisted me in making the
arrest. She was ID'd as Clairann Gallaway.*

In 1990, Clairann Gallaway moved into 544 East Dalton Avenue.
Much to Douglas's growing disappointment and overwrought frustration, she continued working as a prostitute on the Stroll. Clairann knew
some of the other girls there, including Yolanda Sapp, Nickie Lowe, and
Kathy Brisbois. Spokane's sex workers didn't have a lot to work with in
terms of real estate, and at times there was steep competition for johns.
Sometimes Clairann would come home and lament that one of the
group members had been unkind or even roughed her up for one reason
or another, but even so, she still saw herself as a member of the Circle.

Or at least thought she was.

Douglas would tell the police years later that Clairann was insistent on working as a prostitute despite his strong opposition. She was
his. Only his. He hated sharing her with other men. It was a constant
source of angst between them. While he wanted her all to himself, she
obviously didn't feel the same way.

In 1994, Clairann packed up for the coast, as those in Spokane
refer to Seattle.

Or maybe somewhere else.

He never saw or heard from her again.

Douglas was in emotional shambles after Clairann left town. He was
as lost as he ever had been. He ran through various scenarios with his
friends—most notably the trio of Massengale brothers with whom he'd
skirted the law and bought guns. Maybe she was in jail? Possibly dead?
He had no idea. She was the love of his life, and her absence meant there

was no way to fix a relationship as complicated and dangerous as theirs had been. Of all the people he'd ever known, he was sure Clairann's acceptance of his difficult situation was genuine. Clairann had always been his only true advocate. It was true that some of his mental health counselors, social workers, and friends like the Massengale brothers talked a good game. They could be encouraging, even sympathetic, when they listened or observed Douglas's peculiar strangeness.

Or could do a reasonable job of pretending to be.

Only Clairann seemed to really, truly understand.

Her acceptance was something that had eluded him since birth. The connection they shared wasn't based on the never-ending quests for drugs, like so many other couples who'd joined forces to survive the streets. It had been the battle waged against mental illness, one in which they'd both been embroiled in since childhood. Somehow, they'd found each other. No one else could understand the wild mood swings, the terrifying hallucinations, the erratic and dangerous behavior that colored every aspect of their lives.

And now she was gone. He was alone again—with his doubts and demons.

Investigating Clairann Gallaway was part of the detectives' dive into the life of Douglas Perry after he was linked to the murders. Through arrest records, they confirmed that Clairann, then in her mid-fifties, had been working as a prostitute in Malibu, California, as late as 2012. Authorities said Douglas's old love had multiple personalities, perhaps as many as thirty-six. When they tried to reach her at a Los Angeles treatment facility, a doctor said she was presenting as a personality named Beth.

At least, that's what she was doing that day.

It was true that medication helped stabilize her erratic behavior, but only so much. Clairann, the doctor said, was also known as a bit of an escape artist. Whenever she could manage it—which was a lot—she'd bolt from the facility and find her way back to the beach to sell herself for cash for drugs. Her self-destructive behavior was on an endless loop.

While the Spokane detectives were never able to interview her, Jim Dresback and his team continued to be struck by two key dates from her time with Douglas in Spokane.

First, Clairann was arrested by Spokane police for prostitution on February 21, 1990, putting her in jail the next day, February 22, when Yolanda Sapp's body was discovered on the riverbank.

Second, Clairann was picked up again on May 15, 1990, which put her in jail the day Kathy Brisbois's body had been found.

Clairann was in jail and *not* with Douglas Perry on the dates of two of the murders. That was just some kind of bizarre coincidence. Or was it? The veteran detective didn't think so. He felt Clairann's arrests were linked to the murders. He just didn't know how.

Was it as simple as giving Douglas the opportunity to kill while the love of his life was in jail? Was it time away from Clairann so Douglas could procure the services of prostitutes and then, for whatever reason, dispatch them to the river? Did he target the members of the Circle as an answer back to rumors that they had been cruel to Clairann?

Or was it something else?

CHAPTER EIGHTEEN

Jim Dresback had to force himself to sit through the boring hearing in the courtroom in the Thomas S. Foley US Courthouse and Federal Building in Spokane on November 13, 2012. Even when the subject of the proceeding was a criminal in a case he was chasing, he found such legal machinations routinely dull and lifeless and pro forma. The results were almost always exactly as expected, as everyone involved played their roles as required to create the desired court record.

So, even when this hearing was held for the judge to take a guilty plea from Donna Perry to the firearms charges filed against her in March after the ATF raid on her house, Dresback found the event itself cut and dried, and boring. It was of less interest to Dresback, even though it provided his first glimpse of Donna Perry in the flesh, than the fact that the conclusion of the federal prosecutors' business with Perry meant Dresback and Mark Burbridge might finally get access to Perry for their long-awaited interview. Dresback didn't even care that he couldn't get a good look at Perry during the hearing while the judge accepted her guilty plea and set her sentencing for a month later. His real concern was that she might be released from jail pending her sentencing and could elude the crucial in-custody interview that he and Burbridge hoped would provide some answers to their many questions about the murders of Yolanda, Nickie, and Kathy. He was relieved when the judge ordered Perry to remain in jail until sentencing.

When the hearing ended, Dresback immediately approached the prosecutors with more than a little trepidation to ask if they would now allow the interview. He was pleasantly surprised when they readily agreed and then set it for just two days later.

Dresback reserved one of the larger conference rooms at the Spokane County Jail for the interview, rather than one of the small, dingy rooms that would be the usual location for a meeting with suspects or witnesses or felons. He wanted his subject as comfortable as possible for this chat with the cops.

The veteran detective had conferred with an FBI specialist in the Behavioral Science Unit for suggestions about how to interview this unique suspect. The expert, who had consulted on many serial killer cases, said this was the first one he was aware of in FBI history in which the suspect had sex-change surgery between the killings and the arrest. In fact, this case of first impression left the expert with little to suggest, except that Dresback be careful to use the suspect's preferred pronouns during the interview. If Donna Perry presented as a woman and considered herself one, the cops had to be sure to call her "she" and talk about "her" activities. The disrespect implied in using "he" and "him" could be insulting enough to Donna to immediately crush any chances for a cooperative exchange. Dresback agreed and had already made that part of the plan.

He and Burbridge had also decided that Dresback would lead the interview and Burbridge would focus on taking notes, observing Perry, and serving as the "bad cop" if that became a useful tactic.

Cuffs rattling, and wearing a wrinkled, ill-fitting green prison uniform—a loose V-neck top over a white T-shirt and baggy pants—Donna Rebecca Perry entered the room at 9:09 a.m. on November 15. Sheriff's Detective Kirk Keyser, as casual and friendly as could be, ushered her inside and told her to face the wall so he could remove her handcuffs.

"I just have to have them on while I walk you to and from," he said.

As Donna leaned her forehead against the wall, she responded in a flat but friendly tone.

"Well, I'm not going anywhere. I'm too damn old to get in a fight."

"No, I know," he said, with an all-knowing grin. "Well, Donna, I'm too old to fight anymore. So, the two of us together, we're . . ."

"We're just old," Donna answered back.

Donna slid into a chair between a large brown-topped table and the off-white wall in the ten-by-twelve-foot room.

Keyser offered her coffee, pop, or water.

Donna brightened at the mention of a drink. She even managed a smile.

"Yeah, a soda would be cool," she said, thinking. "Classic Coke . . . or a Pepsi . . . Sugar. Lots of sugar."

"Sugar, all right," the detective said. "Just so you know, I have to tell you this room is recorded. I'll go grab you a Coke and be right back with you. OK?"

"OK."

Keyser left and returned with the soda and then left her alone again. Two minutes later, Jim Dresback and Mark Burbridge entered the room.

"Hey," Detective Dresback said in a casual, friendly tone.

"Hello," she said.

"Donna Perry?" he asked.

She looked up. "I am, in fact."

Jim Dresback had seen her from afar only once, and Mark Burbridge had never caught a glimpse of her. They had to admit, at least to themselves, that she was a haggard, rough-looking woman. Her graying hair was parted in the center and hung loosely past her shoulders.

Oh, my God, Dresback thought, *she needs a shave.*

Donna's face appeared to reflect every one of what must have been sixty hard years.

She looks like a meek, mild, doddering old woman.

Detective Dresback suppressed a grimace.

How many drinks would it take to drink her pretty in a late-night bar?

For his part, Mark Burbridge was having a similar reaction. Donna had made no effort to present herself as a woman. No attention to her hair. No makeup. He also noted that she made no attempt to soften her voice. It still registered as male.

She had gone to a lot of effort—surgery in Thailand—to be a woman, but here, at least in the light of a police interview room, she presented no better than an unattractive guy.

As the cops sized up the woman who used to be a man, she offered them nothing but a blank look

Dresback walked around the table to sit on the same side as Donna, close enough that he could have reached out and touched her. Burbridge, in a purple open-necked shirt, offered her a greeting as he sat across the table.

"How are you doing today?"

"I'm good," Donna said. And then she asked, "Who am I talking to here?"

"Well, I'm Detective Dresback and this is Detective Burbridge."

Burbridge offered a friendly smile. "Hi, nice to meet you, Ms. Perry."

"Uh huh. OK."

"You can call me Jim," Dresback said.

"I'm Mark," Burbridge added.

"Mark and Jim," Donna repeated. "What are you interviewing me for?"

"Well, we will get into that," Dresback said, almost as if that topic of discussion wasn't that important. "Would you spell your last name for me?"

"P-E-R-R-Y."

"And the first name?"

"Donna. D-O-N-N-A."

Donna provided her home address and explained that she didn't have a phone anymore and didn't have a job because she was a disabled adult on Social Security disability. When asked to name relatives, she said she didn't have any. Everyone was dead.

"Who did your family consist of?"

"Me, myself, and I," Donna said with a short laugh. "That's it." But then she ruefully added, "My cats. My cats were taken away."

"Oh, you have cats?"

"I *had* cats—plural," she said, with her voice registering regret or grief, or perhaps annoyance.

"How many cats did you have?"

Donna paused a beat, tallying her felines. "Well, I started out with thirty-six," she said, still thinking. "I wound up with ten. Then the other one ran off and it died. And there's at least five out in the backyard."

"You had thirty-six cats? Wow!" Dresback said with an edge of surprise. "How do you keep all them fed and . . ."

"Well, that was the idea, to keep me busy and out of trouble. Had to have a hobby. That was my hobby."

"Do you have any brothers or sisters?"

"No, they're all deceased," she said.

Dresback wondered why she would intentionally omit her sister Karen, who police knew lived in California.

Asked for their names, Donna again omitted Karen as she answered, "Uh, let's see. Brothers and sisters. The oldest one was Lawrence. Then I had an older sister, Katherine, and then there's me. And that's it."

"Were you the youngest?"

"Yes," she lied again.

"Lawrence and Katherine. OK. Can I call you Donna?"

"Yes."

Then it was time to broach the subject of the interview.

"All right," Dresback began. "Well, Donna, I know that you're in jail for some federal issues. We don't want to talk about that. That's not what we're here for . . ."

Donna went right to the point. "Am I being under arrest for something locally here—for something stupid?"

"No, I'm not arresting you."

"OK. What's the pep talk for today?" she said, this time with an edge of sarcasm.

"Well, I want to see if you can help us out. We're working some old cases . . ."

"Yeah?"

"Hoping maybe you can help us clear some things up. OK?"

"How old is old?"

"Well, I don't know. They're '90s."

"Nineties?" Donna repeated with a little uncertainty.

"And before we get into that, I have to make sure that, since you are in custody, even though I'm not talking about any of that, about those federal charges, I do need to advise you of your rights. You know that you don't have to talk to me. You can have an attorney. You're familiar with that stuff, right?"

"Yes."

"That's what I want to cover with you . . ."

And then Donna Perry seemed to swipe the cops' hopes and plans off the table.

"I should probably have an attorney here if you're going to question me about something," she said.

Dresback went ahead and read her Miranda rights.

"I think I should have a lawyer here if you're going to ask questions."

"All right," Dresback said while trying not to register his disappointment and frustration. "And it's 9:18 a.m. on 11-15. See what I wrote here. Your response was, yes, I think I should have a lawyer here . . ."

"Uh huh."

"As far as answering questions. Sign that there . . . Down there at the very bottom. I'll fill that top part in later."

Donna Perry put ink to the form, and Dresback turned to the other item on his agenda. "OK, we have another order of business we have to take care of today. I'm gonna ask for a sample of your DNA. And what I'd like to do is . . ."

She was getting more suspicious. "This is in conjunction with what?"

"Well, it's in conjunction with some old cases that we are investigating, that we . . ."

"Old cases for what? What's the reference to these old cases?"

"Well, I want to make sure that you want to talk to me about this. OK?"

"Well, I should have a lawyer here if you're going to take DNA and all of this."

Detective Dresback explained that Donna had no right to an attorney when he executed the search warrant authorizing the police to take her DNA sample.

"We'll show you the search warrant and go over it with you," Detective Burbridge added. "But you don't get a choice in the matter."

Donna shook her head. "OK. I have no idea what you guys are talking about."

"Well, let me go get the stuff and, uh . . . We'll step out so you can ponder that for a minute," Dresback said.

The pair of detectives stepped out at 9:19 a.m. and went down the hall to the room where the monitor for the camera in the interview room was showing Donna Perry's image as she sat alone. Detective Burbridge thought her face and body language indicated she was thinking about what to do now that the cops were pressing her for DNA but not answering any of her questions. He could see her mind working. Donna was wondering what this was all about.

The detectives returned to the room at 9:23 a.m., and Burbridge offered a friendly "Hi, again" as they walked in.

Donna responded with a flat "Uh huh."

"I'm going to go over the warrant with you in a second, Donna," Mark Burbridge said.

Donna went right back to her main concern. "Why would you want my DNA? For what?"

Detective Burbridge decided to let her know what was really happening.

"Well, this is a search warrant for first-degree murder. We have information you might know some things about a murder. That's why we brought you down to talk to you today. That's why we want your DNA."

"Are you accusing me of murdering somebody?"

"Well, we want to know if we can eliminate you—or exclude you."

"When was this supposed to have taken place?" she demanded.

Burbridge needed to put this discussion in the proper context. "And again, you wanted a lawyer, so I can't talk to you. If you want to talk to us, then . . ."

"Yeah, I need a lawyer for something like this," Donna said.

"Then you need to tell me that."

"This is crazy," Donna said, raising her voice. "Oh, there went my blood pressure! Oh, God!"

Jim Dresback started to open the DNA kit.

"This is the hardest part," he said. "Opening this little box up."

"Yeah, I think I'd better have a lawyer," she said again. "This is crazy."

Dresback nodded. "OK, OK."

Donna looked again at the search warrant. "I can't read this damn thing. I don't have any glasses."

Dresback read it aloud, while Donna kept her eyes fastened to him without saying a word.

"All right," he said, opening the package of swabs. "If you can just hold those and rub them firmly between your cheek and gum."

Donna Perry did as she was instructed. Dresback put the swabs in the box and sealed it.

"Thank you. Now, that is your copy of the search warrant. You can take it with you."

"Am I being accused of murder or something?"

"Yes," Dresback responded without any particular emphasis. "That is the . . . you are the prime suspect in . . ."

"What's this related to?"

"Multiple murders," Detective Burbridge answered, and his partner quickly added, "But several. More than one. I don't really know how many . . ."

"So, when will I know if my DNA matches?"

"Well, I imagine you'll know shortly after I do. It takes a little while to do this. The DNA . . ." Detective Burbridge went on.

"Basically," Donna said, "I'm about ready to crawl out of my tree because I don't understand what's going on."

Burbridge returned to her request for an attorney.

"Again, Donna, we can't talk to you. You've asked for a lawyer. Unless you tell us you want to sit down and talk . . ."

Dresback took over. "And you do understand that the rights of your having an attorney and your right to remain silent—these are your rights. All they do is restrict me. They don't restrict you in any way. You have the right to talk and you have the right to not talk. OK?"

The cops left the room at 9:31 a.m. to let Donna stew for five minutes before returning.

When she spoke this time, her voice was louder, higher, and more emphatic.

"You're accusing me of murder? Of who?"

Dresback wanted to avoid any Miranda issues as he completed the search warrant return. "Um, hold on just a second. Um, I'm sorry. I just can't do two things at once. I'm just writing down . . ."

Donna didn't want to hold on. "So, if my DNA comes back negative, I'm off the hook on this mess?"

"Well, I mean, not entirely," he said. "There are fingerprints involved, too."

"Fingerprints?" she said in surprise again.

"*Your* fingerprints," he emphasized.

"Mine?"

Detective Dresback nodded. "Yes."

"On what?"

"On one of the items belonging to the dead person."

Clearly Donna wasn't getting enough information.

"Does this dead person have a name?"

Detective Dresback was still finishing the search warrant return. "OK, I'm signing here. OK, I'm going to write my name here as seizing officer." He slid the paper in front of Donna. "And if you sign that, it indicates that you have received a copy of this."

She was still suspicious of this entire event. "Am I being formally charged now?"

The detectives answered "no" in unison.

"So, we've got all that stuff we have to sort through," Detective Dresback went on. "And then you add the complication to it that it's more than twenty years old. Are you doing the math in your head right now?"

The cops both chuckled, but not Donna. She was rattled.

And that was a good thing.

"No, my head is completely exploded. I *thought* I was scared," she said. "Now, I'm *really* scared."

As Dresback handed her the search warrant return, she demanded, "Tell me what's going on. I need a lawyer or somebody to explain what actually is going on."

"In 1990, there were three prostitutes murdered in Spokane . . ." Dresback said.

Donna took in that information.

"Three prostitutes murdered in Spokane," she said.

"All within a relatively short period of time. They, uh, just recently, as of, I think it was September of this year, uh, there was . . ."

"More murders and stuff?" Donna guessed.

"There was DNA recovered from one of the prostitutes."

Once again she went right to the main issue. "Was it vaginal or something like that?"

Jim Dresback wondered if that direct question was an admission Douglas Perry had sex with the victims before he killed them.

"No," he said, "that DNA was put into a database called CODIS, which is a state and national database for DNA."

"Uh huh. OK."

"And if you've ever been convicted of a felony in the state, you have to give a DNA sample that then goes into CODIS and that's used to generate hits."

"All that and I've just given you another DNA sample?"

"Well, what I'm doing is, and let me explain. They ran the DNA, a full male profile DNA that was found on the subject."

"OK."

"When they ran it in CODIS, it came back as a match to you. Now, in order for us to make sure that that is your DNA, we needed to come here and get a sample from the person we know to be you to make sure there is not a clerical error or some kind of error in the system that would give a false reading. And then they will take what they know to be your sample of DNA, compare it to a sample that was taken from the dead person and verify that that is your DNA or verify that is not your DNA . . . The fingerprints are on a different . . . are on the belongings of a different person. Um, so that ties you to two, for sure."

"Prostitutes now?" she asked.

"Yeah. So that's what we're investigating. Um, there are obviously . . ."

"So, if the DNA comes back positive, then I'm going to be arrested for murder. Is that it?"

"Well, that's up to the prosecutor, and they look at it and say, 'OK, there's probable cause and we believe that we can prove this beyond a reasonable doubt,' and then they'll file the charge and then you get arrested. And that's, that's how it's supposed to work . . . So, I don't really have that answer for you, because I don't know it yet."

Donna Perry was now a bobblehead. Nodding and shaking her head over and over. "God, I'm paranoid enough. If I go back to my cell,

I'll probably commit suicide . . . I'm already, in my mind, I'm already in the gallows. And I'm just going batshit. I can see it now. I'm in a total panic mode."

"Well, I can see you're upset. And . . ."

"No, but the thing of it is . . ." Her voice shot up in tone and volume. "Murder? Me? Jesus!" She pressed an index finger to each temple to emphasize her shock and surprise.

Neither detective was buying Donna's shock and surprise. Both were convinced she had known exactly why two Spokane cops wanted to talk to her that day.

"We're in a little bit of an awkward spot here because I want very badly to respect your rights, so I don't really . . . I want to answer your questions the best I can."

"I have a million questions," Donna said.

"Well, I have about a thousand," Dresback said. "So, you've got more than me. And like I said before, it's your right if you at any time decide that you want to discuss this, you have the right to do that. But until that happens, I'm not too terribly comfortable asking you anything about it, to clarify things. So that's where we're at. Do you have any other questions for me?"

"What are the names of these people?"

Burbridge said he wasn't comfortable disclosing that.

Dresback agreed.

"Not yet."

Donna shook her head again. "I don't even associate with these people. I have cats. I do need to talk to somebody . . . mental health or somebody. I am really . . . Oh, Lord Jesus!"

"Well, we will certainly pass that information along to the jail people," Dresback said.

"Oh great, now they think I'm a murderer. What next?"

The tone of her voice had begun to register a new level of distress. *Good.*

"If I've done such a horrible deed . . . God, I thought [those] years in a federal lockup for possession of firearms was bad. This is insane!"

Dresback nodded. "Well, it can be a life-altering event, that's for sure. Do you have any other questions . . . I'll tell you if I can answer it. I'll tell you if I can't answer it."

"I can't believe this."

"Well, I'll tell you what we'll do. Why don't you finish your pop, you know, relax here for a little bit. We'll leave you alone for a little bit. Give you a chance to finish this, ah, soda and we'll be back to take you up to your house [her cell]."

"Are you serious? I'm upset. This is insane."

The detectives left her alone at 9:45 a.m. Dresback went down the hall to watch the security camera capturing Donna Perry as she stood and began pacing the small area behind her chair. Dresback considered that a good sign. She was torn between her request for a lawyer and her desire to know what the police knew and what they intended to do.

Donna was back in her seat when Dresback returned at 9:51 a.m. with Detective Keyser, a signal that they were ready to send her back to her cell. Dresback laid his business card on the table in front of her and said, "This is me."

Donna was clearly still in great distress. "If I've done such horrible things," she said, "then I deserve to die. Is that correct?"

Jim Dresback shook his head. "Oh, Donna, I wouldn't say so. No . . ."

Donna upped the ante. "Can I borrow your pistol with one round? I'll settle the whole matter right here."

"I don't think that's . . . no . . ."

"I can't live under this kind of stress . . . I would rather die right now than deal with all this shit."

The detective tried to change the direction and tone of the conversation. "There's a lot better ways to deal with this shit than that."

"I'll save you the problem. Everybody thinks I'm an asshole anyway."

"I don't think you're an asshole."

"Put the pistol here with just one round and then step out," she said. "Then I'll finish it. OK? Please."

"I'd rather you not do that. Seriously, I'd rather you not do that."

"I don't understand." Her voice rising again. "Murder? Are you shitting me? Me? Murder? What date?"

He pointed to the table again and said, "This is my card and . . ."

"I'm scared shitless, mister."

"OK," the detective said slowly. "This is who I am. Take this with you. If you decide you want to talk to me . . ."

Donna finally said the words—the words all the cops want to hear.

"Let's talk. Let's sit down and work this out of my head. Somebody tell me what I did wrong," she said. "Oh, Lord. My God. I can't . . . I just can't believe . . ."

Detective Keyser left and Mark Burbridge stepped back in at 9:53 a.m. as Donna continued her lament. "Oh, my God. My worst nightmare. I can't believe . . ."

"We're here for you," Dresback offered, and Burbridge said, "You can help clear this up for us."

Dresback again: "We're here, sitting down. And maybe the clearing of it up will help you, too."

Donna sought more details. "What date were these murders supposed to be at?"

Dresback wanted to be sure a judge wouldn't later rule that everything Donna Perry would say from this second on was inadmissible in court because the cops violated her Miranda rights. After all, she had repeatedly asked for an attorney during this conversation.

"Before we do that, though, we do have to cover this," he continued. "We still have [to do] this legally, OK? So, what I'm going to do is, I'm going to read you the same rights again. You still have the right . . ."

"I want to know what happened. I don't know."

Dresback went over her rights again.

"With these rights in mind, do you want to answer my questions?"

"I'll try to answer your questions."

Right answer, Dresback thought.

Burbridge spoke up. "Here's the deal I'll make. I'm not going to lie to you and Jim's not going to lie to you, if you don't lie to us. OK? Is that fair?"

Donna nodded.

He pointed to the signature line on the form waiving her Miranda rights. "I need your signature right here where it says, 'Sign.'"

"I just want to know what's going on," she said, signing the form.

CHAPTER NINETEEN

Mark Burbridge looked across the table at Donna Perry and hoped she would stick with her decision to waive her Miranda rights and talk. Fingers crossed. Breath held. And then, quickly, he moved ahead so she wouldn't have time to reconsider.

"So, there are some things that just never go away," the detective began. "I know you've probably experienced that. There are several things. This is something that just keeps hanging out there and hanging out there and hanging out there."

He picked up the collection of photographs of prostitutes that the forensic team had assembled. "I've got some photographs here I'd like to show you that may refresh your memory if that's OK. And the reason why I want to show you these photographs is, I know that in the '90s you dated some prostitutes."

Donna nodded and offered a first step in cooperation and what the cops thought was a significant admission.

"I'm a male human being. I did pick up some prostitutes, yes. But I always let them out and they were alive and well when I let them out."

Dresback thought the way Donna phrased that was odd, and he filed it mentally in case there was a reason to revisit it later.

"And you had a significant other who was a prostitute there for a while. Did you not?"

Donna nodded as she said, "Claire Gallaway."

"Clairann?"

"Clairann Gallaway."

Dresback started handing the photographs to Donna.

"What I'm showing you is a photograph and I've marked it Number One just so I can keep it straight which one I'm showing you. Do you know that person?"

"No."

"And this is Number Two."

Yolanda's mug shot.

"Oh, God, no," she said. "I didn't date Black girls."

The detective let the answer pass without comment and continued to show her photos one at a time. She didn't know Number Three.

"And here is Number Four. I know there's going to be some more Black girls."

"No . . . you can categorize them out. Rule out the Blacks. I didn't date any Black girls."

Donna said she didn't recognize the women in photos Five, Six, or Seven.

"Now, you're thinking back to the early '90s, right?" he asked.

She nodded and offered a surprising acknowledgment. "If I recognized them, my eyes would light up. I don't . . . I've never seen these guys."

"Number Eight?"

"No, no. God, look at me twitch. Jesus, I'm upset."

She didn't recognize Nine, Ten, or Eleven.

"And again, Donna. I'm not necessarily talking about people that you dated. Just people that you recognize from back in the '90s, in that day."

"I only . . . I had Claire Gallaway then and I used to go down and pick her up to get her out of there because I was worried because of the murders that were going on at that time."

"Yeah. Yates was killing people back in those days, wasn't he?" Dresback asked.

"Yeah? I don't know."

He handed over Number Twelve. Donna stopped and studied it. "That's Clairann, isn't it?"

"OK."

"Looks like her," she said slowly before changing her mind. "No, that's not . . . Seriously, is that Clair? I don't know. It looks like she got hit."

"Well, these all tend to be booking photos and they can be kind of, you know, different looking."

"No, that hair is too dark. I don't know."

"Does that look like Clairann?"

"To some degree. But God, it was so long ago."

"And Number Thirteen?"

"She's too young to be a hooker."

Mark Burbridge had a question. "Do you have a prostitute that you favored or that you knew well?"

She answered quickly. "Claire Gallaway. I had a live-in one."

He pushed for a bit more. "Did you ever pick them up on the street? Down on Sprague or anything like that?"

"Most of the time I was up on . . . by the old library, up there on First."

"How many times would you say you dated a prostitute other than Clairann?" Dresback asked.

"Not very many. A couple, two or three times maybe. I didn't have the money. Social Security at that time was only what, just a little over 700 bucks."

"Did you ever take any of these prostitutes home to have sex with them?"

Donna gave a nod.

"Was that normal for you?" Dresback asked as he wondered how anything in this discussion could be considered "normal."

"No. When it got too rough down there, I would pick them up and take some of them home, have sex with them, and then return them."

Detective Dresback dug for more details that would make a stronger connection to the prostitutes on the Stroll.

"See, this is the part where your expertise comes into play in terms of what was the criteria involved when whether or not you . . . had sex right there or took them home."

Donna had her own agenda. She sought to minimize any potential evidence linking her to the murders.

"It wouldn't surprise me if you found fingerprints and stuff on these hookers," she said. "I would have sex with them and release them and go home. That was it."

"OK. And this is a little more personal. I apologize for that. But the sex you had with them, was it kinky?"

"No."

"Rough?"

"No."

"Anybody get hurt?"

"No."

"There wasn't any blood being drawn or anything like that?"

"Huh uh. No way."

"With any of these girls that you dated?"

"No."

"How many times do you think you took girls home to your house?"

"No more than a couple of times a month."

Detective Dresback moved his aim closer to the target. "You like guns, clearly."

Donna hedged a little.

"As I understand the gun issue," she said, "it's backed up in mental illness . . . I'm extremely paranoid." And then she jumped back to the point of this entire interview. "Like I said, if I've done something horrible like this, I deserve to die."

"Well, do you think there's a chance you've done something horrible like this and would not remember it?"

"God, I hope not. That's why I'm scared shitless."

"Well, I know when you were in Omak . . . uh, you . . ."

"I was an avid sportsman, yes."

"And you had a federal firearms license for a while, did you not?"

Donna went off point again, blaming her first federal firearms conviction on the fact that, as Douglas, she owned an old, non-working machine gun from the nose turret of an old B-17 or B-25 bomber airplane.

"I never used it," she said. "I never touched it. But since it was in my possession, I got my ass kicked and lost everything."

Donna stopped talking and tapped a finger on photo Number Twelve.

"That could be Claire Gallaway. It may or may not. It seems like . . . as I remember Clair, she had hair about this color. These other gals, I've never met, no."

And then she offered a statement Jim Dresback knew genuinely came from her heart.

"That's the only person I ever really wanted to have as a girlfriend, was Clairann," she said. "The reason I was down there [on East Sprague Avenue] is I was fishing her out of there while all this other shit was going down and that's how I got stopped [by the police]. I used to have an old Scout. I would go down there and wait and then I would literally manhandle her and put her in the truck and drive off to get her out of there."

Dresback zeroed in on the International Scout, which he thought could fit the description by some witnesses of the vehicle they saw victims getting into. "Well, let me ask you this, since you brought up . . . the Scout. What were you driving back in 1989, 1990, 1991—in that time frame?"

"An International Scout, which I sold."

"To?"

"I can't remember the gal's name. I needed the money to make the rent, for my mortgage payment."

Donna didn't remember driving any other vehicles during that time but agreed she had two motorcycles, which she called motorbikes.

How did Donna get from living for thirty-eight years in rural Omak to living in big-city Spokane? She explained that the federal judge who sentenced her on the firearms charges in 1988 ordered her not to return to her mother's home in Omak. Her probation officer had her move to Spokane for convenience.

Dresback and Burbridge couldn't help but wonder how different so many lives would have been if Douglas had stayed put in little Omak and never discovered East Sprague Avenue or the banks of the Spokane River.

CHAPTER TWENTY

By any measure the Massengale brothers were an odd trio, but they probably knew Douglas *and* Donna Perry better than just about anyone else—and they might have helped her obtain guns illegally and possibly participated in trafficking in guns with her. Jim Dresback thought it was time to see what Perry had to say about her three old friends as she sat forlornly at the end of the conference table facing two skeptical detectives.

"What do you know about the Massengales?" Dresback asked abruptly.

Donna bobbled her head slightly. "The Massengales are more than I understand. There's more to them than just . . . one guy being on disability and another guy working at Huntwood [a cabinet-making company in Spokane]. They live way beyond their means, and I have no idea how they supplement it . . . How did Glen get five brand-new motorcycles in the biggest economic turndown there is? Now he's caught up in credit card debt and that's how I got in trouble this last time."

Donna suggested one of the brothers was schizophrenic and had a friend who kept his guns for him so he wouldn't get in trouble for possessing them. She didn't know the friend's name but said the Massengales called him "Beach." Perry met Bruce Massengale at the Evergreen Club, which she described as a center that helped people with long-term mental illness—"like myself." Her probation officer sent her there, but she was later banned from the club because she wouldn't contribute 10 percent of her income to support it.

Next, Donna shifted into a characterization of her mental illness.

"Psychiatric. In other words, I'll be going down the street and if it happened, where the hell am I at? I probably couldn't tell you. It's all done with instinct. I tried to get into Spokane Community Mental Health five different times and each time they told me to get the hell out or they'd call the police."

Detective Dresback said, "Well, looking back at your history, it looks to me that there were some times when you showed some—I don't know what to call it—anger, aggression, and . . ."

Donna answered with the reason for all of *that*.

"Well, I was raised and beat up as a male human being by my father and older brother."

"How old were you?" the detective asked.

"Between four and seven."

"Did they continue to abuse you in the home there . . . beat you up and rape you? Did they continue to do that . . . the whole time you were living there?"

"Yeah, pretty much . . ."

She went on to say her parents refused to get treatment for her mental illness and dealt with it by leaving her at home whenever they went out.

Alone.

Donna let out a quiet sigh. "I was the kid that didn't exist . . . If you ask them point blank, they will acknowledge it. It's better out of sight, out of mind."

Dresback pushed for details on the things Donna or Doug had done—things that would help build the case against her.

Specifics on the acts of violence that had imbued most of her life.

"I know you got upset at one point with Spokane Mental Health and . . ."

Donna stared into space to answer.

"I wanted to go to Mental Health and avail myself of an educational program and everything else they could help with. They said categorically, no. In fact, the federal judge ordered me to go, and I complied with his orders. Then all of a sudden, here's Mental Health for some reason, they sent a letter to the judge and said, no, they're not going there, and he backed down, the whole thing. I don't know. That's way above my head."

"Well, what were you upset with Mental Health for? I mean . . ."

"Because I wanted to go there, and they said they didn't want me there . . . And I needed to go. When I didn't get to go . . ."

"You threatened to shoot up the place like . . ."

"No, no, no."

"You did make that threat, though. At least they thought you did."

"Well, I probably was using the wrong, what you would call, expressions, at that time. Now, I don't say anything to them. I'm afraid to."

She went on to say she had been mistreated after she mentioned she was suicidal.

"As soon as you mention that word, they strip you buck naked and put you in a yellow suit and sit you in a cell with no, very few clothes on, and you freeze your ass off. So, I can't talk to people. I do . . . they lock me up."

"Did you make a couple of suicide attempts when you were in this jail in the past?"

"Several. Now this has come along."

Dresback shrugged. "Well, what is done is done. I can't make that go away."

He changed the subject and asked about the times she stayed with the Massengales. She denied she ever did. "No, I've always had a place of my own to stay."

"Did you ever buy a house?"

Donna nodded and fidgeted. "I've had several houses and I've lost everything, and now I'm losing my mind."

She said she had lived at 2006 East Empire Avenue for twenty years and was trying to buy it when she was arrested by the ATF in March.

"I've lost that house, too, because of my pettiness. I'm rather disappointed in myself."

Dresback steered the discussion back to the prostitutes. "When you dated these girls . . ."

"I haven't dated any of them. I would have remembered it."

She tapped a finger on the photographs. "These are the girls in question?"

"You're pretty sure you would have remembered dating any of those girls?"

"Yeah, I would have." She looked at a photo again. "This is Claire Gallaway. I'm sure."

Burbridge said, "I want to make sure we're clear. How many total prostitutes do you think you were with over a period of, say, the early '90s from '88 through '92?"

Dresback expanded the time frame to cover more of the murders of prostitutes. "Well, let's go to all, all of the '80s."

"Well, it couldn't have been more than once or twice a month for the simple reason I only got paid every four weeks. Social Security. I've been living on it since '85."

"So, how much would a date normally cost? How much would it cost you?"

"I don't know. This is so stupid."

"When you were living with Clairann, how did you get the girls in the house?"

"Clairann used to be on the street for two or three days at a time. She'd disappear . . . She was having sex for cocaine. She was a cocaine addict."

"What do you think her take would have been if you had brought a girl home and she was there? Would that have upset her or would she be OK?"

"I think it would have upset her. But I was careful enough not to have her in the house at the time when another girl was there."

Dresback sensed Donna was willing to get into the facts of her life with Clairann. "But she was staying with you consistently in the mid '90s? No, in the early '90s actually, because she went to Seattle."

"Yeah, she left in '94. She went back to Seattle."

"I think we have a report from Seattle that Clairann was arrested for prostitution in '91, '91 or '2. I'm not sure when."

"Yeah, I called to see if she was, you know, somebody had killed her or whatever."

"Did you ever go to Seattle to get her out of that scene?"

Donna shook her head no. "Way beyond my means to reach that far. I didn't have the . . . I figured if she wanted to leave, she was free to go."

And then Donna added, "I did cry a lot when she left."

"Did you love her?" Dresback asked.

"Yes, a lot."

"How many personalities does she have?"

"Dozens or more."

"What's her most predominate personality when you were together?"

"Uh, when she had her shit . . . act together, you wouldn't have found a nicer person."

"Was she taking medication for . . ."

"She was supposed to the last time she got out of Eastern State Hospital. I went out to get her and bring her home and, uh, she categorically refused. She was qualified for a disability check. Tried to talk to her and I said, 'Sign up for it. You don't have to be a hooker no more.' And she wouldn't do it."

Donna said Clairann had a serious drug problem that caused friction between them, since she never used drugs.

"I told her categorically, no johns in the house and no drugs . . . She did it anyway."

"It would be a little hypocritical if you insisted she not bring a john and then you bring a prostitute."

"Well, I was a hypocrite. Most men are hypocrites."

"Well, I hear that. That's true enough."

Dresback wanted to nail down this apparent link between Clairann's arrests and the timing of the murders.

"But, OK, so, as I understand it, you would, you would, uh, if you brought a prostitute home, it would have been during a time when Clairann, you believed, she wasn't going to be there for whatever reason."

"Exactly."

Donna said she had not had any contact with Clairann since she left her the last time.

"Is she dead? Is Clairann dead?" she asked abruptly.

"No."

"She's still alive?"

"Yes."

"Where's she at?"

"Malibu, California."

"Did she finally get married or what? Is she still a hooker?"

"She is still a hooker."

Donna again brought the conversation back to her expression of shock and disappointment at being accused of murder. "I'm going to be in prison the rest of my life. Like I said, lend me your pistol and we'll get this over with."

"I don't like to hear it," Dresback said of the suicide threats. "I don't like to hear you say that . . . As long as you're alive, there's a hope."

"Yeah. Once you're in jail, there's no hope."

"Well, you're . . . the Irish have a saying. Long time dead, a long time."

"Well, I have a saying that goes, 'As long as you're alive, you can feel the pain.' You'd do anything to take it away."

"Life is pain, right?"

"Exactly. The pains just keep coming."

"Life is pain for a lot of people."

Burbridge broke back into the conversation. "How come you and Clairann broke up?"

"She was wanting to hit the streets and I said no. I didn't want her to do that. I didn't want to share her with anybody."

Dresback wondered if that level of attachment to Clairann had anything to do with the murders. "And you've never been married?"

Donna shook her head.

"Would you have married her?" the detective asked.

"Yeah, I asked her several times."

"Oh. So, if she had given up prostitution?"

"Hey, if she'd taken her meds and we could travel a lot . . . out into the sunset. I'd have gotten a bigger house. At that time my credit was available. I'd have brought her kids over and we'd all have been one big, ugly family. But she didn't want to do that."

Donna shook her head. "And she's still turning tricks. Ahh, that dumb bitch. It's amazing to me that she hasn't gotten AIDS or something by now."

"Well, I don't know any more about her than that."

"Well, I've known her for thirty years."

"I don't know if all eight of her kids are still alive, but I do know she has children living up here in Washington because the person in the center where she's staying said they want her to come up here and she won't."

Donna shook her head. "She hates Washington because I'm still up here and as soon as she showed up, I'd go get her."

"Is she blaming you for her situation?"

"No, she never blamed anybody. She just had a fascination. She was self-medicating on cocaine to treat her mental illness. I told her, I said, 'It's never going to work.' That's one of the reasons I don't mess with street drugs."

Donna studied the photo again. "That's Clairann Gallaway now that I sit there and look at her. That's her. She looks like she got fat after that."

"Well, now that you've had a chance to look at them again, are there any other girls that you know?"

"Just that. That's Clairann Gallaway and the rest of these, I haven't a clue who they are."

Burbridge tried to help move the discussion away from the suggestion of a visit to Washington State's execution chamber.

"Donna, let's talk about the Dalton house, if we could a bit," he said.

"Dalton house?"

"Think about it. You bought it, lived there for two or three years . . . Can you describe the inside?"

"No, I can't."

"OK. Did you ever take prostitutes there?"

"Not that I know of."

"It's during the time you moved in with Clairann. You said you took them home occasionally. Why wouldn't you take them home during that time?"

"I don't know. I have no idea. Clairann was actually . . ."

"Well, I'm gonna go up to that house sometime in the next few days and take a search warrant up there, looking for evidence . . ."

"It's not my house," Donna said as if to reject any interest in Burbridge's plans.

"You lived there for what . . . while this was going on."

"I lived there for a few . . ." Donna suddenly turned her thoughts back to Clairann. "God, she did get killed, didn't she?"

The cops ignored that and Burbridge pushed ahead. "Let's talk about the house for a while . . . There is evidence that shows you were with these girls and DNA wasn't really known back then and it wasn't used really by law enforcement too deeply. There were some items left with one of these girls that came out, out of the killer's house, and we're testing that now. I think that's going to lead to you, too. And belongings from the prostitutes . . ."

Donna seized on Burbridge's conclusion about her house on Dalton Avenue.

"Killer's house? What would be . . . what date of the murders are you guys investigating now?"

"Well, we're talking about 1990."

"The early '90s?"

"The actual year of 1990, which is during the time you were on probation from the '88 charge, and you were living in Spokane . . . You were driving that International Scout. We're trying to help you get back into that point where you recall . . ."

"The only thing I remember from those days was Clairann. I'd say I can't really recollect to what was happening. Hell, I can't even tell you what I had for dinner yesterday. I can't . . ."

Dresback tried to relate, a not-so-easy task. "Well, I can't tell you what I had for dinner yesterday, either, but that's not . . ."

"We're talking about killing somebody twenty-two years ago," Burbridge said to put the question into a stark context. "I can tell you about the first buck I killed when I was twelve."

"I can't," Donna said, and she took the chance to redirect the discussion. "I only poached deer in the wintertime when we were broke."

Dresback tried to get the conversation back on point. "So, in 1990 you were living at West 18th—8th. Do you remember where else you lived?"

"Huh uh. I can't."

"Now, when you say you can't, is it . . . is it that you can't remember, or you don't want to?"

"Well, I can't remember. The thing of it is, I lived in West 18th—8th and then I went to jail." Donna changed the subject again. "Why would the Massengales say I lived with them?"

Dresback quoted the Massengales as saying Donna was supposed to stay with them for a few days after she got out of prison but stayed for three months. He said he wasn't sure of the dates. "It's a little more difficult for me because I didn't live this like you did," he said.

"It's getting tough for me to bring back old memories," Donna explained. And then she moved the discussion into new territory. "See, what happened was, when I did the gender change, my brain completely is rewired for something else. I take estrogen every day and I got . . . You talk about masculine things like guns and stuff . . . there's terrible gaps in there. And why in the hell did I go out and was shootin' goddamn guns? Scared, I guess."

"Well, you . . . you had dozens of guns and thousands of rounds of ammo almost every time ATF arrested you. I know that and . . ."

"Yes, and it's part of the mental illness because they told me I'm paranoid. They said I'm paranoid and I don't know any better and I don't grab a whole bunch of stuff and sit in the house . . . I've done it three times and it's ridiculous. Three times. It's not a love affair with guns. Let me clue you. It's something much deeper than that. I'm afraid somebody's gonna hurt the gals down there and I got old enough . . . now I'd just like to end the whole thing."

"Well, are you afraid in the jail?"

Donna nodded as she said, "Worse."

"Who do you think is gonna hurt you in the jail?"

"Anybody. Everybody."

"The jailers? And anybody say anything to you that would make you think that?"

She shook her head. "It's my fault. I'm a coward. I know this."

"I don't know. I'm not a psychiatrist. I'm not a psychologist. I can't help you that much in terms of, you know, what you're going through . . . what you've been through, what your life has been like. But I know sometimes that, that, many, many . . ."

"My father put the fear in me about him and a fear that was deep enough. And I have a police experience that hasn't made me—how would you say it?—compliant? . . . It's all added to those fears. I'd just like it to stop."

"So, you want it to stop?" Dresback saw the opening to move the discussion in the right direction.

"Well, I don't know how to make it stop."

"I do."

"How?"

"The truth."

Donna knew where Dresback was going, and it was time for her to put an end to this whole thing.

"I didn't kill those girls."

"No?"

"What do you mean, no?" Donna demanded.

"You remember what happened. I can tell you remember what happened." Dresback handed Donna the photos of Nickie Lowe, Kathy Brisbois, and Clairann Gallaway.

"Those are the two girls, right? This is Claire Gallaway. I . . . I slept with her. These two I've never slept with . . . nothing to do with them. How they got DNA on them or hair fibers, fingerprints, whatever . . ."

Burbridge stepped in. "Your belongings were with them."

"My belong . . ." Donna's tone turned indignant. "What kind of belongings, sir?"

Burbridge shook his head. "I'm not going to tell you that, but your DNA's gonna be on those belongings. There's no doubt in my mind."

Donna's tougher tone continued. "Well, I guess my life is pretty well over. You've already reached your conclusion."

"Well, the conclusion may be there, but the why is important to me. Is that important to you?"

"No."

"The why is very important. It'll make determinations for, like, what the prosecutors do, what judges do, and people who want to help you do."

Donna moved again to the extreme. "If you have that kind of evidence and you feel that I've hurt somebody, then I can say this: Give me your pistol."

Dresback hoped to get Donna away from the suicide threats. "Well, the problem . . . Yeah, the problem is, that wouldn't work for us. You know, if you're convinced it would work for you, I have no say about that. But I know it wouldn't work for me."

"I don't want to spend the rest of my life . . ."

"I don't want to spend the rest of my life with the memory of you doing that to yourself, OK?" Dresback hoped he sounded as sincere as he felt.

"Well, if you have proof that I've murdered somebody . . ."

"I don't have . . ."

"And I can't remember it . . ."

"Here's the deal, though. I don't understand how your DNA and your fingerprints . . ."

"Somebody set me up again."

"Again?"

"Well, the Massengales . . . The Massengales bought the guns and ammunition and gave them to me. I was not allowed to bring out that as a witness in my own defense of this last charge . . . The lawyer I have said he knows because, hell, they can't run the serial numbers on those guns. I know who bought them, but for some reason everybody wants me in jail . . . The only thing I can think of is somebody wants me out of that house."

"I think what we need to focus on in here is what you can do for you. OK, now you have tried a lot of different things."

"Oh, yeah?"

"I mean, in a lot of respects, you've lived a troubled life. I don't pretend to know . . ."

"That's a cliché in this day and age."

"Yeah, but true nonetheless and I don't."

"Well, my mother used to say, 'Gee, Douglas, you've lived a hard life. Feel sorry for me now. Get your ass out and go to work for me.'"

"That didn't seem to work out, did it?"

"Well, I went and got to work. Didn't get anything out of it because the orchard was cut down and the property sold. I got $20,000 and a lifetime worth of work, and that was the end of it."

"There were things in our discussion here . . . there are some things that we have talked about that you acknowledge . . ."

"We have two possibilities," she said. She nodded toward Burbridge. "The gentleman over there wants me dead. I can feel that already. Why don't we just get it over with?"

Burbridge shook his head. 'I don't want you dead."

Dresback echoed, "He doesn't want you dead."

She seemed to be reaching a new low point. "I want me dead. If I . . . if I've actually done something horrible like this . . ."

Dresback hoped to salvage the conversation. "Let's try something different."

"What?"

"Let's try facing up to what you know."

Donna was steadfast as she gestured toward the photographs of Nickie and Kathy. "I don't remember these two females . . . I remember this one because I used to sleep in the same bed with her."

Dresback tried again to redirect her. "Now, listen. Let's try a little bit of a different approach."

Donna didn't wait before casting doubt on Burbridge's claim of evidence from her belongings. "Now, I screwed several girls then . . . But clothing . . . from a prostitute . . . I don't think so. No."

"I didn't say clothes," Burbridge corrected.

"Or anything like that. Clothing. Any personal items. No. Huh uh."

Dresback said, "Let's look at what did happen."

"What did happen?"

"Yes, that's the question."

"Uh huh," she said as if to dismiss the suggestion.

"Until you face what did happen, it's gonna be a rerun of the same thing over and over and over again, whether your life . . ."

"When I had sex with the girls . . ." she interrupted.

"Ends tomorrow or twenty years from now."

"I had sex with them. I turned them loose. They were fine the night . . . the night they left."

Dresback decided it was time to challenge Donna's story. "And Donna," he said firmly, "that's not working for you."

"But that's what happened."

"That is what you're saying, Donna, and that is not working for you."

"No, the reason I want to die is because, if I've done all kinds of horrible things, then I should be punished for it."

"What I don't know, and as Mark would say . . ."

"Well, you got the DNA and stuff. I would imagine the prosecutor is gonna jump down my throat and say that I'm an asshole one more time. So, now they're gonna fight back and, if I'm lucky, I'll go to a mental hospital. If not, I'll wind up on death row."

"Really? Are you a victim?"

"No, I don't know what a victim is."

"Are you a victim or did you make a victim? That's the question here."

"Am I a victim of what? . . . What are you getting at? How would I be a victim?"

"Because you're saying the prosecutor is going to do this and do that one more time."

"Well, they will. They will."

"I don't know what they're gonna do. That's down the road and, as it goes in life, you deal with things as they come up. This is time to deal with this, because it isn't going away."

Donna's denial was just as strong as before. "I didn't kill those women." But then she made a potentially important concession that could put her close to the victims. "I may have slept with them."

Encouraged by that much of a confession, Burbridge pressed her again. "Here's the real thing. The question for me is, people that kill people, multiple people over periods of time, they generally keep going once it starts. So, the question for me as a law enforcement officer who's studied this in depth . . ."

"Uh huh."

"What made Donna stop? So, then I asked myself . . ."

"Douglas didn't stop. Donna stopped it. The gender change operation."

Dresback thought Donna Perry had just walked right up to the edge of a confession. Did she intend to say that Douglas couldn't stop the killings, but Donna did? Dresback thought that was closer to being a confession without being a confession than anything he had ever heard from a suspect.

Burbridge had the same thought, and he pushed for more. "Do you think that's what stopped it?"

"I have . . . yeah . . . I'm convinced of it."

Dresback stepped in. "I hadn't thought about that. That's a good question."

Burbridge added, "Well, here's . . . here's another one. I'm wondering, too, is, where is he?"

"There's no more testosterone to fuel the anger," Donna said.

Burbridge sensed an opening. "Well, so, do you think that changing from Douglas to Donna stopped your anger and . . ."

Donna Perry had tiptoed to the edge again, but then she stepped back. "I'm paranoid as hell and as emotional as hell, but I won't hurt anybody. Now, I did . . . like you said . . ."

"There's something that changed in your life at that time," Burbridge suggested.

"Make goofy statements and shit like that. I don't do that anymore . . . I'm on estrogen and stuff. I'm a harmless, quiet woman."

"Tell us about Douglas's anger."

"I can't relate to Douglas anymore because I'm a woman. You want me to take my pants off and show you? I'm not a guy anymore."

Neither cop wanted that. Burbridge said firmly, "I believe you."

Dresback's reaction was a little more colorful. He immediately recalled the line by Tommy Lee Jones in the movie *Men in Black* when Jones lamented being swallowed by a giant space roach—as one of countless things he'd rather forget. Dresback was perfectly satisfied to take Donna's word for the extent of the surgery.

"I had the full surgery," Donna continued.

"And I'm . . . I respect that," Burbridge said. "I'm calling you Donna and Ms. Perry."

Donna nodded. "I appreciate that greatly. Thank you."

"And I respect that. But here's . . . here's what else changed in your life . . ."

Donna pointed to one of the photographs. "This is what changed."

"You came to Clairann?"

"Maybe I came to Jesus. Did you ever think of that?"

"Absolutely. That could have happened. Clairann was in your life. A lot of frustrations. From her choices with the prostitution . . . She leaves your life and the killing stops."

Donna realized where Burbridge was going. "Killing stops? In other words, you're saying I killed them."

Burbridge nodded. "I've said that all along."

"You sure I did it?"

"Yeah, no question. The question is why and that's what's important to people that can help you make a difference."

Donna wasn't biting. "I'm not going to admit I killed anybody. I didn't. Donna has killed nobody."

Burbridge tried to get behind Donna's meaning again. "Douglas did?"

"I don't know if Douglas did or not. It's twenty years ago and I have no idea whether he did or didn't."

Donna had pulled back from the brink of a confession about Douglas and was moving on. "I do know this much. People have slaughtered my cats. They stood right there with a club, held the cat up and crushed its hindquarters and then turned around and said, 'Now, what are you going to do about that,' and turned around and left me with a dying cat in my hands."

"If Donna has seen how to be . . ."

"Of what? How to be how?"

"How to act, how to listen . . . How to not let your temper get the best of you."

"There is no temper."

"Donna has seen that. My question is, how does Donna . . . how does Donna reconcile what Douglas did?"

"Douglas had walked away from it," she said.

"Can he do that? I mean, that's fine until today and I know you're comfortable. I know you're comfortable. You are completely comfortable with what the ATF has done and your ability to deal with that and go on with your life. I know that and I know that's why you want to keep going back and talking about . . ."

"I would still like to have the trust and the honor of carrying a handgun or a rifle . . . But I'll never have it back."

"Well, maybe not, maybe not."

"It's a very great disappointment."

"But you can deal with what ATF has done. That's your comfort zone. That's where you are, actually."

"No, I just shut up and don't want to say anything, the wilder and stupider it gets. I did not kill those two people. I don't know why . . ."

Burbridge took another run at pinning the murders on Donna's former identity. "Douglas did."

"What?"

"Douglas did."

Donna didn't bite. "No, Douglas didn't do it. As far as I know, Douglas didn't kill these people.' She gestured toward the photographs. "The rest of these people . . . this is the only woman I recognize, right here. She looked like she got the shit pounded out of her."

Dresback forced Donna to confront the damning evidence again. "How do you explain then the DNA and the fingerprints?"

Donna made even more of a concession. "Well, maybe I slept with them a time or two. I have no idea." She had finally offered the possibility that she had direct contact with Nickie and Kathy. "Girls they say, well, Clairann used to have a half a dozen [sexual partners or contacts] in one night down there on Sprague to pay for her cocaine. That's my guess. Now, I'm not an expert. You guys are the experts. Explain it."

Dresback tried to push Donna to confront the murders. "I'd like you to try and look back and see what really has happened that's not gonna go away. That is . . . that you're dragging around with you . . . like an anvil everywhere you go that you have taken some real positive steps in trying to change . . . but it's not really gonna go away."

"It is away, because how can I confess to something when I didn't do it?"

Dresback decided to press Donna harder.

"I'm sitting right here. It's right here between us. It's here now. It'll be there when you get back up in your jail cell. It'll be between you and the guard when you talk to them. It'll be between you and whoever you converse with. It's gonna be here. It won't go away, and I appreciate that you've taken all these steps to try and make this go away. What I'm asking you to do is to, is to—and you're gonna have to dig deep here to deal with it—to face it."

"I'd like to know what you want."

"It's here, in front of you right now."

"Called a what?"

"It's here in front of you now."

"No, it isn't. What?"

"The truth."

"These two people . . . I have no . . . no . . ."

"These two girls, not being alive anymore and what happened to their family and what their family is living with because of that . . . You loved Clairann. If somebody that dated her had killed her, that would have broken your heart. There are people . . ."

"I wondered if she would get killed if she stayed down there."

"There are people, as we speak today, there are people who are living that very nightmare, and you can . . ."

"I wish I could help you."

"If you can't do anything for yourself, you can do something for the people that loved these girls. You can do that. Nobody else can do that."

"I can't help them. I'm sorry."

Burbridge leaned in. "I've interviewed literally hundreds of people like you that sit here and deny and deny and deny. And eventually, in the end, the vast majority of them come around and tell the truth. And you know it."

"And marching to the gallows and they die."

"No, no. I've never had a death penalty case in my life. In the end, do you know what they do? When, after they tell the truth about what happened?"

"Uh huh."

"They go, 'Wow, I feel so much better.' And a week later, they call me and ask me to come back and talk to them. I sit down with them and they go, 'You know, I'm sleeping at night . . .'"

"I'm sleeping at night, too.'

"'I feel so much better. I'm just starting to feel whole again.' They carried this huge, horrible secret with them. I think you tried to get control of what Douglas was doing . . ."

"I think so, but it wasn't for that reason."

"I don't know what happened with these . . . with these girls," Dresback said. "I don't know if it was . . . I'm not saying that you went out there looking to hurt anybody. It was just another day. But somehow things turned sideways, and I would like to know, and their families would like to know, what happened here. Things got out of hand, you know. I'm not making any judgments on you and I'm not painting you as an evil person. But things definitely got out of hand and these families have to live with this. And you're the one that can give something back to them that's worth living for."

Burbridge tried to suggest a scenario that would let Donna claim something other than premeditated murder. "You know, if they attacked you and tried to rob you . . . that happens. Hookers do that."

"Like I said, you asked me to remember what happened twenty years ago. I don't know . . ."

Dresback tried to put the guilt in Donna's hands again. "Donna, you know what happened. You don't forget this kind of thing."

"Yes, I can."

"Douglas doesn't forget this kind of thing."

"Douglas doesn't exist anymore."

"Douglas knows."

"I left him in Bangkok."

"And he knows exactly what happened. He's still a part of you."

That struck at the core of Donna Perry's transformation to a woman. To Donna, it wasn't just a matter of anatomical alteration. And she wasn't going to let Dresback limit her profound conversion from Douglas to Donna.

"No, that's where you're wrong," Donna said. "He's not here anymore, and I try to make a life as Donna Perry. Changed my name, changed my gender. I live a clean, productive life, and here I am in jail again. I'm the stupid ass. Donna even . . . I've missed one thing. I got rid of the violence with the sex-change operation. The only thing is the emotional response is ten times more . . . what would you call it?"

"You got rid . . ."

"Powerful?"

"You got rid of what Douglas did?"

"For twenty years."

"Yes, yes. You didn't . . ."

"And now I get hauled up in front of this again for something I didn't do."

Dresback wouldn't let Donna off the hook that Douglas had set. "You didn't get rid of what Douglas did before the sex change—and that remains."

"No, it's not."

"Maybe nothing else of him remains, but that does."

"And you're going to punish Donna for it? Is that it?"

Burbridge thought Donna had just revealed the reason for the sex change. She hoped to avoid responsibility—and punishment—for the murders Douglas committed by becoming Donna. He wanted her to know that wouldn't work. "Yes, the body is accountable for its actions."

And Dresback agreed. "Yes, that is it. That's the truth."

Donna asked, "Why does it mean the same thing?"

"And that's the truth," Dresback said again.

"Well then, I'll do the rest of my life behind bars again."

"And you know that it's right."

Donna's experience couldn't let that pass. "No, you don't torture somebody by leaving them in a concrete room freezing their ass off where that's not enough heat."

Burbridge renewed his warning. "I'm not kidding you, Donna. I've got a warrant for the house on Dalton. I'm going there. I think you killed at least one or two of these girls in there and I think I'm gonna find bullets and their blood underneath that carpet and hardwood flooring and subflooring. There's no doubt in my mind, when I peel that house apart, I'm gonna find out, because I'm very, very thorough. I don't miss nothing."

"OK. I didn't have any guns. At that time, I wasn't allowed to have one."

"You had guns your whole life."

"I know I've had guns my whole life, until I got to Spokane, and they were all taken away."

Dresback offered to accept part of Donna's story about the guns. "OK. It's the Massengales then. I get that."

Burbridge hoped to catch Donna in the mistake of knowing too much. "I never said these girls were shot. What would make . . . make you think these girls were shot?"

"I guess . . ."

"They could have been stabbed, strangled . . ."

"No, it could be strangled."

"You clearly said . . ."

"No, I didn't."

Dresback pushed the need to give the victims' families closure, but Donna wasn't accepting the cop's premise. "I don't know these women. I don't know their families. I don't see how I could have empathy with them unless I actually knew them. I don't."

"You can't relate to somebody you don't know?"

"That's it."

"And as long as you don't know them, whatever you do to them is all right?"

"No, I didn't say that. I said I don't know their families and I don't know these people."

"Donna, how do you . . . how do you reconcile . . . How do you come to grips with what you actually did? Whether you know it or not?"

"Did I? Did what?"

Burbridge couldn't let her plead ignorance. "You know."

"I didn't kill anybody . . . I didn't kill these two women."

Burbridge again: "Douglas did, absolutely killed them."

"No, Douglas . . . I don't know if Douglas did or didn't."

Dresback thought that was at least a small crack in her wall of denial.

Burbridge remained tough. "There is absolutely no question that Douglas did it and that you, Donna, know what happened."

"No. I will say this, in my own defense. I'd rather go live in a mental hospital, be under a doctor's care. Now, can you help me with that, guys?"

Dresback pointed to the photographs of Nickie and Kathy. "I don't know. Maybe they'd like to do that, too, but they can't. Maybe she'd like to live in a mental hospital. Maybe she'd like to have kids. I don't know. But they can't. And that's Douglas's responsibility. And it's a responsibility that you inherited."

Donna didn't accept Dresback's assignment of inherited guilt. "I have no idea what you are talking about. I inherited what?"

Burbridge thought Donna looked shaky. "You doing all right?"

"What time is it? I've got to take my medications."

"Do you have your medications with you?"

Donna preferred to pursue the conversation. "No, no, no. The thing of it is, if this is the case, now, if you feel that I've done this and I trust your judgment, then I should have a bullet through the head and let's end it. What do you say, guys?"

Burbridge didn't take the bait. "I say the family deserves to know the truth and I think . . ."

"I told you the truth."

"I think that Douglas . . ."

"I'm looking you right in the eye and I told you the truth. I didn't kill these bitches, period."

Burbridge was surprised at Donna's characterization of the victims. "Why are they bitches? Did they do something to you?"

"It's a term. Whores. They call me a bitch and I'm proud when they do that."

Burbridge pointed at one of the photographs. "So . . . let's say that maybe she's not a drug addict. Maybe she's got kids. Maybe she's struggling for rent. Maybe she's just a woman that's so down on her luck that's her only choice. Does that make her a horrible person?"

"I have no idea. I didn't know her."

"Does she deserve to die?"

"We're all gonna die sooner or later. I'd rather do it sooner than later."

Burbridge pointed to the photo again. "We're talking about her."

"I have no idea what she . . . what she wants."

"Douglas was saying it was time for her to die and I want to know why," Burbridge demanded. "Was Douglas so angry for a reason?"

"But I don't think Douglas killed anybody. I doubt it. Not those two because I don't recognize them."

Was that another backdoor confession? If Donna had recognized the women in the photographs, would that mean Douglas might have killed them?

Donna kept talking and was advancing another goofy conspiracy theory about why she could be facing murder charges. "I do know that the people trying to get me out of that house and now they figure out the federal judge is gonna kick me loose and I'm gonna go back to the house. Now they think they got me on a murder charge that all of a sudden just pops up out of nowhere. It's weird. It's totally weird."

Burbridge ignored that idea and tried to connect Donna directly to the murders again. "I think you've been dreading this day for twenty years."

"No, I haven't dreaded any day." She looked into Burbridge's eyes. "You seem like a decent sort. I'd be glad to have you as a neighbor."

Burbridge ignored the odd comment. "No, I meant you were dreading the day that the police were gonna come knocking on your door and talk to you about these dead girls."

"Well, right now, I wish to die. Can you help me out with that?" She fell back on her mental illness. "God, I'm so paranoid now. That's the way it is."

Burbridge tried to play to her excuse of mental illness. "You say you want help to go to a mental institution? The truth will get you there, to how this all happened. How . . . how . . ."

"No, they'll have it back in the newspaper . . . 'Donna's a monster again' and away we go. One of my mother's favorite sayings was, 'You're a monster. I should have dropped you on your head when you were a baby.' So, that's what I grew up with."

"So, the mental institution you want to go to, they're gonna want to know the truth and the only way you're gonna get there is the truth about how Donna tried to get ahold of Douglas by turning, becoming the woman she felt she was inside and maybe that's the anger that Douglas felt."

"No, no . . ."

"To try and get that out?"

"Because the timing of it was, I found out psychotropic drugs would basically limit my abilities and stuff on the motorcycles and the car. That's grounds for the state of Washington to take your driver's license away. I chose the sex-change operation as a permanent way to control any violence. God, with that record [Douglas's record], when one goes from male to female, there's a marked and very great downturn in violence towards people. Part of the violence in Douglas's life was the fact that Douglas was acting like a woman and getting called on the carpet for it. Now that I act like a woman, it all fits together. That was the basic premise of the sex-change operation. It had nothing to do with violence. It had something to do with me. What's going on up here [*pointed to her head*] matches what's going on down there [*pointed to her lap*]. It's called brain sex. When I was [living as a man], his penis and testicles were female-like instead of masculine-like."

Donna was really getting to the basis for the sex change as Burbridge said softly, "OK."

"And that's why I switched it. And the violence tendencies, whatever Douglas had from God knows what, and I'm not an expert at it . . . that was little . . ."

"What kind of violent stuff did Douglas do?"

"Hitting people, cussing, violence, stuff like that."

"Did he get in fights?"

"No, just with the family. Also, when I became a woman, people left me pretty much by myself. I'm an ugly old woman, sixty years old. Nobody's gonna bother me. Doubt it. No, no. So, I really like . . . and I like being a woman because I am domestic. I like to stay by myself. I like to raise cats and things. I like to watch TV and I'm a political junkie. I like to watch the elections and things like that and you're not supposed to do that. My father had a different image of what I should have been and I couldn't be what he wanted. So, what did he do? He beat the crap out of me and said, quote, 'I'm gonna make a man out of you.' Instead, he pushed me further into being a woman. If he were alive today, he'd probably reach over the table and break my neck for being a woman. And now, I'm supposing this . . .

"I had two sets of genitalia at one time because there was scar tissue between the scrotum and the anus about yea big around," she said, demonstrating by making a circle with her fingers on both hands, "where the vagina should have been at. Somebody removed it. But when I had the surgery in Bangkok, the world-class surgeon damn near had me bleed to death on the operating table because certain arteries had been moved where they shouldn't have been at and he took his laser to make me into a woman and cut them in two and I damn near bled to death in Bangkok. So, yeah, I learned a lot of screwy things."

Donna launched into her argument about being a disappointment to her parents, especially her father, because she was born a "morpho-dite" child when he wanted a son. "So, he decided to make me Number Two son and guess what? It didn't work out. That was the basis of the anger . . . So, eventually, I got up enough courage to realize I had taken all the psychotropic drugs and whatnot, and I went and, uh, that [the sex change] was the only thing that was left. And it worked. It stopped the violence cold."

Dresback wanted to get down to the basics with Donna about the murders. "Donna, what do you think . . ."

Donna cut him off. She wasn't done.

"Please," she said, "it [the sex change] stopped the acting out. It stopped me walking up and threatening to punch somebody in the face . . ."

"Donna, what do you think should happen to the person who would do this . . . who killed those people?"

She didn't hesitate. "Death. I said so. Death."

"And you're correlating that with you wanting to kill yourself?"

"No, I'm correlating with the embarrassment and all of a sudden, I'm being charged with first-degree murder."

"And who do you think . . . who is it that you're worried about that you're gonna be embarrassed to?"

"Myself. My own self-respect. I . . . If you have proof that I actually did this—I have no recollection of it. If I actually did this, then I think I should have a bullet to my head. It's the humane thing. Bang and it's over with, and we'll test the religious theories that I've been studying all my life."

"Like what?"

"I'll have a chat with God, and we'll see where I'm going after that. OK?"

Burbridge tried to help her with the concept of guilt and responsibility. "But Donna, you are not mentally . . ."

"I can't help you with that "

"You can by telling the truth."

Dresback said, "Whether you know them or not, you can help them. You can help you . . ."

"I have asked for help from strangers and basically, they told me no."

"Well, here I am," Dresback said to offer his help if she told the truth.

Donna shrugged. "It's too late."

"We [had not] met until today."

"It's too late now."

"For them?"

"They're gone."

"But not for you."

"They're out of it. I'd like to be gone myself. I'm losing the house and during the three . . . three different times getting arrested for guns . . . You're right. The guy in Carswell said you just don't get it through your head. No, I'm scared shitless from one day to the next and you just scared the shit out of me one more time. OK?"

"This is serious," Burbridge said.

"It's very serious—and I can't help you, sir."

"It's not gonna go away."

"I know."

Dresback pushed once more. "You're not ready to tell the truth yet?"

"I told you exactly. I do not know these women."

"I know what you said."

Burbridge weighed in again. "I believe you don't know them."

"And I probably had sex with them, but I did not kill them." Another important concession from Donna that put her and the victims together.

Dresback said, "Well, what's interesting is the DNA is not in the location that would be expected to be found from somebody having sex."

Donna didn't know what to think about that. "I . . . I . . . You're talking Greek to me."

"I know. I know I am. I get that and that doesn't matter, because what matters here is that you know what Douglas did . . . You know what he did."

"If I had contact with these people, it was probably with a date." Another concession.

"You not only know what you did . . . and you've gone to great extents to hide it."

"I have no recollection of killing these people. None. I don't even know them. And how they . . . you could get DNA or my clothes or my fingerprints on these people—I haven't a fucking clue. I don't recognize these people at all."

"And if you keep saying that, do you think it'll be true?" Dresback asked to challenge her again.

"No, I'm telling you the truth. I did not hurt these women. I dated a lot of girls out there. When I had Clairann, eventually when Clairann would come home, that would be the end of the dating, period."

"And when you do die, because everybody does, and you do see God and you do have a conversation with him to see where you're going next, what is that going to sound like? Because he's not me."

"True."

"He's way smarter than me."

"I'll bet."

Dresback tried to extend the conversation about a reckoning with God. "He already knows what Douglas did. He knows what Donna did. He knows what your dad did . . . He knows what Clairann did. He knows what everybody in the family did. He knows exactly the life you've had. He knows exactly your motivations. He knows what Douglas did in this situation and he knows that you didn't confess to the fact, and you didn't own up to it. He knows that. How do you have a conversation with that? That's what's coming and that's what's dragging you around. That's not the way it's supposed to be in the human experience. And if we're . . ."

"Well, if I've had any experience in these conversations, I could . . . like, you know what my mother did once upon a time ago. She slapped my face and made me confess to stealing a bottle of pop and then like two hours after I sat there and cried and I hid on the steps of the basement, she came by later and said, 'Well, your brother finally confessed that he took it.' Now, how do you think I . . . We're going right back to this again. I'm being accused of something."

"We're going back to this again, but this is not that," Dresback argued.

"Well, I'm trying to use the example," she said.

"That's a way different example," Burbridge explained. "There's actual evidence you're involved."

"I can't confess to something I didn't do."

"I wouldn't want you to—and you can deal with this right now," Dresback said.

"And like I said . . . If you have the evidence, you've already convicted me. Put a bullet through my head now. I'm expecting it."

"Who can you *not* fool about this?"

"Me, myself, and I."

"Me, yourself, and God, you can't fool. You can fool me. Oh, you might be able to fool the court. You might be able to fool a jury. You might be able to fool your lawyers. But you can't fool you and you can't fool God . . . with that, and you, those carrying this around."

"What kind of life does Mr. Yates have?" Donna asked in a sudden reference to the imprisoned serial killer.

"I have no idea," Dresback said in surprise.

"Pretty horrible, isn't it? There's worse things than death."

"But I do know that that life he was gonna have very well may have been made much better, easier, because of what he was willing to own up to."

"Did he actually confess to the murders then?"

Dresback and Burbridge said yes in unison.

"Really?" Donna seemed surprised.

Dresback said a person's quality of life is something beyond the location where it is lived or even the people it is lived with. He told Donna she would have to continue dragging an "anvil" of guilt around if she didn't do what was necessary to cut it loose.

"I have no anvil I drag around."

"That's it right there," he said as he pointed to the photographs on the table. "You're looking at them."

"You say that it's . . ."

"That's the anvil."

"But I'm not . . . no. Huh uh."

Burbridge tried to cut through the BS. "You know when we first came in here today and Jim started talking to you about why we were here and wanted to read you your rights?"

"Uh huh."

"I was watching you and you started hyperventilating and I could see your heart pounding out of your chest."

"Uuuhh . . ."

"Let me finish. There is no doubt you've been dreading this day for twenty-two years. It's been a nightmare for you and trying to plan what to do and how are you gonna react. Wow . . ."

Donna gestured toward the jail escort deputies outside the closed door. "Yeah, she's got a gun. He's got a gun. It scared the shit out of me."

Burbridge responded, "I don't have a gun on."

"He does," Donna said as she pointed to Dresback. "That can scare anybody."

Burbridge nodded. "It's . . . It's big."

"It scared the hell out of me."

"Like I told you before . . . the way you're gonna help yourself in making a determination about where you go and what your life is gonna be like beyond this is . . ."

"I won't have a life. You'll put me in prison for the rest of my days."

"We're not kidding you about being . . ."

"You'll never let me out now."

"That's going to be up to the prosecutor and the judge."

"They'll never let me out."

"Well, we're not kidding you about the DNA and we're not kidding you about the belongings and we're testing . . ."

"Belongings? Like clothes? What? Tell me?"

"You know what."

"What kind of clothes. What? DNA? Hairs? What?"

Dresback added, "Donna, do you really think we'd lack evidence here?"

"I don't know. What kind of evidence do you have?"

"Do you really think . . . we'd have this case here and we're talking to you, and we just don't have any evidence? We've got evidence. That's not the point. That's a distraction to the point. You know what the point is. The point is the same thing that's been here."

"I have . . . I have no recollection of even being with these women, so how could I have killed them?"

"I want to know what Douglas knows about this."

Dresback couldn't tell what it was that flashed across Donna's face—anger, frustration, resentment. "Douglas doesn't know shit and I don't know shit—period," she snapped. "I did not kill these women. I didn't. Honest, I didn't kill them."

"You control what your life's gonna be like beyond this day."

"I can't help some . . . I hope I get out so I can go back to my house and raise cats. According to you gentlemen, I'm never going to. I understand that much. [*She pointed to the search warrant.*] I read that. It says first-degree murder. That's death penalty shit."

Burbridge tried to explain the complicated process involved in securing a death penalty for a defendant. "There's gonna be more than one court. There's gonna be multiple courts . . ."

"Yeah, death penalty shit."

"You know, it's . . . I mean, it's your choice. Your life is a reflection . . ."

"Where was the DNA found at? That's what I'd like to know. If I get an attorney, he's gonna know and he's gonna tell me. Where's the DNA coming from and all this happy shit."

"Well, we . . ."

"I'm angry now."

"Good, because that's what it takes. That's what it takes to get yourself in a position to make things better."

"All I want to do is live quietly and peacefully. And people just want to hurt my cats."

"You want peace?" Burbridge demanded.

"Yeah, I want peace."

"Seriously?"

"I want people to leave me alone."

"How do you have peace under these circumstances?"

"I have peace."

"How do you expect that?"

"Well, what you're doing now is just ripping my mind to pieces . . . You're accusing me of being a murderer."

"I'm not victimizing you. I'm giving you an opportunity . . ."

"And I want the opportunity to die by my own hands."

Burbridge seized on the death wish and asked, "Douglas and Donna together feel bad about what happened here?"

"No . . ."

"Let me finish."

"We're both scared at . . ."

"Let me finish."

"This is what makes me go out and buy a gun . . ."

"Let me finish."

"To protect myself."

"A gun won't protect you from this. At least, it won't go away. I don't intend to . . ."

"It's went away. It's gone."

"It's back."

"Because the simple reason is, I didn't hurt those women."

"You did. Now, if Douglas/Donna feels really bad about what's happened here and wants to kill themselves . . ."

"Because?"

"The state could do that for you, if you want the death penalty. Let's talk about it."

"No, I really want to do it myself."

"Why?"

"Because I want to be in control of my life just one time. And I'm going to reserve the right to kill myself. I don't want somebody else to do it."

"Do me a favor before you do it," Burbridge said.

"Uh huh?"

"Write me a letter and tell me the truth about Douglas."

"You have DNA or whatever that I'm supposed to have murdered these two women. I'd like to see it. I'd like to know what you've got."

"The time will come."

"Yeah, I'm scared shitless about this whole proceeding. I killed somebody? Are you serious? Oh, my God! No, I didn't kill any of those women."

Burbridge now had the chance to reveal his conviction that Donna Perry had killed more prostitutes than the three he and Dresback were there to talk about. The cop took that directly to her. "See, I don't think the number's two. I don't think the number's three. I think the number's more like five girls."

"Where? Show me."

"I'm not gonna show them all to you. The reason is, I don't want to feed you information and have you repeat it to me. I want it coming from you. That's why I'm not telling you what other evidence I have. I'm not telling you where the DNA was. I'm not telling you some things that happened. That's why we didn't tell you how they were killed."

"I don't know."

"You did volunteer that to us. There's no doubt in my mind when I get up to that house on Dalton that I'm gonna find twenty-two-year-old blood in that house, that I'm gonna find bullets, that I'm gonna find other things."

"Well, I was out of the house a lot of those times. Somebody could have come and did whatever."

Burbridge decided to ridicule Donna's suggestion that she was framed. "So, let me make sure I understand your argument. Somebody came in my house, killed hookers, put my DNA on these hookers, took my belongings with them, and dumped them in different places. That's gonna be your defense at trial?"

"I have no idea. I'm not a lawyer. I'm not a police officer."

"No, but you are Donna. You know the truth."

"I know Donna tries to mind her own business and tries to live a quiet, simple, straightforward life."

"How mad is Donna at Douglas?"

"She's not. She's amazed at . . . Why me? Why me?"

"Can Donna make up for what Douglas did?"

"No, if they're gonna put me in prison for the rest of my life, evidently not."

"How do you think Donna should make up for what Douglas did?"

"[If] Donna actually did things she should . . . go to a mental hospital and try to treat the mental illness."

"What if Douglas did it? Same?"

"Same . . . same thing."

Dresback asked, "So, there is a . . . there is actually a real thread between Douglas and Donna here?"

Donna was emphatic. "Huh uh. No. That's where you're wrong. Female brains operate totally different than a male brain does."

Burbridge didn't want to let Donna Perry escape responsibility for what Douglas Perry did. "Those memories are there," he said.

"No, I have no memories."

Dresback began listing her memories. "You remember motorcycles. You remember what you drove. You remember hunting. You remember growing up. You remember . . ."

"Yeah, because I did those things. I don't know anything about this."

"So, what do you think of the Spokane River?"

"I don't even go down to it."

He asked if there were any bodies of water in Omak. Donna said the kids used to swim in an irrigation ditch. She said she didn't like living there, partly because it was always too hot in Omak.

Then she said, "God, I'm shaking."

Burbridge didn't doubt that. "I don't blame you."

Dresback added, "And that's not uncommon, being in your position."

The stress of the interview was clearly getting to Donna. "I'm just about ready to start screaming. Get some kind of release from this."

"That's what I keep referring to as the anvil that you're carrying around."

"No, I'm not dragging an anvil around."

"You can release it."

"There's nothing to release, except that you just scared the shit out of me. You wouldn't believe it. Before I have a stroke or heart attack . . ."

"Are you weighing the options here?" Dresback asked in hopes of lightening the tone.

"No, I'm just trying to get my headache and stuff to . . . If you close your eyes, you can listen to people a lot better. That's one of the things they taught me. I hurt nobody. But I do thank you about the information about Clairann. I always wondered what happened to her."

"Now, I can show you a most recent picture of her."

Donna seemed excited. "Would you, please?"

"We'll have to go get it."

Dresback and Burbridge left the conference room at 11:24 a.m., after nearly two and a half hours of tense interviewing. Donna knocked on the door ten minutes later to ask to use the restroom. She was back in the conference room when the cops returned at 11:38 a.m. and handed her a photograph of Clairann Gallaway.

"This . . . ?" Donna asked in surprise.

"Yeah," Dresback said. "She's got like thirty-two different personalities and when we called down there, the lady said she was calling herself Betty at that time."

Donna shook her head. "That's not Clairann."

"Crazy, huh?"

"You change," Burbridge said. "Some lead hard lives."

Donna seemed insistent. "This isn't Clairann . . . I don't know."

While she continued looking at the photograph, Dresback asked, "In, um, '94, you recall the ATF arrested you in '94 and you talked to Agent Lance Hart?"

She said she did.

"And I had forgotten about this, but apparently you told him that you went down dressed up like a girl and went down on Sprague and prostituted yourself out for money for guns."

"I wanted guns back," she said. "I did dress up as a woman at the time, but not as a prostitute. Yes, I may have drove through there in women's clothing and stuff like that, but not as a prostitute."

"So, you never actually . . ."

"No, never."

"Turned any tricks?"

"No, I was experimenting with clothes and stuff. I have all my life. I got caught doing it in my mother's bedroom. Got my ass whipped."

"All right then."

Donna returned to her doubt that the woman in the photo was Clairann. "God, I didn't recognize . . . It doesn't look like her."

Detective Dresback assured her it was Clairann and added, "I know. It's crazy. She doesn't look anything like she used to."

"She had multiple personalities?" Donna asked.

"Yeah, some thirty-two of them. It's just a little bit extreme, I think." Dresback moved directly into a question about Donna's vehicles. "You talked about your International Scout. Did you have a Pontiac LeMans back in those days, a 1970 green Pontiac LeMans?"

"I can't remember."

"Or a Catalina?"

"I can't remember . . . they're all gone."

"Well, believe it or not, we found the Pontiac LeMans . . . It's down in Spangle, south of town there. Some farmer's son has it and they are restoring it."

"Good luck. It's costly."

"It's what?"

"I said when the gas prices went over two and a half dollars a gallon, I couldn't afford to keep it."

Donna must have suddenly remembered the LeMans.

By then, Dresback knew he and Burbridge had everything they were going to get from Donna Perry. It was time to wrap this up. The detectives stood and Donna joined them. She stepped behind her chair and rested her forearms on top of its back.

"Well, I appreciate you taking the time here and talking to us," Dresback said.

"Sorry I can't help you," Donna replied. "You've just scared the shit out of me."

"For the sake of the victims' families and your own soul, you could still talk to me and I'm available to you any time. OK?"

"After going through this, I understand why I want to die. I . . . This is horrible. This is terribly horrible."

Donna lowered her head onto her arms on the back of the chair and began to whimper.

Dresback said, "I understand that and you can get through this, but you . . ."

"Yeah, right." Donna looked up and directly into Dresback's eyes. "I'm sitting in my cell thinking you guys are gonna come in and murder me now . . . I'm paranoid as hell. I do irrational things."

Dresback spoke very quietly. "At least do me the honor to know that I would never do anything like that to you. That's not . . ."

"Well, like I said, I would like a bullet in the head right at the moment, 'cause if I have done something this horrible, I deserve to die." Donna put her face back down on her arms as her voice cracked and again became a whimper.

The detectives cast a quick glance at each other before Dresback said, "I don't know what you deserve, but I know that you can . . ."

"My poor cats. They're gone," she whined with her head still face down on her arms.

Dresback was taken aback by the unexpected lament about her cats. But he still wanted to offer to help her unburden her soul with a confession.

"I know you can make this better," he said. "I've seen it happen literally dozens of times."

Despite the tears, Donna was resolute about the murders—and her cats.

"I didn't kill anybody. I didn't kill anybody. They killed my cats instead. They took them away and killed them. They hurt me really badly."

Dresback tried to focus on the idea of getting a confession.

"Isn't it time to let it go, finally?"

Donna stayed firm.

"I have never killed anybody, damn it. No, never."

Burbridge passed over a copy of the search warrant with Dresback's card attached.

"I don't want it," she said as she pushed it back across the table. "It'll just drive me crazy knowing it exists."

Burbridge indicated he would have it put in her file at the jail.

Donna didn't want any part of that.

"I'm going to destroy it," she said, and began tearing it up, claiming that having the document lying around could get her in trouble.

"They're gonna beat the shit out of me for something I didn't even do."

Burbridge turned to Donna as he swung open the door to leave.

"You sure you don't want to keep this card in case you decide you want to call us and come out and have another pop with us?"

Dresback smiled and added, "That kind of hurt me a little bit when you tore up my card."

Donna, looking forlorn and resigned, stared at the cops.

"So, now you know what my mother did to me," she said. "She would accuse me of things like this and come back a day or two later and say, 'Gee, I'm sorry. I just ran you through a wringer.'"

And with that, the interview was over.

CHAPTER TWENTY-ONE

Donna Rebecca Perry wasn't a numerologist, but the tally of numbers didn't sit well with Jim Dresback and Mark Burbridge.

And didn't bode well for her either.

She denied killing Yolanda, Nickie, or Kathy twenty-six times during the two-and-a-half-hour interview with the Spokane detectives.

She muttered nine times that she would deserve a bullet to the head if she had killed them. Five of those comments included a suggestion that the detectives give her a pistol so she could shoot herself.

Five more times she directly threatened to commit suicide over the allegations that she was the serial killer who murdered three prostitutes.

Five other times she said she deserved to die if she were guilty.

At least four times she expressly said Douglas Perry did not kill the women, although she seemed to hedge a bit by saying she had put an end to violence by Douglas.

Those were not the kinds of incriminating statements Detectives Jim Dresback and Mark Burbridge hoped to get from Donna Perry when they finally interviewed her. They thought new forensic evidence all but proved she was the Spokane serial killer who struck at least three times in three months in 1990—more than twenty-two years earlier.

Yet despite the overwhelming number of statements declaring her innocence, the interview had not been a total failure. Dresback believed he had heard a statement closer to a confession without being a confession than he had heard in his long career as a detective. Thanks to what Dresback thought was a brilliant question posed by Burbridge, Donna Perry had essentially said her female identity had put a stop to the violence—and perhaps she even meant to the killings—committed by her male identity.

Burbridge had expertly delivered what police interrogators call an alternative question. That's usually a way to offer a scenario indicating guilt while giving the suspect an opportunity to explain why the actions weren't as bad as they seemed or weren't intended to have such a serious outcome. *"Could you have been acting in self-defense? Were you trying to save someone else's life? Did you not intend to hit the other person so hard? Did you lose your temper?"*

In this case, Burbridge set up his question by noting that serial killers generally continue to hunt and murder once they've started. Then he asked the question Jim Dresback thought was genius.

"What made Donna stop?"

Donna's response to that one was almost an admission that Douglas was the serial killer and only the sex-change operation allowed Donna to end the killing.

"Douglas didn't stop. Donna stopped it. The sex-change operation," she had said.

Burbridge followed it up.

"Do you think that's what stopped it?"

"I'm convinced of it," she said.

As Burbridge drilled deeper, Donna explained when Douglas was gone, so was the violence that came with his male hormones.

"There's no more testosterone to fuel the anger," she explained.

Those statements by Donna Perry demonstrated an awareness of her own guilt, Dresback thought, even if she denied it in other statements. But he also knew that, while her comments could be used against her at trial, they did not amount to proof beyond a reasonable doubt. Even combined with the DNA and fingerprint evidence, he worried they might not be enough to convince a jury to convict Donna Perry of murdering three prostitutes.

The investigation into Douglas Perry and, by an unprecedented and extraordinary extension, into Donna Perry would have to continue. But finding people who knew Douglas or Donna Perry in the years before and after the murders wasn't a simple task. It was too long ago. Dresback decided to send out a call for help from the public through the media. He released the affidavit he wrote for his application for the search warrant at 2006 East Empire Avenue. The affidavit set out all the facts in the murders in 1990 and, more importantly, cited the very recent DNA and fingerprint matches that linked Douglas/Donna Perry to the crimes. And, of course, it explained that Douglas became Donna after gender-reassignment surgery in 2000. Dresback also made one of Douglas's booking photos available.

The detective got the result he hoped for. *The Spokesman-Review* ran a front-page story under the headline "Woman Linked to Prostitute Killings: Suspect Was a Man at Time of '90 Crimes." It was a detailed account of the murders and the investigation that had led to Douglas Perry. To the newspaper's credit, the sex change was not treated sensationally and was essentially reported as just another fact in the case. Dresback was pleased that the story said the police wanted to talk to people who knew the victims or had any contact with Douglas in the late 1980s and early 1990s, or who purchased a gun from him during that time. That was the point of getting the story out there. Surely, he thought, a story about a likely serial killer who had a sex change would draw a lot of attention and maybe even some valuable tips.

The day after the detectives talked to Donna, Dresback and Johnston tracked down Kathy Brisbois's sister Debbie Bailey. Finding out more of who the victims were was part of finding out how and why she might have been killed. This was not part of a blame game played out by law enforcement, but another step in catching the killer. Debbie had an important perspective. Not only was she a sibling, but Debbie had real knowledge of what her sister had been up to over the years because she'd also been in the life. She conceded right away that she was involved in prostitution with Kathy for a while in the 1980s. She wasn't proud of it. It was the way things were. She'd been out of the life and told the cops she had not heard that her sister and other prostitutes had formed the Circle. When Dresback held out a booking photo of Douglas Perry from 1989, she identified him as someone she'd seen around the Stroll, but she didn't know him personally. She did recall, however, that he drove a white van that looked like a Volkswagen and would stop and ask prostitutes if they wanted to watch him masturbate. Debbie said Kathy was using heroin that she bought from a woman named Aloha.

Before the detectives left, Debbie said she would reach out to Aloha and see if she would talk.

A couple of days later, Dresback and Johnston met with Aloha Ingram at her pine-and-juniper-shrouded house in the Comstock neighborhood of modest homes south of the city. It was not a long interview. It didn't need to be. After all, Aloha didn't have the time to beat around the bush. She'd been through too much for that. She admitted right away she had not only sold heroin to Kathy but also used it with her, as she did with several people during the time she was working the area around Trudeau's Marina. Looking at Douglas Perry's photo, she said he was vaguely familiar, but she didn't know anything about him. She was much better acquainted with serial killer Robert Yates, whom she considered a loving and gentle date.

Ironically, a "safe" date.

Aloha said Yolanda, Nickie, and Kathy knew each other, and she remembered seeing them together once at a bar. Aloha also said she knew Yolanda and Darrel "Doc" Thomas were a couple, and she always suspected he had killed Yolanda because the two of them had some terrible fights.

News reports also led to a call from Cathy Dorn, Douglas Perry's neighbor from across the street when he lived at 544 East Dalton Avenue. She remembered the ATF raiding Perry's house in 1994 because they evacuated all the neighbors before they went into the house to arrest Perry. Dorn said she never saw Perry at that house again. She said she and her husband had seen Perry digging in his front yard one time before the raid. When her husband went over to ask what he was doing, Perry "snapped" at him and told him to mind his own business. She said she never saw signs that anyone else ever lived there with the suspected killer and never noticed him having any animals. She thought he might have had a night job because she would often see him leaving at night on foot or in the International Scout.

While such leads painted a picture of who Douglas Perry was, they didn't advance the investigation by linking him with the murders.

And just who Douglas was, well, the same word that came up in Omak topped the list from neighbors in Spokane.

Arlen Garlich, who lived just a few doors down the block on East Dalton, called Detective Dresback to say he always thought the guy was "weird."

Really weird.

Garlich had once seen Douglas Perry in his front yard dressed as a woman. He went on to say he talked to him several times, but the odd fellow was a "loner" who was not at all sociable. He never saw other people, especially women, at Perry's house, nor had he seen any animals. He remembered seeing him driving an off-white or gray International Scout and had a vague recollection of seeing him with what might have been a green 1970s Pontiac LeMans. The neighbor also remembered finding an empty box for a Ruger 10/22 or "Mini-14" rifle after Perry threw the box in the trash. And when the ATF raided Perry's house, he recalled peering over the fence to see agents carrying out "a lot of guns and crossbows."

Weird.

A loner.

True and interesting, yes. But not all that helpful in building a murder case. The DNA evidence was key, but more was needed. Dresback, like others on the case, knew investigations require patience when on the hunt for evidence.

This was one of those.

When reviewing tips from the original police investigation in 1990, Dresback came across a report from a Spokane police officer who said he saw two women—Patsy Johansen and Gloria Allen—get out of a white van at East First Avenue and Madelia Street not far from the Stroll area about a week after Yolanda was murdered and posed by the river.

The officer cut short his interview with the women to answer a radio call about a shooting.

Dresback wanted to know what that was all about, so he and Johnston tracked down Patsy Johansen, who admitted she had worked as a prostitute in that area, but never worked with Gloria Allen, whom she knew as the sister of Yolanda's boyfriend, Darrel "Doc" Thomas. And Johansen said she had never been in a white van with Allen. She recognized the photo of Douglas Perry as someone she had seen walking around the area with his hands shoved deep into his pockets but had never seen him in any vehicle. Disappointingly, she did not recognize the photo of Clairann Gallaway. Nor had she ever heard of the Circle.

Where was Clairann? And how did she fit into the puzzle Spokane law enforcement had been putting together?

When Detective Johnston finally tracked down a doctor who had been treating Clairann Gallaway in Los Angeles, any hope of answers about Clairann, the Circle, and what role, if any, her very existence played into the murders, faded immediately.

The doctor said his patient's mental health was so poor that she had been made a ward of the state by the California Mental Health Court, which also placed her under court-ordered supervision and control, called a conservatorship, that would be in effect for at least a year. The supervisor with the Los Angeles County Department of Mental Health overseeing her care told Johnston his request for police to interview

Gallaway would have to be approved by the public defender who was representing her in court.

After the public defender reviewed Johnston's request and Clairann's file, he decided not to allow the interview.

Hearing from Clairann, as central as she was, was never going to happen.

When Mark Burbridge kept his vow to Donna Perry and led a search of the house at 544 East Dalton Avenue, he encountered one of those unpredictable twists that drive cops wild. The current owner of the house had ripped out and replaced the hardwood floors. The old floors where the Spokane detective hoped to find bullets or bloodstains from the murders of Yolanda and perhaps Nickie were long gone. Remembering that neighbors had reported seeing Douglas Perry digging in the yard at the home, Burbridge led his team to dig a number of holes in areas they thought might have made good hiding places for whatever Perry would have wanted to bury. Except for a surprising and inexplicable number of forks and spoons, the effort went for naught.

Meanwhile, Johnston spent hours and hours tracking down the two vehicles they knew Douglas Perry was driving at the time of the murders: a white 1969 International Scout and a green 1970 Pontiac LeMans. The Scout was now owned by a couple in Woodland, a suburb north of Portland, Oregon, which was just barely still in the southern part of Washington and 373 miles southwest of Spokane. The police in Woodland had the Scout towed to the Washington State Patrol Crime Lab in Vancouver, where Dresback and Johnston completed a detailed search in hopes they would find evidence like long-dried bloodstains that could be traced to one or more of the victims. It didn't happen. The only interesting item was a rusty, corroded .22-caliber cartridge that Dresback found in debris in the front passenger-side floor of the vehicle. It was the same caliber as the bullets that killed the three prostitutes, and Dresback was certain it had belonged to Perry. All the owners of the vehicle since Perry said they never had any kind of ammunition in the Scout. But after twenty-two years, there was no way to link the bullet to Perry or the murders.

After Johnston located the LeMans with new owners in teeny tiny Spangle, eighteen miles south of Spokane, the cops got another search warrant. Dresback, Johnston, and Burbridge, accompanied by forensic specialists, recovered significant amounts of hair, fibers, and debris from the car that would be tested for any matches to the victims. But again, there were no traces of blood that could provide the kind of damning evidence against Perry the cops hoped for.

An ATF agent later called Johnston to see if the police wanted to retain any of the firearms seized when they arrested Perry in March. Johnston said he would only be interested in the .22-caliber weapons they confiscated. But the agent explained that the three .22-caliber guns seized were all manufactured after 1997, and therefore none of them could be the murder weapon from 1990. Johnston passed on the offer.

On December 14, 2012, a federal judge sentenced Donna Perry to two years and three months in prison for illegal possession of a firearm and ammunition by a felon. The judge filed a recommendation with the Bureau of Prisons that Perry be held in a facility that could provide her with appropriate mental health treatment.

CHAPTER TWENTY-TWO

Charlotte Schell's office was in a busy center hallway in the Spokane Falls Family Clinic, a medical center on Mission Avenue in the center of the Lilac City. The forty-eight-year-old was a welfare-eligibility specialist for the Washington State Department of Social and Health Services, which had arranged the small satellite office for her in the clinic as a convenient location for the public in need of her services. Charlotte's open door made her visible from the hallway and was meant to be a welcoming invitation for anyone looking for welfare assistance. Through 2007 and 2008, one woman would drop in almost weekly for extended chats about life in general when she came to pick up her prescriptions. She liked Charlotte, telling her she was the only woman who had any brains and was worth talking to.

The visitor's name was Donna Perry.

Donna and Charlotte quickly discovered mutual interests in motorcycles, guns, and shooting and enjoyed their conversations about almost every other aspect of daily life. Donna detailed her gender-reassignment surgery and her time in prison, and Charlotte offered a nonjudgmental ear for discussions about those complications in her life. Donna started talking about how her life had seemed out of control—wild, as she deemed it—before prison and the surgery, and she said something about being involved in shooting people.

Suddenly, Charlotte was all ears.

"What do you mean, shooting people?" she asked, studying Donna carefully. "I thought you went to prison for other reasons."

Donna must have realized she might have shared too much and quickly backpedaled.

"Well, yeah, but that was back when things were wild and out of control before my surgery."

Charlotte realized Donna hadn't denied shooting people but had immediately changed the subject and made it clear she wanted to talk about something else. She certainly didn't say anything about who she might have shot. She had done something similar to that on other occasions when talking about intimate details and events in her life, as if she realized, *Oh, I've said too much,* and she would try to change the subject quickly. That happened before when Donna had said something about "my gun-running days."

During another conversation later, Charlotte tried to reopen the topic of shootings by saying, "About, you know, shooting people, what's that all about?" Perry tried to shrug it off, saying, "Oh, that was all part of the past. That was before my surgery."

Charlotte made note of how Donna clearly divided her life into separate chapters before and after the surgery.

"This is the point at which my life was completely out of control and wild and then I had the surgery," Donna said, "and then after that, I became controlled and, you know, able to lead a pretty regular life."

Donna also told Charlotte that some people wondered why she had undergone the sex change and sometimes asked if she was gay or straight or which sex she preferred to be with. Donna sometimes would chuckle about that.

"Here's the thing," she explained on another occasion. "My life was getting out of control, and I knew that I was either going to end up dead or in prison again if I didn't do something about it. So, I had the surgery, just like you geld a horse, and I got my life back under control."

"What about the sex?"

"I'll let you in on a little secret," Donna said. "I'm celibate. I don't have boyfriends, girlfriends. I don't even go there."

Charlotte came to believe Donna didn't seem to care much for women in general.

One time Donna dropped into the office, angry and agitated. She said a refugee family from Somalia had moved next door and she was becoming more and more upset about that. She obviously didn't like that they were Black. And she insisted they were constantly watching her. She began talking about how, from certain windows in her house and locations in her yard, she could shoot them.

"But Donna, you've been in prison," Charlotte said. "You don't want to go back to prison. You don't want to do that."

Donna looked at her calmly. "It's not that bad. I wouldn't have to worry about keeping up the house payments."

She proceeded to list the things in her life that were causing her stress and said they wouldn't be problems anymore if she went back to prison. She insisted it wouldn't be such a bad thing after all.

Charlotte took all that in.

Shooting people.

Not afraid of going back to prison.

It was troubling, and scary enough to fill out a departmental incident report and express her fears to a social worker that the potential for violence by Donna Perry was very real and needed to be on everyone's radar.

And she called Detective Dresback to tell him all of that after she read the newspaper story quoting him as looking for information about Donna Perry. He believed every word of Charlotte's story.

What she recounted during that conversation dovetailed with everything he was learning about Donna Perry.

CHAPTER TWENTY-THREE

The early months of 2013 rolled by quickly as the detectives tried to check off items on their to-do list and find more evidence that would support murder charges and a conviction by a jury for Donna Perry.

One item they marked off was Perry's allegation that a friend of the Massengale brothers was keeping guns the brothers had for sale off the books so they would not be in possession of them if the police checked. Dresback got a call in February from Bruce Massengale's live-in girlfriend, who wanted Bruce to talk to Dresback about a man named Beach. She put Massengale on the phone, and he said the man was Glen Beach. Beach didn't have any of Massengale's guns, he said, although Beach had kept some for him many years ago. He said Beach only owned a .44-caliber pistol and a 30-06 rifle now.

Asked about Clairann Gallaway, Bruce Massengale said he remembered she was Douglas Perry's girlfriend and was a "hooker" with "three, four, or six kids." He said Douglas did not want Clairann working as a prostitute because he was afraid someone would kill her.

Dresback and Johnston then talked to Beach, who confirmed knowing the Massengales for more than thirty years. He said he had only seen Donna Perry perhaps three times, but that was enough to conclude she exerted a lot of control over the three Massengale brothers. He denied that he ever received or stored guns for the Massengales or Perry. Beach said he had a .22-caliber rifle, but it was very old and had belonged to his father. Beach didn't know anything about Clairann Gallaway.

More reports found their way to Dresback's office. One came from the Washington State Patrol Crime Lab regarding the pink panties recovered at Perry's former home on East Empire Avenue. The technicians found no trace of blood, but DNA recovered was a mix of two donors, the major donor being Perry or a male in his genetic line and the minor donor remaining unidentified. It was not, however, from Yolanda, Nickie, or Kathy.

The lab also said DNA found in a vaginal smear collected from Kathy Brisbois matched Perry. Dresback considered that proof Perry had sex with Kathy. Not only that, it explained why Perry—when told about DNA samples by the detectives during their interview in November— immediately asked, "Was it vaginal or something like that?"

In March, the crime lab dispatched a similar report concluding that material in a vaginal smear from Yolanda Sapp also matched Perry or a male in his line. Proof, Jim Dresback believed, that Perry also had sex with Yolanda, despite his seemingly racially charged denial of ever dating Black prostitutes.

Next, the analysts at the lab concluded that the major DNA contributor to the stain on the floral blanket found near Yolanda's body matched the DNA profile for Douglas Perry. That particular profile did not occur more frequently than one in 3,300 males in the US population. It wasn't an astronomical number, like one in a million, but it was something a jury could consider when weighing all of the evidence.

Suddenly, after all the years—the coming and going of the men and women who worked the case since the first body was found—Detective Dresback had the long-sought trifecta in the serial murder cases that haunted the banks of the Spokane River since the winter of 1990.

Douglas and Donna Perry were unquestionably, undeniably, and abso-fucking-lutely linked to all three members of the Circle. Yolanda, Nickie, and Kathy were gone, but they were not forgotten or relegated to a cardboard file box that was sifted through every few years when budgets allowed or departmental PR flacks thought relaunching an investigation would get brownie points.

The women of the Circle and their loved ones had waited long enough.

PART THREE

DONNA

CHAPTER TWENTY-FOUR

The Federal Medical Center in Carswell rises over the flat Texas horizon like a fortress, its beige, sun-bleached walls topped by curlicues of razor wire. Inside, a disparate mix of women, from notorious killers and drug kingpins to white-collar criminals and those with dire mental illnesses, do their time under the care of doctors of all varieties as they serve out their federal sentences.

It was never an easy place to be. Over the years, the facility was home at one time or another to would-be presidential assassin Lynette "Squeaky" Fromme and "Angel of Death" nurse Kristen Gilbert. Wanda Barzee, the kidnapper of Elizabeth Smart, would be under fire for rampant sexual abuse of the women incarcerated there.

The cure for some? Worse than the affliction that got them there.

By June 2013, Chero Everson had managed to survive at Carswell and was a short-timer with only weeks to go on a five-year stretch for possession of drugs with intent to distribute in Iowa. Having been diagnosed as bipolar and suffering from PTSD, the thirty-five-year-old had been held there since 2009. She also had a litany of other health issues such as migraines, seizures, nerve damage, and more. Unable to perform a job on a work detail, Chero spent most of her time in the exercise areas, or working on little craft projects, or reading in the library. She loved God and Johnny Cash, and she served her time.

The calendar had only one more page to turn and she'd be free to start over.

One morning in early June, while Chero waited in the pill line to get her daily meds, a stone-faced and disinterested guard asked her to escort a new inmate to the fourth-floor dispensary for the newcomer's initial medications.

Chero glanced over, her eyes landing on the newbie. There was a lot to take in. The woman didn't just stand out—she clearly seemed out of place, like a puzzle piece forced into the wrong set. Her face was a pale road map of hard living. Her long graying hair hung lank around her shoulders and cast shadows over sunken cheeks. She hunched her shoulders forward and avoided eye contact.

Chero couldn't look away. The new woman wasn't just strange looking—she was unsettling in a way Chero couldn't quite put her finger on. She clearly needed help.

Inmates like this lady don't survive without help, she thought.

The inmate introduced herself as Donna Perry.

Chero gave her a friendly smile and guided her up the stairs.

Later, she'd chalk up that moment as being one of the biggest mistakes in a life full of them.

Donna was assigned to a room across the atrium from Chero's. Each room housed four inmates in two sets of bunk beds. None had doors, so there was little or no privacy. Donna seemed to interpret this concept as an invitation, slipping in and out of Chero's room whenever the spirit moved her. Before long, Donna was a constant and slovenly presence—lingering in her room, hanging around her in the common area, or shadowing Chero around the outdoor track. Donna smelled bad and her nose ran like a faucet when she ate. She took every opportunity to brag about having an IQ of 180, though alternately saying she still felt ignorant.

Donna was human Velcro. Wherever Chero went, she was right there.

And then without any warning, and without the privacy of even a whisper, it started.

The talk.

Donna said she had been diagnosed as a sociopath, with schizophrenia and hallucinations. That wasn't unheard of in a place like Carswell, and Chero was sympathetic. Drugs could help, but never really fix her strange shadow.

Donna soon dropped the bombshell.

"I'm a contract killer," she said—or rather *announced*. And without the slightest bit of compunction, she explained how she had killed nine women—prostitutes, she clarified—calling the murders "just business."

She also murdered some men too.

Chero was unsure whether to believe Donna or dismiss her accounts as delusions from a damaged mind. The more Chero heard, however, the more she was inclined to accept Donna's story. Her accounts seemed so precise. So full of detail and, yes, professional detachment. She described selecting her victims, watching them, learning their routines. And the coup de grâce was the feeling that came with the outcome.

"When you kill someone," Donna said, a faint smile crossing her lips, "they never believe it's going to happen. They're always surprised."

She dumped bodies by rivers, sometimes in cars, and showed no concern for evidence left behind—a bullet, a casing, a body flung out like trash.

Most of her contract killings took place in Spokane, Washington.

While she professed to be very good at her work, Donna had mellowed with age and no longer felt the rage that fueled her vocation. She told Chero that she didn't work alone, that a Spokane cop hired her to get rid of the prostitutes in the area.

She was spilling so many things that Chero had a difficult time keeping up.

"Why are you telling me all of this?"

"You remind me of my mom," Donna said.

CHAPTER TWENTY-FIVE

Chero Everson's unease simmered for days. Donna's stories, chilling as they were, had initially felt distant, like dark fantasies from a troubled mind. Yet the more Chero listened, the more she realized these weren't just macabre tales spun to pass the time—they were confessions, each word dripping with a calm, calculated truth that made her stomach turn.

And as terrifying as the past that Donna described was, it was the future that kept Chero awake at night.

This woman with the bad hair and strange affect wanted to kill.

More than that, really.

Loved to kill.

Donna's voice softened when she spoke of murder, like recounting an old love affair. Chero couldn't shake the feeling that Donna's time at Carswell was only the press of a pause button, a holding pattern before she could act on her urges again.

It wasn't a matter of if, but *when.*

Chero realized then she'd opened a door that she would wish later had been dead-bolted. Better yet, soldered shut. Her feelings of empathy for the strange misfit had brought her in proximity to something very dark. Chero knew a thing or two about the seedier side of life, but it wasn't the space she sought to inhabit. Not only was she clean in prison, but she intended to stay that way when she got out. The drug world was not going to suck her back down again. She had kids. She had plans.

But Donna Perry, well, she was something else. She was dangerous. Threatening too. She coolly said she didn't worry about Chero disclosing any of the incriminating things she offered up on their walks.

"No one will believe you because of your mental health issues."
Oh really now.

Not sure of the end game, Chero decided to document Donna's bizarre story in the pages of a journal hidden in her room.

She wrote out her first entry on June 8, 2013, chronicling how, as the pair walked the track and before catching a softball game in the yard, Donna dropped another bombshell.

> *She told me she killed 9 women, prostitutes. Shot them twice in the head. Her weapon of choice is a 9mm Beretta. That killing women is not personal, its business. She began to confide in me a couple days ago after I was told to take her to get medical attention. She's been attached to my hip. The murders have happened as far back as 22 years . . . as she presented herself as a man.*

As she wrote it all out, Chero worked hard to process what Donna was really saying. It wasn't easy. Some of it was confusing. Some of it was scary.

> *She refers to herself as either a woman or man also says she is like Hannibal Lecter and changes her styles of killing from guns to a knife as well as bare hands. She used a saw blade modified sharpened serrated edge so when the throat was slit that it cannot be stitched up.*

Donna was also upfront about her sexual situation. She said she had gender-reassignment surgery in Thailand thirteen years ago. Her penis and scrotum were removed, she said, and "plastic inserts" were added to enlarge her breasts.

Chero wrote later:

> *Penis was small but masturbated and achieved and ejaculation constantly. Said her hole (vagina) was in working condition and big enough to put a fist in. (gross) She desires companionship but has an aversion to sex but is attracted to women . . . Wants to write a book. Still has the urge to kill when someone is being loud, obnoxious, passive aggressive . . . a black lady threatening and insulting the Hispanics was agitating her.*

In stunningly short order, and in every sense, Donna Perry managed to monopolize Chero Everson's every waking or *sleeping* moment. Even in slumber, thoughts of Donna raced through her mind. At once, she was enthralled and sickened by her new, uninvited bestie.

And she was scared too.

Chero wondered what someone like Donna would do if she knew how afraid of her she really was.

One morning Donna made her way uninvited into Chero's room with a suggested plan for their day together, as though Chero didn't have a say in any of it. It was picture day at the facility, and Donna wanted to make sure she and Chero would get a picture of the two of them together. Donna was unkempt as usual, wearing the same barbecue sauce–stained shirt she never seemed to change.

Tidy in her appearance, she wasn't.

Chero once remarked on Donna's hygiene, so this time Donna volunteered right away that she'd showered. Chero had serious doubts about that. She wondered if Donna had really ventured upstairs to the showers or had done what Donna called a "whore bath"—a quick wipe with a wet washcloth.

First breakfast, followed by the pill line for medication, and then pictures.

Throughout all of that, Donna yammered about everything. Chero studied Donna carefully as she talked about hallucinations she was having. Things she was seeing were bothering her, making her agitated.

Sometimes they came during the day, though mostly the hallucinations came at night.

"When I lie down," Donna confided to Chero, "I see a big orange, feral cat. Sharp fangs. She lies right down on top of me and opens her yellow eyes."

Chero didn't say a word. Listening was her role in their increasingly unsettling relationship.

"The cat's so close it tickles my nose."

Chero nodded, because she didn't know what to say or how she was supposed to react.

She knew cats were important to Donna. She told Chero that at one time she had thirty-six of them.

Chero wondered if she had so many cats, why she didn't think to have them fixed.

Donna lit into the suggestion. She didn't believe it was right to neuter or spay a feline. It was mutilation.

Chero gave her a little room on that.

"But why so many?" she asked.

"Because of what I did to them," she said, segueing from the cats she loved to the cats she killed on the farm. Too many to count, she said. She killed them in different ways. With her hands. Mostly with guns.

"Daddy got me the bullets," she said. Before the cats, and the women she killed, Douglas Perry used his little sister Karen's Barbies for target practice.

In the afternoon, Donna and Chero lined up with the others for picture day. In the portrait of the pair, Donna lurks behind Chero with a blank look in her eyes. She is drab from top to bottom. Her graying hair hangs in oily strands. She wears no makeup. No glasses either. Chero, without question, made the effort. Her hair is perfect and her makeup just right.

Outside of police mug shots, Donna told Chero that this was the first portrait for which she'd posed since high school.

On the way back to their rooms, Donna launched into recollections about the Massengale brothers. Donna told Chero that the men were in a gay relationship, despite being brothers.

She also said that while identifying as a woman, she occasionally posed as a man named Don. Don picked up prostitutes and brought his favorites home for sex.

"And to cuddle on my lap while watching TV," Donna said.

As she listened, Chero thought she was going to have a lot to write about that night. It was getting weirder and weirder.

Donna said that a single hair tied her to one of the prostitute murders, but the state had lost the evidence. Further, when her guns were confiscated and destroyed by the feds—the reason she was in prison— they destroyed evidence connecting her to the killings.

Freely and nonchalantly discussing murder each day, Donna described the grim details of brain and bone matter and some basic anatomy like where major arteries are located and how fast one will die when they're severed.

The smell of blood too.

And while she talked a good game about the killings in Spokane and the knowledge she had on guns of all kinds—while walking around the track, she pointed out which trees were good sources for a shotgun or rifle gunstock—Donna was worried about what was going on back home.

Her dreams haunted her too.

Chero wrote in her journal: *"Last night the orange cat came back and early this morning instead of opening her eyes and being face to face to some fearsome critter's rear end was backed up and sprayed her all over the face neck and upper body. She decided to call the cat Barf. I am often speechless when she says things."*

She added later: *"Perfection is hitting a target or bullseye from far away 4 people deep moving and not having any collateral damage."*

Each time Chero returned to her room, she exhaled. She was on a kind of mission—stealthily interviewing Donna and logging it all in her journal—but it was unnerving her. Part of it was the guilt that came with the deception of pretending to be Donna's friend. She also felt sad about Donna's complicated and messy life. But it went further than that too. Donna was suffocating her and creeping her out. She learned from others in the prison that Donna was lurking outside her cell in the middle of the night.

She wrote in her journal: *"I wish I would have never been nice to her!"*

The most unnerving part wasn't Donna's past—it was the present. Donna confided to Chero she'd waited fifty years to meet someone like her.

"I want to marry you," she said.

Chero didn't want that but didn't know what to say either.

Donna spoke of a life together after prison, painting a vision that was equal parts delusional and sinister.

"I'll protect you," Donna said. "I'd kill for you."

Her actions matched her sentiments. Donna threatened guards when they got too close to Chero and chased off other inmates who tried to carry on a conversation with her.

Chero slept on what to do about Donna. Or at least tried to.

"Spokane was hot," Donna told her one morning, referencing police attention on some unsolved murders there, which she said was part of why she had transformed herself from Douglas Robert Perry to Donna Rebecca Perry.

She had the surgery to evade law enforcement.

"A disguise," she said, adding that no cop would consider an old woman when looking for the killer of some hookers.

Donna had become more demonstrative too. She began to share other ways to kill—lethal techniques she'd somehow mastered. Like delivering a single, fatal blow to the face. Once, mid-conversation, she suddenly demonstrated, her hand stopping just short of Chero's face.

It was enough to send a shiver down Chero's spine.

All this unwanted extra attention scared the young woman who'd just about completed her time—and none too soon. Chero had to tell someone. The next day, she ditched Donna and made a collect call to her mother. She unloaded everything and asked her to see if she could confirm any of the stories Donna Perry was dishing out.

Her crimes were way up north in Spokane, Washington.

CHAPTER TWENTY-SIX

The woman on the phone from Corpus Christi, Texas, had a lot to say, and Jim Dresback was all ears. Gloria Toelle was worried about her daughter's safety because of a bizarre and ultimately frightening relationship she'd made with another inmate in federal prison.

"Donna Perry is her name," she said.

As Dresback took it all in, the concerned mother shared what Chero had disclosed and how she thought the information she had could help the investigation of the prostitute murders in Spokane. And from what Gloria was saying, it might even be bigger than that. Much bigger. She explained that her daughter, about to be paroled on drug charges, had befriended the suspected serial killer in the prison's medical clinic and was now having serious second thoughts about it.

"She's scared," she said.

Gloria was married to a cop and had always stayed on the right side of the law. Her daughter had stumbled—mostly because of the drugs that came with a bad pick of men—but she was a good person and knew right from wrong.

And this Donna Perry was all kinds of wrong.

"She said she killed a bunch of people . . . as many as forty."

Jim kept writing it all down. It was hearsay, of course. But good hearsay that could lead to something.

"She said she's a professional hit man," Gloria said.

He wrote that down too.

And there was more.

A lot more.

Gloria went on to say Chero had been keeping a journal because what she was hearing was so bizarre and frightening.

The detective didn't need to think twice. He knew he and Mark Burbridge needed to get to the informant as soon as possible. He immediately called Carswell Federal Medical Center in Fort Worth to make arrangements to see the reluctant friend of a potential serial killer.

In the world of law enforcement, things seldom get better than that.

A week after talking to Gloria Toelle, Burbridge and Dresback caught a flight to Texas to interview Chero Everson. It was a hideously humid day; Dresback later likened the walk to the rental car to making his way across the bottom of a swimming pool.

Dripping wet five seconds out of air-conditioning.

At thirty-five, and despite her health problems and the circumstances, Chero was a vibrant woman, with long dark-brown hair falling over her shoulders and framing olive-toned features. Her brown eyes, highlighted with pink eye shadow, sparked intelligence—and worry.

Chero repeated some of Donna's comments and stories as the detectives made notes and recorded audio, almost dumbstruck by the bold admissions and bizarre claims made by the first transgender serial killer in American history.

It wasn't lost on anyone in the room that Chero was scared about her "friend" Donna and what she might do if things didn't go her way.

"She told me she was a sociopath and that she was proud of that," she said.

A proud sociopath? That was one neither detective had heard before. Then again, they'd never heard of a transgender, weapons-obsessed, hit man serial killer either.

In many ways, Chero was quite impressive. She was obviously smart. She knew specific names and concrete details that only someone who'd managed to get close to Donna could possibly know. And since Donna was disclosing directly to Chero, the hearsay rule didn't apply. She also had a moral compass in a place where few existed.

Chero said Donna was in love with her. She wanted to marry her and move with her to Corpus Christi where her family lived. Chero didn't like that plan one bit. First, she wasn't gay. Second, she didn't love Donna. And third, Donna was completely and utterly dangerous.

Over the course of the interview, Chero spilled Donna's secrets. She recounted the conversations she had with Donna as they walked around the track, sat in the social room, walked the halls, or ate meals together.

Dresback brightened a bit when Chero mentioned Donna had wanted her to write down her story.

"Is that something you would do?"

She said she would, though admittedly she felt conflicted about it. She'd been listening as a friend, and doing something like snitching on her was troubling. Seemed like she was more a Judas than a friend, but the stakes were high. The woman who wanted to move to Corpus Christi and marry her wasn't just crazy.

She was dangerous.

"Get her to give you intimate details. 'How did you kill them? What did you do with this one? When was, what was the first one you ever killed? What happened?'"

Chero agreed, though she suggested another way.

"There an easier way of doing this, like, um, can't I be like, wired or somethin'?"

The detective insisted that wouldn't work. Not in a federal prison.

Chero saw helping the Spokane detectives as not only ensuring that Donna Perry stayed right where she belonged but also fixing things in her own shattered life. Her stepfather had a long and distinguished career in law enforcement serving the people of North Platte, Nebraska—a connection she never talked about inside the walls of the facility.

"I have a lot of respect for him," she said of her stepfather. "I've made a lot of really bad choices at a time in my life. Because I'm in prison . . . that is not who I am. Out of respect for my parents and the law and what is the right thing to do, I felt it was important to tell my mom and you."

"These are murders we're talkin' about. This isn't jaywalkin'," Burbridge said.

Chero understood.

"She hated those women," she said. "She *hated* them. They were nothing, nobodies."

Chero also told the detectives about her journal, which they recognized could be an important piece of collaboration to her testimony in a trial. She said she would give her journal to the detectives as soon as she got out of Carswell in about two weeks.

After the interview, the cops returned to the airport, lost in conversation about the catalog of near confessions collected by this invaluable new witness. Their dissection of this new evidence continued as they sat in the airport awaiting their flight home. Going carefully through their notes, they worked to identify which statements Chero related that fit exactly with the facts in the confusing, twisted sixty-year saga of Douglas and Donna Perry and the murders of three young women. She had admitted targeting prostitutes—women she considered worthless "pond scum"—and selected victims carefully. She shot them. She threw their bodies out of her car and left them on the riverbanks. She lacked remorse and regret. She had a girlfriend named Claire Gallaway, who was a prostitute.

Dresback and Burbridge knew Donna Perry's confessions to a fellow inmate were not enough to convict her by themselves. But if they could get Chero to deliver her account of Donna's statements from the witness stand, that might be enough, added to the DNA and fingerprint evidence, to convince a jury of Perry's guilt.

Juries like a story. Juries like a motive. Chero Everson had something that no one else had. She had both.

Despite her promise to help the detectives—and her sincere desire to do so—Chero Everson found herself growing increasingly anxious and decidedly more terrified. The visit with the detectives had put the kibosh on any thoughts she might have entertained that Donna was making up anything when she spun her stories of violence and murder.

Chero went to prison officials and said she was scared for her life while Donna had free access to her at all hours of the day. She said she felt like she was being hunted and asked if they'd move Donna somewhere—anywhere—away from her.

On June 12, she wrote in her journal about a conversation they had at lunch that day. *"Donna mentioned rape and beatings from ages 5 to 14 and a reference that she did what she did years ago because couldn't breed or have a family."*

Their relationship—one-sided as it was—was going further south. Chero, who had been fighting a migraine for days, also suffered a seizure, and Donna was still making everything all about herself. She ignored whatever advice Chero dispensed.

She wrote on June 13: *"She is upset with me for my tone of voice and frustration."*

The next day, more of the same. Donna kept coming around to check on Chero when she was at sick call for a much-needed migraine shot. When Donna found her, it was not to check to see how Chero was doing, but because Donna needed a hug.

Chero wrote: *"Neighbors say she's been at my room a thousand times and is upset and I not being there. I told her we would talk after count. Its rack up time and she just leaves her room whenever she feels like it to talk to me.*"

Donna showed up at her door at eight the next morning, wanting a Band-Aid for her feet.

It was always something.

And it was always creepy too.

She told Chero that she thought she deserved a nickname.

"How about Nipper?"

Chero didn't like it.

"Chief?"

Chero didn't go for that one either. She didn't want a damn nickname. She wanted to get away from Donna.

At lunch that day, Chero broached a subject that the detectives from Spokane wanted her to ask.

"How many people have you killed?"

Donna thought about it for a beat.

Counting in her head, maybe?

"I stopped counting after ten," Donna finally said, pausing and adding, "could be as high as twenty or thirty."

Chero couldn't imagine being so casual about killing people that one could lose track of how many lives they'd taken.

She wrote in what would be her last entry on the afternoon of June 15: *"Also, her mom tried to pour Drano down her throat at age 3. She was left to fend for herself . . . neighbors too treated her bad. She said they created what she became."*

That same day, officials transferred Donna to solitary confinement and moved Chero to a different wing so Donna would not know where the target of her constant stalking was housed. Chero didn't see Donna again before she was released to a halfway house on July 2.

And that was more than fine with her.

Jim Dresback was all about Chero's journal.

While some of Donna Perry's disclosures were prior to Chero's nighttime diary entries, some were contemporaneous—and backed up in real time what the serial killer had said about what she'd done and, more importantly, why.

Pond scum.

After Chero was released from Carswell, Detective Dresback had serious difficulty reaching her. After multiple attempts, when he finally reached her by phone, Chero said her aunt Flossie had the journal and she promised to get it.

But then nothing.

Weeks went by.

He got Aunt Flossie's phone number from Chero's mother, Gloria Toelle, but after three tries, there was no answer.

Where is she?

He tried again and again.

We need her.

On October 1, Dresback reached the front desk of a Dismas Charities residence in Corpus Christi, Texas, a halfway house with a jobs program where Chero had been staying while she got back on her feet.

She wasn't there.

He left a message asking her to call him.

Her disappearing act didn't make sense. Her stepdad was a cop. She'd sought out the Spokane police because it was the right thing to do. She knew how evidence worked.

Where was she?

CHAPTER TWENTY-SEVEN

With essentially all of the evidence the police had been tracking and collecting now secured in the case file, Jim Dresback finally felt qualified to offer a motive—an explanation for why, on three cold nights in early 1990, Douglas Perry made dates with three prostitutes from the East Sprague Avenue Stroll, had sex with them, shot them to death, and then dumped their naked bodies near the banks of the Spokane River.

Detective Dresback believed the motive for the killings was embodied in one other prostitute, Clairann Gallaway. She was, in Donna Perry's own words, the only woman Douglas ever wanted as a girlfriend, ever loved, and wanted to marry. She was the only woman he didn't want to share. He would have done anything Clairann asked of him—bought a bigger house, moved her children in, make one big family, anything—if she would have given up her life as a prostitute, given up cocaine, stayed on her meds, and been his alone.

That last one might have been the most important of Douglas's requirements. His behavior suggested he wanted to possess Clairann.

When she refused to make any concessions, his only chance at winning her—and monopolizing her—was to eradicate those he thought were helping her stay in the life of prostitution and drug abuse. He wanted to eliminate his competition for his fantasy life with Clairann.

The problem was the Circle.

Douglas Perry selected nights when, for two of the murders that Dresback could document—Yolanda Sapp on February 22 and Kathy Brisbois on May 15—Clairann was locked up in the county jail. She wouldn't be at home, and she wouldn't be on the street. With her absent, Douglas could execute his plans without her knowledge.

Dresback also thought it was likely Clairann was in jail when Nickie Lowe was murdered on March 25. While he couldn't unearth arrest or jail records for that date, he found documents showing Clairann had pled guilty to a misdemeanor assault charge two days after Nickie's body was found.

So, he surmised, Clairann was likely under arrest and probably in jail when Nickie was killed.

Dresback also knew there was more justification to rid the world of those women in Perry's mind. They were wasting their ability to procreate and make families—the things Donna might not be able to do as a transgender woman but could have when he was a male and with Clairann.

Yolanda, Nickie, and Kathy had squandered their God-given biological ability to have children. It was one possible motivation for the murders.

When broaching the subject with Burbridge or others on the case, Dresback hesitated to conclude Douglas Perry killed the women for love—it was too messed up for that. Yet with his mental illness, it was possible that Douglas may have seen the murders exactly that way.

Dresback remembered the diagnosis delivered by doctors at Eastern State during one of Douglas's stays at the mental hospital. He had paranoid personality disorder, which they defined as lacking the ability to be sensitive to the feelings and thoughts of others whom he committed offenses against or placed in danger.

As such, he would not have worried about taking the lives of Yolanda, Nickie, and Kathy to try to keep Clairann in his life.

In October 2013, Jim Dresback took the step that—over the last twenty-three years—dozens of detectives before him had been working for and the families of three murdered women had been praying for. He referred the murders of Yolanda Sapp, Nickie Lowe, and Kathy Brisbois to the Spokane County prosecuting attorney with a request for a three-count murder warrant charging Donna Rebecca Perry.

The Spokesman-Review published a story naming Donna Perry, age sixty-one, as the suspected killer.

CHARGES SOUGHT IN 1990 KILLINGS

The Spokesman-Review

November 1, 2013

It had been twenty-three years since Yolanda Sapp left Doc Thomas in their motel room to go to work on the Stroll, since Nickie Lowe told Gorden Lucas they'd meet up later that night, and since Kathy Brisbois told the cops she was scared about the murders of her friends. The families of women in the Circle had waited such a long time for even the slightest hope that their mothers, daughters, sisters, and friends would get a semblance of justice. It brought a flash of joy.

And then more waiting.

Finally, in January 2014, Spokane County Prosecuting Attorney Steve Tucker filed three counts of first-degree murder against Donna Perry. The arrest warrant ordered Donna Perry held on a $1 million bond until she could make an initial appearance before a judge.

That, too, would take a while.

Donna Perry was still in Texas serving her time in the custody of the federal government. It would take two more months before she'd be released to Spokane.

And that didn't mean a speedy trial either.

Donna Rebecca Perry was a very complicated woman.

CHAPTER TWENTY-EIGHT

The accused Spokane serial killer settled into the middle of the row of three seats on the airplane for the flight from Dallas to Spokane on March 14, 2014. Donna Perry had completed her sentence for the 2012 federal firearms and ammunition charges, but she wasn't free. She wore handcuffs as she sat between detectives escorting her back to the Lilac City to face three counts of first-degree murder. On the left side of the prisoner sat Spokane County Sheriff's Detective Jennifer Sutter, and on her right was Sheriff's Detective Damon Simmons. Spokane city police Detective Barbara Byington sat nearby in another row.

Given the circumstances, Donna seemed surprisingly chatty to her traveling companions. She talked about her past as a motorcycle mechanic and engaged in some fiction as she claimed she had been a private security guard for a wealthy person, a job she said allowed her to travel through airports while armed. She described her affinity for guns and ammunition and impressed one of the detectives with her knowledge of them. She mentioned she didn't like Glock handguns, the kind Spokane County Sheriff's Detective Sutter carried.

She talked about spending time at Eastern State Hospital for treatment of her mental illness. She leaned close to the detective several times, conceding she knew the outcome.

"I'm screwed," she said. "They might as well dig a hole and put me in it . . . There's no way I'm getting out of this."

"You want to know something?" she asked a beat later.

"Sure."

"By the time I learned to control myself, it was too late."

Donna said she didn't have the money to pay for her medication. And she asked if Detective Sutter had seen the movie *Sling Blade*, remembering the main character's sad fate staring silently out of the window of a mental institution.

"That's going to be what happens to me," she said.

The group changed planes in Phoenix, and on the second leg of the flight to Spokane, Donna sat in the window seat with Detective Barbara Byington in the middle and Detective Sutter on the aisle.

This time, Donna chatted up Spokane city Detective Byington.

"You know, I'm on medication now," she said. "I'm not violent now."

Interesting.

The detective saw it as an admission that Donna had been violent in the past.

"I'm never going to get out of this," Donna went on. "Instead of jail, I hope they send me to Eastern State Hospital."

After she was quiet for a while, Donna brought up Spokane's most recent and notorious serial killer.

"Whatever happened to Robert Yates?" she asked.

Detective Byington said he received life in prison for the murders in Spokane, but she wasn't sure about the disposition of the murder charges in Pierce County.

It was clear that Donna wasn't fangirling on Yates. She wanted to know who his lawyer had been and whether he got the death penalty.

She was thinking ahead.

CHAPTER TWENTY-NINE

PERRY DENIES HER ROLE IN 1990 SLAYINGS

The Spokesman-Review

March 18, 2014

Donna Perry might have been thinking ahead, but she wasn't alone in that endeavor.

The Spokane County DA's office was deep into ensuring the murdered women would, at long last, get the justice that they deserved.

The assistant prosecuting attorneys assigned to the case—Sharon Hedlund, Tom Treppiedi, and Rachael Curtis—knew they had a unique challenge in taking this case to a jury. Serial killer cases were exceptionally rare and difficult to prosecute for a thousand reasons. Cold cases that were twenty-four years old meant lost evidence, faded memories, and missing—even deceased—witnesses.

The motive behind the murders of these three prostitutes was uncertain. There was literally and figuratively no smoking gun. There were no eyewitnesses. The forensic evidence linking Donna Perry to the murders committed as Douglas Perry was good, but it was open to challenge.

And complicating matters to the nth degree was that the alleged killer had been diagnosed as mentally unstable.

A good prosecutor could usually address those kinds of trial hurdles with proper presentation of the evidence and witness testimony.

But this case had a wild card—a really *wild* one at that.

No one had even heard of a serial killer who had a sex-change operation ten years after the murders and more than ten years before the arrest. How should a prosecutor factor that into the plan for presenting the case to a jury? Was that a major factor in the crimes, or was it just a bizarre element that had no relevance to guilt or innocence? Should it be emphasized repeatedly to the jurors or just explained once?

Would it be difficult for jurors to accept that the alleged killer was a man named Douglas but also a woman named Donna sitting in the courtroom? And were they really the same person all the time? Dresback and others wondered what the jury would make of the gender switch. Would those seated want to convict a woman for crimes committed while she was a man?

Attitudes about gender dysphoria were slowly beginning to shift from disgust and outrage to something close—but not quite—to sympathy.

And while prosecutor Sharon Hedlund was more than competent to win a conviction, that didn't mean the cops especially liked working with the Spokane native. Despite her deep experience, the detectives disliked Hedlund's tendency to push them to do additional investigating and to take extra steps they thought were unnecessary. One cop described a typical Hedlund demand as "I want to know who so-and-so's uncle's third cousin was." The cops usually refused to chase her more extreme demands, saying that they would investigate them when they came up in court.

Not before.

Dresback worked closely with the prosecutor's office to make sure the team had the evidence to convince the jury. He knew he and the prosecutors differed on motive, but that was fine. Prosecutors didn't have to prove motive, although jurors always wanted to hear a reasonable explanation for why the killer killed. For Dresback, Clairann Gallaway was the key to motive: He believed Douglas Perry wanted to eliminate the people Clairann spent time with—the women of the Circle—so he could have her all to himself. Dresback knew the prosecutors would argue their primary theory that Douglas Perry killed the prostitutes because they disgusted him, and they wasted their ability to have children—an ability he envied.

Despite such differences, Dresback respected the prosecutors' role, and he stayed in his lane as the investigator who could advise about the facts of the case and produce the evidence. His job was to support the prosecution, and he was dedicated to ensuring Hedlund and her team had the DNA, fingerprints, witness testimony, and all the rest to prove to a jury that Donna Perry was the killer.

The three prosecutors made an interesting and capable team.

Sharon Lee Hedlund was fifty-one and had been an attorney for twenty years. She often wore her light-blond hair pulled back in a ponytail or a bun pinned to the back of her head, which—when coupled with one of her court-ready dark suits—gave her an all-business appearance. A smart, tough, and detailed prosecutor, Hedlund was also seen as totally committed to her local community, having served on several civic committees and, most notably, as a court monitor for Spokane's widely regarded Hoopfest basketball program—something she never missed for two decades.

Thomas Nicholas Treppiedi was thirty-six and had been practicing law for eleven years since he graduated from the Gonzaga University School of Law in Spokane in 2006. He was a husky young man with dark hair and a beard.

Rachael Curtis had long, wavy blond hair and wide-ranging experience for such a young attorney. Before joining the DA's staff two years earlier, she had served as a paralegal in the US Navy's Judge Advocate General's Corps, a certified legal intern in the San Diego County District Attorney's Office, and a law clerk in the US District Court for the Eastern District of Washington.

The first hearing in the *State of Washington v. Donna R. Perry (aka) Douglas R. Perry*, Case Number 14-1-00190-9, was scheduled for Monday, March 17, 2014. But as should have been expected in an ever-evolving case, there was a glitch. Perry's court-appointed attorney, Assistant Public Defender Anna Nordtvedt, had to explain to Judge Greg Sypolt that her client would not be attending the hearing and that she had not even been able to talk to her yet. The judge rescheduled the hearing for the next day.

Prosecutors filed a motion before the hearing, arguing Judge Sypolt should keep the defendant in jail without bond because the crimes charged involved the use of a firearm or other deadly weapon, because Donna Perry posed a danger to the community, and because she was a flight risk. But when Perry attended the next hearing on Tuesday—looking tired and haggard in an orange jail jumpsuit—the judge set bond at $1 million. Perry couldn't come up with the cash, so she remained in the Spokane County Jail, pending her arraignment on March 25.

The media used stories on the hearing for the first in-depth discussions of the defendant's sex change and its effect on the triple homicide case. Reporters pounced on her comments in the interview with detectives that Dresback included in the affidavit he filed in October in support of his request for murder charges. Most experts consulted for the stories agreed that the sex change should not have any effect on the trial or the verdict, and that the gender change did not insulate Donna Perry from crimes committed by Douglas Perry.

As the executive director of the National Center for Transgender Equality noted in one story, "This doesn't seem like a transgender issue to me . . . This is not about that part of [Perry's] identity, it's about being a murderer."

News reports quoted Perry's denials that she killed the women as Douglas or Donna.

One story cited her response when asked how Donna stopped the violence—"Douglas didn't stop. Donna stopped it."—suggesting Donna blamed Douglas for the murders.

Dresback hated to see Donna's important comment interpreted that way because she never outright blamed Douglas, and the media's suggestion that she did might create false expectations among the public for a quick guilty verdict. Dresback knew the closest Donna came to incriminating Douglas was to say she didn't know whether he did or didn't commit the killings. And on several occasions, she outright denied that *he* killed anyone.

The experts in the stories also disagreed with one of Perry's baseline pronouncements—that a sex change from male to female reduces violent or aggressive tendencies. There was simply no scientific or medical evidence of that, according to the experts.

Kathy Brisbois's brother Dick—one of three brothers and four sisters—attended the hearing and said seeing Donna Perry in court brought him a sense of closure.

"It's good to see and hear that [Perry is] in jail and will be staying in jail," he told *The Spokesman-Review.* "We're all really happy to have some closure even after twenty-four years. It still brings tears to my eyes . . . My heart gets heavy when I think of my sister. I miss her."

The court system seems to accommodate—if not build in—delay after delay in complicated criminal cases. In Perry's case, Judge Sypolt approved the defense's motion to delay the arraignment until he could decide whether Perry was mentally competent to stand trial, based on a competency exam yet to be conducted. The judge also agreed to delay the trial to take evidentiary depositions from witnesses the prosecutors feared might not be available when the trial started. They included ninety-two-year-old Catherine Crisler, who was sixty-seven when she found Yolanda Sapp's body in 1990; Gorden Lucas, Nickie Lowe's boyfriend, who was sixty-four and experiencing health problems; and Perry's former fellow inmate Chero Everson, who now lived in Texas and had been difficult to communicate with recently. If they weren't available to testify at the trial, their videotaped depositions could be presented to the jury instead.

In April, the judge approved a motion by defense attorney Anna Nordtvedt for Perry to be evaluated by a sanity commission, a three-member panel of experts appointed by the judge to determine if she was competent to stand trial. Dr. Nathan Henry interviewed her three times while she was staying in the Eastern State Hospital between July 7 and August 8, when she was returned to the county jail. On August 15, he filed his report, concluding that Perry was competent to stand trial because she understood the charges against her and the nature of the court proceedings.

The other two commission members agreed and soon filed their unanimous reports.

Dr. Catherine Miller's report noted that Douglas Perry was diagnosed in 1988 with paranoid schizophrenia. He also had been diagnosed with mixed personality disorder, which meant he showed traits of other mental disorders but did not meet the full criteria to be considered to have any one of them. Dr. Miller noted a history of self-mutilation, poor relationships, and anger and impulse issues.

Dr. Miller's final diagnosis was that Perry had two additional conditions. First, she listed malingering dysthymia. Malingering refers to reporting false or intentionally exaggerated physical or mental problems. Coincidentally, medical literature says motivations for malingering can include evading criminal prosecution. Dysthymia is a level of depression less than major but still accompanied by persistent feelings of mild depression or irritability that can become severe at times. If dysthymia is not treated, it can lead to more serious mental health and behavioral problems.

The second condition Dr. Miller cited was Personality Disorder NOS, Cluster B. Medical literature says a personality disorder is caused by an unhealthy pattern of thought and behavior that makes it difficult for people to interact with the world and conduct themselves in social situations and relationships. Cluster B is a collection of disorders that affect the ways people behave, meaning Perry could have difficulty regulating her emotions and behavior, which could seem to others to be erratic, dramatic, or emotional. Cluster B includes four disorders, but Dr. Miller said Perry suffered from the antisocial disorder.

On December 9, 2014, Judge Sypolt cited the commission's findings to rule Donna Perry was competent to stand trial. The judge lifted the stay on the proceedings and conducted the long-delayed arraignment. In the courtroom, a sullen, quiet Donna Perry pled not guilty to three counts of first-degree murder.

CHAPTER THIRTY

Except for the assignment of the respected Superior Court Judge Michael P. Price to preside over the Donna Perry trial, there was little activity in 2015 until prosecutors filed a motion in November alleging a conflict of interest as grounds for the judge to remove the public defender's office and its assistants who were representing the defendant. Prosecutors cited Assistant Public Defender Anna Nordtvedt's request for public disclosure of documents from the case against Spokane serial killer Robert Lee Yates, whom the public defender's office also had represented. Prosecutors believed Nordtvedt's request suggested that the defense would name Yates as an alternative suspect. The alleged conflict involved Perry's attorneys gaining access to the documents from Yates's files in the public defender's office, which could be seen as a violation of Yates's rights by Perry's attorneys, as well as a violation of office rules.

While that confusing issue was still pending on March 7, 2016, Prosecuting Attorney Steve Tucker filed amended murder charges, adding that the crimes were part of a common scheme or plan involving more than one victim and the use of a deadly weapon. The new language upped the ante on the sentence by eliminating the possibility of parole from the mandated life sentence. The judge allowed the amended charges, which required him to conduct another arraignment. Donna Perry attended the hearing and pled not guilty again.

At a hearing on March 10, Public Defender Thomas Krzyminski argued that there was no conflict for the public defender's office to represent Donna Perry. None of the attorneys assigned to her case had represented Yates, and the office had installed a robust screening process for any employee seeking confidential information from case files. The judge agreed and rejected the motion to remove the public defender's office.

On April 14, the defense mounted a major assault on the case against Perry with a motion to sever the three murder counts and force a separate trial on each one. The defense argued the evidence against Perry on each murder individually was weak, and if each count were tried separately, Perry could be acquitted.

The motion included detailed attacks on the evidence in each murder. For example, in discussing the fingerprint on the tube of lubricating jelly found with Nickie Lowe's possessions in a dumpster, the motion noted there were unidentified fingerprints on other items in the dumpster. In a rhetorical question edged with sarcasm, the defense motion said, "One wonders if the State had the identity of the donors of those fingerprints if that would be sufficient to also charge those individuals with Ms. Lowe's murder." The motion also pointed out that the DNA samples found on items of Nickie's that contained Perry's DNA also contained mixtures of several other donors who remained unidentified. The DNA found on Kathy Brisbois's vaginal smear had a profile not expected to occur in more than 1 in 3,300 males in the United States but had been located 7,364 times in the US database. And someone other than Perry left a fingerprint in blood and fluid on a plastic bag near Kathy Brisbois's body.

Prosecutors opposed separate trials, arguing the evidence in each murder charge was strong, and each count was supported by at least one significant piece of direct evidence connecting Perry to the crime.

Just five days after filing the motion for severance, the defense asked the judge to exclude all evidence and references to Perry's conduct or convictions that occurred before or after the murder charges were filed on January 14, 2014. Prosecutors naturally opposed any restrictions on the use of any of the evidence or inappropriate conduct, arguing that all of it was necessary and proper to prove a common scheme or plan involving more than one victim, which were elements of the crimes charged.

The judge had not yet ruled on those motions when a new development shook up things dramatically.

On April 28, the three assistant public defenders representing Donna Perry withdrew because of what they called an ethics violation they had just learned of that day. The violation was said to be that the attorneys' investigators had looked through other public-defender case files without permission, presumably to get information on other cases to assist in defending Perry.

Although appointing new attorneys would force a substantial delay of the trial, the judge had no choice. He appointed Bryan Whitaker and C. Patrick Donahue, attorneys in private practice who contracted with Spokane County to serve as defense attorneys when the public defender's office had a conflict. He set the trial for June 5, 2017.

On October 7, the new defense attorneys filed documents in support of their predecessors' motion for separate trials, arguing that trying the three charges together was "inherently prejudicial" against Perry. The new prosecuting attorney who was elected the prior November, Lawrence H. Haskell, responded that there was no proof that one trial would be "so manifestly prejudicial as to outweigh the concern for judicial economy" in conducting one trial rather than three.

Judge Price, always a calm and serious presence with his shock of almost snowy hair and angular features, heard arguments on October 12 and 13, including new defense motions asking the judge to bar prosecutors from using any of Donna Perry's statements to Dresback and Burbridge when they interviewed her in November 2012, to Chero Everson while she and Perry were in prison together in June 2013, and to the detectives who accompanied her on the flight from Texas to Spokane in March 2014.

The prosecution and defense played the video of the police interview for the judge so he could determine if Donna Perry's comments were voluntary and could be used in a trial. Prosecutors then put Detective Dresback on the stand to testify that he never had any discussions with the defendant other than what was shown in the video. Detectives Jennifer Sutter and Barbara Byington testified that they didn't question Perry during the flight, and all her comments to them were unsolicited and voluntary. Under cross-examination, all the detectives said they were aware Perry was taking medication to deal with her mental condition but didn't know if she was properly medicated when they talked to her.

And then Donna Perry took the witness stand to testify that she didn't believe she was getting her medications correctly when she talked to Dresback or the detectives on the plane. If her medication wasn't taken correctly, she said, it wouldn't work, and she would "run off at the mouth like a ticky [*sic*] little bird," saying almost anything that popped into her head. With the proper medication, she would be more able to control herself.

Defense attorney Bryan Whitaker, a husky man with close-cropped gray hair and a goatee, asked if her medication was sedating.

"Most of the time," she said. "If you keep your mouth shut, they don't even know you're there."

"Sometimes, the statements that you're making, are they fabricated?"

"In my opinion, they're not, but probably the rest of the world wouldn't understand what I'm doing."

"Why would that be?"

"I'm schizophrenic. I'm just not mouthy or violent."

Under cross-examination by Treppiedi, Perry said she had tried to control her conversation on the airplane because she didn't want to attract attention while she was wearing chain restraints and possibly scare the other passengers. Treppiedi asked about her thought process when she was talking to the detectives on the plane.

"I was visiting. I was just sitting there shooting the breeze with somebody to pass the time," she said.

In arguments to the judge, Whitaker said Perry's statements during the police interview should be suppressed because she asked for a lawyer five times, but the detectives kept conversing with her for forty-five minutes until they confused her enough that she agreed to talk to them without an attorney.

Treppiedi responded that the law requires a suspect's request for counsel to be "unambiguous," but Perry's comments were equivocal. The detectives had the right to continue to ask if Perry definitely wanted an attorney. During that discussion, Perry voluntarily decided to talk without an attorney.

Whitaker's attack on the use of Perry's comments to Chero Everson was simple. Her meeting with detectives in prison made her an agent of law enforcement, and Perry's comments to her should be barred unless Perry was informed of her rights first.

Treppiedi said Everson talked to Perry before she met with the detectives, and she never acted as their agent at any time. Everson should be allowed to testify about anything she heard Perry say.

When he argued for breaking the case into three trials, Pat Donahue—a tall, slim man with dark hair and a goatee—said the evidence, especially the DNA evidence, was weak in the cases related to Yolanda Sapp and Nickie Lowe. But jurors could be improperly influenced by stronger DNA evidence in Kathy Brisbois's case.

Prosecutor Sharon Hedlund rejected Donahue's characterization of the evidence, especially the DNA. She said Perry's DNA on Yolanda's blanket was mixed with hers. And she added, "Quite frankly, it's the State's position that the blanket was utilized to drag her out of the car and dump her down the hill like a piece of trash."

Hedlund's response to the defense's claim that trying all three murders together was prejudicial to Perry was classic. "Evidence is prejudicial to the defendants. That's kind of the point."

Judge Price immediately denied all the defense's motions. He found no indication that Perry's rights were violated when she talked to the police, to Chero Everson, or to detectives on the airplane, or that she was in any way coerced to make any statements.

The judge also denied the defense motion for three separate trials. He ruled that the evidence on each charge was strong but so intertwined that severing the counts would require three full trials with similar evidence, mostly the same witnesses, and a significant amount of court time for each case.

In some places, it's called the SODDI defense, which refers to the guy charged with the crime pointing his finger and saying, "Some Other Dude Did It." It's a difficult defense to use in a trial, and a judge has to approve it by ruling there is enough evidence against the other "dude" to demonstrate he had motive and opportunity—in other words, to make him a realistic suspect.

On April 4, 2017, just two months before Donna Perry was scheduled to go to trial, her defense attorneys filed a motion to invoke the SODDI defense by naming two men as alternative suspects in Nickie Lowe's murder.

The first was Michael Lee Haney, the drug dealer whose name had come up twenty-six years prior in the investigation by Detectives Jim Hansen and Jim Peterson. They had been told that Haney, who was forty-seven in 1990 but had since died, had claimed he killed the three women because they owed him money for drugs. He'd already admitted to the police that he'd lied about this to scare people into paying their debts to him. Haney passed two polygraph tests in which he denied any role in the murders or knowing who committed them. The defense noted that Gorden Lucas had suspected Haney in Nickie's murder.

The defense also wanted to suggest that Gregory Ross, Haney's cousin or perhaps nephew, might have killed Nickie at Haney's request because she owed him $500 for cocaine. The defense said Ross had a reputation for being Haney's "hit man," who would do anything for him. Haney and Ross, the defense attorneys said, had motive, opportunity, and incentive to kill Nickie and should be presented to the jury as alternative suspects.

Deputy Prosecutor Rachael Curtis argued there was no evidence connecting Haney and Ross to the murder or indicating Ross even knew Nickie or had ever committed any crimes for Haney. The law, she said, required alternative suspects to be linked to the crime by direct evidence that was "nonspeculative," and that was not the case here.

Three weeks later, the judge denied defense attorneys' request to name Haney and Ross as suspects based on what he considered "wildly speculative evidence," most of which would not be admissible at trial. The judge went one step further. He barred Donna Perry's attorneys from *suggesting* to the jury that there was evidence that someone other than the defendant murdered Nickie Lowe.

The SODDI defense was out.

Spokane Street Motel manager Linda Rose bought a new outfit at the downtown Macy's for the Donna Perry trial. Despite the sketchy reputation of her establishment, Linda understood the importance of appearances before the court. Indeed, the summons to testify brought back a flood of memories. The courtroom was the same one where she'd found herself facing off with her brother, Frank Pozar Jr.

Frank and Tessie Pozar, Linda's parents and the owners of the Spokane Street Motel, vanished in the fall of 1984 while preparing for an annual trip to Hawaii, where the self-made couple had accumulated twenty-four lots of property with plans to retire there. They never dropped off their dogs, boarded their flight, or arrived in Hawaii. Almost right away, suspicion fell on Linda's brother, Frank Pozar Jr., who had been estranged from their parents for poor financial decisions he'd made with properties they'd given him. Junior announced that they'd patched things up and moved into the living quarters his parents kept at the motel.

Linda, who had seen her parents a few days before their disappearance, knew something wasn't right. Her parents never mentioned any reconciliation whatsoever. The next thing she knew, her brother started cashing in her mother and father's savings bonds and forging their names on credit purchases to fund an ill-fated computer magazine he'd sought to publish. Linda's testimony on those forgery and fraud charges helped send her thirty-four-year-old brother to prison, but didn't bring a true resolution.

Frank and Tessie's disappearance case has never been resolved.

Linda Rose knew exactly how it felt to wait for a long time for justice, like the families of the Circle.

She was still waiting.

On June 6, 2017, *The Spokesman-Review* that landed on Linda's front step offered up a reminder that was hardly needed by any of those who knew and loved the murdered women found along the river.

CHAPTER THIRTY-ONE

TRIAL OF SUSPECTED SERIAL KILLER TO PICK JURY

The Spokesman-Review

June 6, 2017

The Spokane County Courthouse dominates West Broadway Avenue with its off-white brick façade, blue slate roof, and nine-story central tower—a distinctly European design described as French Renaissance Revival. Behind the five-story building, built in 1895 and marked by four turrets with pointed roofs across the front, is a complex of modern buildings that house offices and court activities.

Behind those walls and in one of the somewhat crowded courtrooms, a trial unlike any ever held anywhere commenced on Friday, June 9, 2017. Spectators would see a courtroom with the three prosecutors sitting on the left and two defense attorneys flanking the defendant, Donna Rebecca Perry, on the right. The podium from which the attorneys would question witnesses filled the gap between either side. There wasn't much room between the attorneys' tables and the desk where the court reporter sat to the left of Judge Price on his elevated bench. Along the left wall at the front of the room were the rows of chairs behind a railing—the jury box.

Opening statements by the prosecutor and the defense offered two wildly different interpretations of the case they'd present a jury of a dozen people, plus alternates, culled from more than 370 called into potential service. They disagreed not only about what the evidence proved but also about how the now-famous sex change from Douglas Perry to Donna Perry fit into this unprecedented and bizarre story of a serial killer.

Deputy Prosecuting Attorney Sharon Hedlund, wearing a dark suit with her blond hair pulled back, said the evidence would tell the story of a man named Douglas Perry who was so disgusted by the lifestyles of prostitutes that he murdered three of them in 1990 and left their naked bodies on display on the banks of the Spokane River. Ten years later, she said, the killer underwent gender-reassignment surgery in Thailand in the belief that it would end his violent tendencies by transforming him into a woman named Donna Perry.

Hedlund said the defendant's guilt would be proven by Perry's DNA found under Kathy Brisbois's left middle fingernail, Perry's DNA mixed with Yolanda Sapp's blood on a blanket found near her body, and Perry's fingerprint on a tube of lubricating jelly among Nickie Lowe's belongings. The three murders were clearly committed by the same person, who shot all three with a small-caliber gun, stripped their bodies, and dumped them "like trash."

"In prison, she bragged about killing women and dumping them in a similar manner," Hedlund said.

Defense Attorney Pat Donahue rejected that characterization of his client. He said the evidence proved that Douglas Perry and his live-in prostitute girlfriend, Clairann Gallaway, were associated with a community of prostitutes who lived and worked along Spokane's East Sprague Avenue. Their association with the prostitutes could explain the coincidence of Perry's DNA and fingerprint on the women's items found during the investigation.

"They found her DNA in her community and now they're trying to hang three old murders on her," Donahue said. He offered a similar analysis of Perry's fingerprint on the tube of lubricating jelly "dug out of a dumpster . . . more than a mile away from where Ms. Lowe's body was found . . . More than two decades later, the State cherry-picks evidence that puts Ms. Perry in the middle to make it all fit."

Donahue also rejected the suggestion that Donna underwent a sex change to distance herself from Douglas, to reduce violent tendencies, or to attempt to conceal her identity so she would not be held responsible for violence by Douglas.

"The evidence will show exactly the opposite," he said. "Donna and Douglas are the same person."

Donahue used an unusual prop as he tried to explain the standard of reasonable doubt required to prove a defendant's guilt. He held up a bottle of Tylenol and asked, if the Tylenol was thirty years old, what level of reasonable doubt a parent would have to exceed before opening the bottle to give to their child.

A reference to the cyanide-laced capsules that left seven dead in Chicago in the autumn of 1982.

Or maybe not.

In a pose Donna Perry would maintain throughout the trial, she sat quietly at the defense table with her eyes downcast, wearing headphones to assist her hearing and offering no reaction to what was said in the courtroom. To some observers, the defendant was a lot like Norman Bates in Psycho in the final scene of the film. Donna's clothes were drab, her hair barely brushed. She kept her body tight and looked utterly helpless. She couldn't hurt a soul. Not even a fly.

One of the first witnesses called to testify had known the victims, their lives, and their deaths.

Linda Rose was no stranger to the witness stand. On that day, however, Linda was in court not for her mom and dad, but for the Circle.

She told the jury she had begun renting to "street girls" sometime before 1990 after a new expressway reduced the traffic by Canadians driving into Spokane, which had been her major source of guests. She knew what the prostitutes did and told them they were not allowed to practice their profession in the motel rooms.

Linda said Yolanda Sapp, her boyfriend Darrel "Doc" Thomas, and Kathy Brisbois lived at the motel, but she did not recognize Nickie Lowe's name.

Prosecutor Hedlund asked, "Do you recall Doc's demeanor, Darrel Thomas's demeanor, when discussing Yolanda's disappearance?"

Linda nodded. "He was real upset about it."

"And did he ask you for anything or did he try to get any money from you?"

"I believe that he asked me for a little bit of his rent back because he wanted to go searching for her or something."

The defense attorneys had no questions.

The first trial of an alleged transgender serial killer in history did not slip quietly through the weekend. The story in Saturday's *Spokesman-Review*—under the headline "Heated Start to Triple-Murder Trial"—managed to present all the unprecedented aspects of the case in straightforward but still surprising, even gripping, detail. The drama inherent in the basic facts was simply inescapable. The story highlighted some of the questions that had long worried cops like Hansen and Burbridge. The charges said a man named Douglas Perry killed three prostitutes and dumped their naked bodies on the banks of the Spokane River twenty-seven years earlier. The person sitting before the jury now, however, was a woman named Donna Perry.

Was this woman legally liable for the acts of that man?

And what did it mean that the man had been living with another prostitute at the time of the murders? What about the mental condition of Douglas/Donna Perry—the person who defense attorneys said was raped by his father? Abused by his brother, mother too? Would a jury be able to sort through all the layers of human conflict and the number of tragic victims to determine if anyone was responsible for everything that had happened in this case?

When the trial resumed on Monday, June 12, the prosecution began an effort to bring the victims to the jury as real people trying to live their lives the best they could. Yolanda's daughter Marika—ten when her mom died and now thirty-seven—identified a photograph of the two of them taken when she was three.

"Just trying not to cry," she said, almost in a whisper.

In a halting and anguished voice, Marika testified she and her younger sister had been staying with their maternal grandmother in the Tacoma area while their mom was living in Spokane with Doc. Her mom would travel back and forth to visit them, sometimes staying a month or two. Her goal had been to get permanent custody of her daughters and move them to Spokane with her, but she was murdered before she could do that.

For the second time, defense attorneys had no questions.

Next, Chilesa Patzer took the stand to talk about her aunt, Nickie Lowe, her mother's older sister. By the time of the trial, Nickie's mom, Diane Matney, had passed at sixty-eight. So had Nickie's sister, Jackie. Though Chilesa, twenty-seven, was just seven months old at the time of the killings, she easily identified a photo of the aunt she never knew. She said her aunt had no children of her own but shared two stepchildren with her common-law husband, Gorden Lucas. She had plans for the future. Chilesa confirmed that before her murder, Nickie had obtained a dog groomer's license and had made plans for a mobile grooming service.

Again, no questions from the defense.

And really, courtroom observers mused, any questions from the defense could only come off as victim blaming or shaming. That wouldn't help Donna Perry. Not in the least.

And then Kathy Brisbois's youngest daughter, Kathleen Mewes—eleven when her mother was murdered, and now thirty-eight—took the stand to identify a photo of her mother with her when she was just six. Her older sisters were fourteen and nineteen at the time.

"Did your mom have any plans for the future right before she was killed?" Prosecutor Rachael Curtis asked.

"Yes," she said, her voice charged with emotion. "She was in contact with our caseworker. She was trying to get visitation rights to visit me and my sister."

The defense had no questions for the third victim's daughter.

Then it was time to talk about murder.

Retired Sheriff's Detective Larry Miller took the stand to identify photographs he took at the scene where Kathy's body was found. Hedlund had him mark locations where various pieces of evidence were found and then cut open sealed evidence bags to show the jury a gray tweed jacket, a left shoe, and a multicolored sunsuit.

"The bloodstains and hair samples that we located were mainly on the roadway leading from where the coat was located down the curve, down the roadway that connects with the main road that parallels the river. It was like there was drops or patches of it as it went down like the victim had been carried down to that location or dragged down to that location," Miller said.

Next, Hedlund called John Graves, a local bail bondsman who had done business with Yolanda Sapp and Darrel "Doc" Thomas "off and on" for several years. He said he ran into them on February 21, 1990, outside of a motel. They asked him to loan them some money. He didn't say how he responded.

"Did you ever have any contact with [Thomas] after Yolanda was found deceased?" Hedlund asked.

"I had contacted Doc, yes . . . He just came to me and said, 'They killed my baby.'"

Whitaker's cross-examination was quick.

"Did Yolanda and Thomas need money often?"

"Yes."

"Do you know if they were in debt to anyone at that time?"

"I have no idea, sir. Not to me."

CHAPTER THIRTY-TWO

On day two of the trial, Gorden Lucas told the court he was living the thug life while he and Nickie Lowe tried to carve out a life together for more than a decade.

"I did a lot of robbing, a lot of illegal stuff like that . . . Ran massage parlors," he said.

Lucas described how he and Nickie met in the late 1970s when they both worked at a massage parlor in State Line, Idaho. Sometime before 1990, they ended up moving in with Nickie's mother in Spokane and "working the streets." He called that their "last resort" and said Nickie was a prostitute to get money to buy drugs.

Hedlund asked him to describe his personal relationship with Nickie.

"It was like a normal life as anybody else," he said. "It's just that it was against the law. I mean, we had a normal life other than that. I mean she was a loving person, very. When she worked, she worked, and when she didn't, she didn't. And you know, it was a normal life."

Nickie's brutal murder sent Lucas on a downward spiral ending in 1991 when he went to federal prison in Oregon for bank robbery. He served three years of a seven-and-a-half-year sentence but said that incarceration helped him go straight after he was paroled. He had a good job and had gotten married.

"I haven't had so much as a speeding ticket since then," he said, a little wistful pride seeping into his words. "Got it right finally, which was too late and I'm sorry about that."

He said learning that Nickie's murder and the other two cases were being reopened caused him some emotional upset, implying that he returned briefly to drug use.

"Why is that?" Hedlund asked.

"Well, I would have liked to have been the one to, at that . . . point in time, you know, to deal with it instead of the courts. We wouldn't be having this court date today."

At her seat at the defense table, Donna Perry, dressed in slacks and a pale-lavender blouse, kept her eyes down and offered no reaction to Lucas's implication that he would like to have killed her.

Hedlund had Lucas identify several photos of items Nickie had with her when she disappeared and were found in a dumpster off East Sprague: her shoes, her wallet, and a tube of lubricating jelly that bore Perry's fingerprint. He also identified photos of Yolanda Sapp and Kathy Brisbois, explaining that he and Nickie knew them well, that the women often rented a room together at the Spokane Street Motel and worked together when customers wanted more than one girl.

"They trusted each other," he said, "and they worked together that way."

He said he thought something unusual had happened that made the women afraid.

"There was [something] . . . at that point in time, when Yolanda got murdered, and Nickie kept saying she was next, and her and Kathy were tight at them times and ran together a little bit there. I couldn't get much out of them as far as, you know, when they said that, I said why, what did you do . . . and I never did really find out."

"And what about after Nickie died? Did you have any communication with Kathy about it?"

He said he saw her at the motel.

"She was uptight, too. Very uptight, like something was going to happen."

Finally, Hedlund showed Lucas a photo of Douglas Perry.

Lucas indicated he'd seen the defendant at a house near the motel shortly after Nickie was killed.

"I've seen him around and that's all I can say," he said. "I did not know him, and we weren't friends."

Under cross-examination by Whitaker, Lucas said he did not know if Nickie owed money to anyone. He agreed with the defense lawyer that there were times when people who believed they had been ripped off or wronged took matters into their own hands.

"Is this what that felt like to you?" Whitaker asked.

"Sure, it did. Something was not right."

Though some three hundred miles away in Tacoma, the story of who their mother was that was being played out in the courtroom and long before during the seemingly never-ending investigation was extremely hurtful to the family of Yolanda Sapp. Repeatedly, the media denigrated Yolanda Sapp's memory by referring to her solely as a drug-addicted prostitute.

Like she was nothing but *that*.

The truth was, Yolanda was like Kathy Brisbois, a mother looking to make her way back home to her girls.

A mother who loved her kids.

Yolanda's murder by the river's edge put an end to the possibility— the *hope*—that everything would be okay someday and a happy ending was possible. When one of her daughters saw other children with their mothers at school, she still had hope for a reunion.

A chance to be like the other kids.

No one had a right to take that away from Yolanda's girls.

CHAPTER THIRTY-THREE

From his seat on the bench behind the prosecutors' table, Detective Jim Dresback hoped the testimony he was hearing from the stand on the third day of trial—June 13, 2017—would create a huge leap toward a conviction of Donna Perry. To Dresback, the testimony by forensic scientist Mariah Low of the Washington State Patrol Crime Laboratory was the most exciting and the most incriminating.

Listening to Low now, Dresback could easily remember their phone call on September 14, 2012, when she announced that the DNA profile she created from blood and material under Kathy Brisbois's fingernail got a "cold hit" in the national DNA database, matching it to a man named Douglas Perry—a man who soon turned out to be Donna Perry. That was the first payoff for the cops and their predecessors who had been chasing a serial killer for twenty-four years.

As he listened to Low's account of the testing that led to the DNA match, Dresback was hoping the jurors were also appreciating her testimony and what he considered was its near destruction of Perry's claim of innocence.

Testimony early on the fourth day of trial, however, concerned a less impressive event by the crime lab. Spokane Police Sergeant Kip Hollenbeck told the jury he was assigned in 2008 to review the Yolanda Sapp and Nickie Lowe murder files as cold cases. He learned some pieces of evidence from the Yolanda Sapp investigation had been mistakenly destroyed in 1999 while the crime lab was undergoing renovation. Included among the items incinerated by the lab were the green army blanket that was wrapped around Yolanda's legs, a blood-soaked towel, a wig, a necklace, two rings, some carpet samples, and some trace evidence like hair and fingernails.

Prosecutor Tom Treppiedi asked facetiously, "Sergeant Hollenbeck, is it a good thing that items of evidence were destroyed?"

"No, sir."

"Was there still evidence for you to pursue, then, in reviewing this case?"

"Yes, there were several other items."

Cross-examined by Whitaker, Hollenbeck said the destruction of the evidence was reviewed, and another officer wrote a report that concluded, "A subsequent investigation found that there was no malicious intent to destroy the evidence."

The fifth day of trial, June 15, featured a parade of retired detectives offering their memories of the investigations into the three murders before the court, as well as the long list of other prostitutes murdered in Spokane in the '90s.

As retired Sheriff's Detective Jim Hansen was sworn in, he got his first look at Donna Perry—a strange experience after all these years of not seeing the face of the serial killer he was chasing. In fact, as he testified, he realized he was having a hard time keeping his eyes off of her and his mind off of her sex change as she sat almost unmoving with her head down at the defense table. He had worried about whether the unique complication of a sex change for a serial killer would derail the trial by giving the defense the ability to argue that the person charged was not the same person who committed the crimes. Hansen had little faith the system could overcome that kind of hurdle and deliver what he thought was the appropriate justice—three murder convictions. He just hoped the courts and jurors would see the sex change for what he believed it was—a scam she created specifically to enable her to avoid responsibility for the murders.

While all of that was rattling around in his head, Hansen tried to focus on his testimony to explain he had worked on the city-county task force through the end of 1990, and then he and city police Detective Jim Peterson took over the investigation into all three murders in January 1991. He listed some of the people they interviewed, including some more than once, and talked about the evidence they sent to the crime lab for analysis in the days before DNA became such precise and damning evidence.

Under cross-examination by Whitaker, Hansen said he never heard the names of Douglas or Donna Perry or Clairann Gallaway in all the years he investigated the cases.

CHAPTER THIRTY-FOUR

One of the few comments the jury would hear about Donna Perry's gender identity came from an ATF agent early on the sixth day of testimony, Monday, June 19, 2017.

Agent Lance Hart testified he and the Spokane police executed a search warrant at Douglas Perry's house on East Dalton Avenue on June 30, 1994, to seize firearms the defendant was illegally accumulating.

Hart said he asked Douglas Perry how he had the financial means to acquire the thirty-three rifles and pistols the police had just seized.

"He told me that he would dress up as a woman and he would go onto Sprague Avenue, and he would engage with customers as a prostitute, and that he would make his money that way to purchase firearms."

Prosecutor Treppiedi did not ask Hart any more questions about that, but it surely grabbed the jurors' attention.

And the next witness certainly held their attention too.

Valerie Katrell said she was a "working girl" on the Spokane Stroll when Douglas Perry picked her up for a date on New Year's Eve, December 31, 1998, and took her to his house on East Empire Avenue.

Treppiedi asked, "What struck you or why does that time stick out to you?"

"Because it was the strangest . . . when I walked into his home, I looked around, and I said [to myself], 'Whatever you do, you do whatever you have to, to get out of this place alive,' because he was extremely creepy. There was mannequins and crossbows and weapons and things everywhere in his house, everywhere. And it was just the creepiest thing I've ever been through in my life."

"Did he say anything to you?"

"He was petting my face and telling me, 'I could never hurt you. I could never hurt you.' It was the creepiest thing because, petting my face. That's all I remember. That's all I could remember him saying."

The defense had no questions for the witness.

The officer who stopped Perry that morning after talking to Valerie Katrell was Corporal William J. Hager, who testified the defendant was armed with two knives and a taser. He said the defendant gave him permission to search his car, and he found several documents in the glove box.

"They were some attorney papers that had the name Douglas R. Perry on it and basically in the highlight it said that Mr. Perry had a gender psychosis disorder."

That drew an immediate objection to hearsay testimony from the defense that the judge quickly sustained.

Treppiedi then had Hagen testify that he found other papers in the car "that showed the proper steps on getting a sex change." That line went by without objection.

The defendant's omnipresence on the Stroll was also confirmed by city police Captain Thomas J. Hendren, who was on patrol in 1998 when he stopped the defendant on East Sprague Avenue at 1:30 a.m. Hendren testified that all he entered on a field-interview card was that Perry "was hostile and wearing a four-inch-long blade knife and a stun gun on his belt and I had questioned that individual about if they were involved in prostitution activity and they denied it."

No charge, he said, was filed.

Next, Sharon Hedlund turned the jury's attention to the defendant's ownership of guns that could have fired the bullets that killed the prostitutes. ATF Special Agent Michael Northcutt testified that two

.22-caliber rifles—a Remington Arms model 597 and a Ruger model 10/22—were among the twelve firearms seized when ATF and Spokane police raided the Perry residence on East Empire Avenue in March 2012. When the eleven-year ATF veteran ran a trace on the Ruger, records showed it had been shipped to a sporting goods store in Coeur d'Alene, Idaho, on April 17, 1989, where it was purchased on May 4, 1989, by a man whose name appeared in the records as Bruce Earl *Massengate*. Northcutt said he determined that name was a misspelling, and the buyer was Bruce Massengale, one of the brothers thought to have bought and kept guns for Douglas while he was banned from owning firearms.

Under cross-examination by Bryan Whitaker, age fifty-six, Special Agent Northcutt said it was May 19, 2017, when he ran the trace on the Ruger model 10/22 rifle that was seized in 1994.

"So, last month?" Whitaker asked.

Northcutt nodded. "Correct."

"Twenty-three years later?"

"If the math is correct, yes."

Pressed by the defense lawyer, Northcutt told the jury he was not familiar with the ballistic reports in the murders and could not speak to whether either of the rifles he mentioned had anything to do with the case.

Three bullets were recovered from two of the victims: one from Nickie Lowe and two from Kathy Brisbois. The three bullets killing Yolanda Sapp were never recovered. The bullet found in Nickie's spine was virtually intact. One of those from Kathy was still most of a bullet, but the other one was more damaged. Both were badly distorted.

Gaylan Warren, a former forensic scientist from the State Patrol Crime Lab who now operated his own lab, Columbia International Forensics Laboratory, testified that he couldn't provide complete analysis of the bullets because there was no gun to test. He concluded, however, they were all .22-caliber long-rifle bullets. Classifying them as long-rifle bullets didn't mean they were fired by a rifle—it denoted the size of the cartridge.

Warren testified the bullet from Nickie and the better bullet from Kathy could have been fired by the same gun. They shared characteristics of being fired through a rifled barrel that had six lands and grooves with a right twist. That means the grooves cut into the inside of the barrel that makes the bullet spin and stabilize had six raised portions— the lands—and six grooves, all of which made the bullet spin clockwise, which is the right twist. The barrel of the gun that fired those bullets would have to match those characteristics.

But Warren testified the two bullets recovered from Brisbois did not share characteristics and had been fired through different barrels. That could mean they were fired by separate guns, but they also could have been fired by a gun that had multiple barrels, such as a double-barreled derringer.

The next witness was Glenn Davis, a firearms expert from the State Patrol Crime Lab who said his analysis of the three bullets was similar to Warren's conclusions. But he said he believed all three bullets could have been fired by the same gun.

He said he provided the police with lists of dozens of manufacturers that made guns that could have fired the bullets—pistols, derringers, and rifles. City police Detective Michael Drapeau testified he found records of two purchases by Perry of .22-caliber handguns, one made by Rohm and the other by Iver Johnson. He said he did not know exactly when the defendant made those purchases, but all guns seized by ATF were purchased between December 3, 1973, and February 21, 1979—roughly eleven to sixteen years before the murders.

Drapeau also testified that part of his responsibility in the first phase of the investigation was to document Perry's background and personal history. Hedlund used that opportunity to address Perry's sex change, asking Drapeau, "Were you able to discern a change in Mr. Perry to Miss Perry or Ms. Perry?"

He looked down at the papers in front of him.

"Yes," he said. "During the background reviewing his case file—let me find it here—on about January 31, 2000, Douglas Perry, while on probation, flew to Bangkok, Thailand, and got a gender-reassignment surgery."

There it was. It was out in the open now. Donna Perry had no reaction as she remained frozen at the defense table. Hedlund didn't dwell on it, quickly asking Drapeau if he assisted in the interviews of the Massengale brothers. He said he did, but Whitaker again objected to testimony characterizing the Massengales in any way.

The judge overruled the objection this time.

Hedlund asked Drapeau for his impression of the Massengales, and he mentioned something that had been the subject of discussion among the cops for some time. "It sat in my mind that [Mark Massengale] wouldn't say the word 'prostitute.' He just kept saying 'working girl.'"

"And that seemed odd to you?"

"Seemed odd to me."

CHAPTER
THIRTY-FIVE

The seventh day of trial was consumed by testimony by forensic scientists who performed fingerprint comparisons after Douglas Perry was identified as a suspect. The scientists used Perry's fingerprints from his "ten print" or "ten card"—the single card bearing prints for all ten fingers—to compare to prints on evidence from the murders.

Kristen Storment, a forensic scientist with the state crime lab, testified that in 2012, Detective Mark Burbridge submitted five items believed to belong to Nickie Lowe, which were found in the dumpster, for fingerprint comparisons. The witness matched the defendant's fingerprint on a tube of lubricating jelly.

On cross-examination, Whitaker tried to minimize the value of matching the fingerprint on the tube to his client by asking the witness if she could tell how old the fingerprint was.

Storment said fingerprints cannot be aged.

Carrie Christen, the retired manager of the forensic unit for the Spokane police, testified she also matched the defendant's prints to those on the tube, confirming Storment's conclusion. She said a fingerprint on the envelope from the state welfare office also found in the dumpster drew a match with another man through the Automated Fingerprint Identification System known as AFIS in 1996. But she said the man's fingerprints did not appear on any other items in the investigation, and he did not become a suspect in Nickie Lowe's murder. The man told police he discarded the envelope after opening it and reading the contents as he passed by the dumpster.

Many observers from the public sector—trial junkies, as they are known—hold a fascination for DNA and its growing role in forensic science. It's incontrovertible. It is what it is and nothing else. For those watching the Donna Perry trial, however, it wasn't the most important part of the state's case.

They weren't there to figure out who Donna Perry killed. They were there to figure out just who this woman was.

What was her story?

What made her tick?

CHAPTER THIRTY-SIX

Social worker Danielle Arndt told the jury on the eighth day of trial—June 21, 2017—that Donna Perry had been pleasant and cooperative as Arndt began conducting a "psycho-social assessment," but became "more angry and upset" as she insisted on talking about the murder charges against her.

"She would not redirect from that topic and appeared to me that she was attempting to prove her innocence," Arndt said.

Arndt had been assisting in a court-ordered mental competency evaluation in the summer of 2014 when Perry was admitted to Eastern State Hospital. The witness said her goal was to collect information on the defendant's "background, drug and alcohol history, family history, previous mental health history, pretty much all history, background. Also, I go through the police reports, document that. I interview the patients, ask why they are there, why they think they're there, things like that."

The defendant told her that the only reason she was caught was because her DNA was found under a prostitute's fingernail. And she had harsh words for that prostitute, who was one of three Perry was charged with killing.

"She slept with eight other people that day. She turned tricks. You know what people who turn tricks are? Fools. Jokers," she recalled Perry saying of the victim, who turned out to be Kathy Brisbois.

When it was his turn, Whitaker focused his cross on the fact that Arndt's report only had quotation marks around the word "fingernail," but she testified the entire comment by the defendant was a direct quote. Arndt agreed she should have put quotation marks around the entire comment when she wrote the report. Whitaker asked if the lack of quotation marks would have been a "glaring error" when she reviewed her report after writing it in 2014.

"Probably," she said.

The interview with Donna Perry that Detective Mark Burbridge related to the jury was entirely different from the social worker's, and it led to some disagreement between Burbridge and Defense Attorney Bryan Whitaker.

Whitaker asked if Burbridge had employed the "Reid interrogation method" when questioning his client. Burbridge almost chuckled when he said he had attended training on the method some twenty-four years earlier and didn't even remember what it was about. Whitaker provided his description as "Where you set some bait so the person will speak to you, get them to loosen up. For instance, how many times did my client ask for a lawyer before she agreed to speak to you that day?"

"One time, I believe."

"Okay. Now, after the person has done that, you confront them with a tidbit of information to get them to talk to you, correct?"

"No."

"You don't then leave the room, so they think about it and come back?"

"Well, we left the room to get the search warrant, to execute a search warrant on her . . . We executed the search warrant and then we left the room so the transport people could take her back to jail."

The detective insisted his goal in an interview is to seek the truth.

Whitaker challenged that simple definition.

"And so, when someone says that they didn't do something, according to your training, what are you supposed to do in that particular situation?"

"That depends on if we have evidence that says they are lying or not, and then we continue to try to find ways to get them to talk about what happened."

"So, you presume they are lying and any answer they give is incorrect?"

"No. That's not accurate."

"During this interview, how many times did you hear Detective Dresback tell my client she was denying the truth? Do you remember?"

"Dozens."

"And each time, it was in a direct response to having been told, 'I didn't do this'?"

"Yes."

Mark Burbridge said he never has an agenda or tries to get the answers he wants to hear. "But if I have specific evidence that someone is not telling me the truth, I confront them on that. I'm not there just to accept anything anybody says. And you can find ways to get people to get around whatever issue it is that they are not wanting to talk about or trying to make themselves look better."

Whitaker said that sounded like the goal of an interrogation, not an interview.

"It starts out as an interview and turns into an interrogation," the witness said.

"So, we should just stop calling it an interview?"

"No. There's two parts to it."

"I know," Whitaker said before ending his questioning with "we'll discuss that later, but not with you."

Sheriff's Detective Jim Dresback finally took the stand to set the stage for the jury to watch the video of the interview/interrogation of Donna

Perry he conducted with Mark Burbridge nearly five years earlier. With his hands folded calmly on the edge of the wooden stand in front of him, Dresback thought how different this felt from the countless times he had testified in other criminal trials. Not only was this the culmination of decades of good police work, years and years of intense investigation, and amazing levels of law enforcement dedication, but it also was the last time he would testify. He was retiring in six days. And this last testimony wasn't for just another case. It was for his last and most haunting case. It was a final push for justice, and he had to get it right, not only for the victims but for their families and their communities that had waited so long for answers.

Dresback told the jury his involvement in the case began when he was assigned to Major Crimes in 2004.

The detective told the jury the whole story—how matching DNA under Kathy Brisbois's fingernails to Douglas Perry's DNA in 2012 finally delivered the break needed to solve a very cold twenty-two-year-old case. He explained that tracing Douglas Perry's DNA led police to Donna Perry as the first-ever transgender serial killer. The cops learned about Perry's doomed love affair with Clairann Gallaway and her eventual departure from his life. They established the intriguing timing of the murders of Yolanda and Kathy on days when Clairann was in jail. They discovered the connection of Perry to other prostitutes on the Spokane Stroll and the times he had been stopped there by the police. And they learned about the mystifying sex-change operation. But they had never heard Douglas Perry's name before 2012.

With that background and introduction, the jurors watched the two and a half hours of conversation between the defendant, Dresback, and Burbridge. They heard Donna express absolute shock at being accused of murdering anybody. But if she did, she said repeatedly, she should be shot in the head. She denied she killed anyone—either as Douglas or Donna—and then she would say something like "I don't know if Douglas did or not. It was twenty years ago, and I have no idea whether he did or didn't." She drew a curtain between her life now and her past life as a man.

"Douglas doesn't exist anymore . . . I left him in Bangkok," she had said.

After denying ever meeting the women, the defendant finally admitted she might have had sex with Nickie and Kathy—"a time or two"—but didn't kill them.

And then the jury heard the question and answer that Dresback thought captured the entire story of Perry and the murders: "What made Donna stop?" and her response, "Douglas didn't stop. Donna stopped it. The sex-change operation." She would say later about the surgery, "It stopped the violence cold."

Dresback felt the exhaustion creeping in as he left the stand. But he wasn't just tired. He was ready to move on. He had spent a career chasing justice—and thirteen years pursuing this serial killer—and now he was reaching the end of the line.

This is it for me. I'm done, he thought.

CHAPTER THIRTY-SEVEN

The bodies of Yolanda Sapp, Nickie Lowe, and Kathy Brisbois told forensic pathologists the facts of the brutal and merciless murders, and on the ninth day of trial on June 22, 2017, John D. Howard, from the Spokane County ME's office, relayed those grisly details in clinical terms to the jury.

Prosecutor Hedlund led Dr. Howard through the murders in chronological order.

Yolanda died from three gunshot wounds from small-caliber bullets that Howard said "entered her back, went through the chest causing internal organ and aorta—the largest artery in the heart—damage and then exited through the front . . . three separate wound tracks . . . three entrances, three exits . . ." There was no evidence to indicate how close the gun was when Yolanda was shot.

He also said her body showed "some blunt injuries in the form of abrasions or scrapes, particularly in the forehead and around one of her armpits."

He didn't speculate about how she might have suffered those injuries.

Nickie was second. She also had been shot by a small-caliber weapon. This time, however, a bullet had been recovered that "passed through her skin, hit her diaphragm, her liver, went through her aorta, again the largest artery of the body, and then struck the bone of her spine and came to rest in the bone of the first lumbar vertebra or the lower back vertebra."

Dr. Howard said there was a bullet hole in her shirt and in her jacket, indicating she was shot before they were pulled up to expose her breasts. As with Yolanda, there was no physical evidence to suggest how far the gun was from her body.

Severe marks on Nickie's back indicated she had been dragged over a rough surface, probably after her shirt and jacket had been pulled up. He told the jury that the marks were probably made while she was alive but could have been postmortem.

The most severe injuries had been inflicted on the third victim, Kathy Brisbois. Howard said she had suffered at least eight blows to her head from a blunt object that caused a cut to her forehead and seven separate lacerations at the locations of impacts from hard bashes to the right side, the back, and the left side of her head.

"It could be a so-called pistol whipping where the butt of the gun or some part of the gun strikes the head," Howard said, "but it could be some other object, too. It could be a rock. There's nothing specific like a hammer blow, but two-by-fours, rocks, any kind of blunt object, as well as a gun, could produce these."

Asked if the blows would have been fatal, the medical examiner said they "would be painful but not necessarily cause death by themselves but could have some concussive effect . . . I think she was alive when these injuries occurred, based on the amount of bleeding that's associated with them."

And then there were the three gunshot wounds. Next to the cut to her forehead was a wound from a bullet that ripped through her forehead and into the cranial cavity, damaged the brain, and then came to rest at the very back of the inside of the skull, where it was recovered. Judging by the soot deposits and gray discoloration around the bullet wound from the gunshot residue, Dr. Howard described it as "a very close-range wound, less than an inch."

Another bullet fired from very close range struck Kathy in the center of the chest, "damaged ribs, hit her heart, passed through the diaphragm, hit her liver, went through the stomach, entered the part of the chest cavity on the left side . . . and then exited the body" on the lower left side. That bullet was not found. "The muzzle was either touching or less than an inch away when the gun was fired," the doctor said.

A third bullet "passed through her shoulder area, struck her fourth rib, went through the upper lobe of her right lung and lodged in the lower lobe of her right lung." That bullet was recovered.

She also suffered abrasions and bruises, as well as what were assumed to be injuries from being dragged on her back—marks like those on Nickie.

Howard testified all three women had scars on their lower abdomens indicating they had undergone Caesarean birth procedures. There was no explanation why Nickie had such a scar when she was reported to have had no children. Howard also said Yolanda had undergone surgery to have her fallopian tubes removed or tied off to prevent pregnancy. Yolanda had two children and Kathy had three.

When Hedlund completed her questioning, defense attorney Bryan Whitaker had nothing for the witness who had documented the brutality attributed to the defendant.

It was time for the gun evidence—evidence that not only pointed to the defendant and the victims she'd been charged with killing but also tracked with the kind of violence with which Douglas, and later, Donna, had become so entwined.

CHAPTER THIRTY-EIGHT

Deputy Prosecuting Attorney Sharon Hedlund planned to show that Donna Perry had two brothers buy guns for her after she was prohibited from owning them because she had been convicted on federal firearms charges. Getting those two to confirm that from the witness stand, however, was no easy endeavor.

Bruce Massengale repeatedly explained that he suffered a stroke several years earlier that made it difficult to remember the things Hedlund was asking about. He agreed he knew the defendant before the sex-change operation transformed Douglas into Donna.

"I knew her as a man and I knew her as a lady," the witness said. He remembered meeting Douglas Perry at the Evergreen Club in Spokane, a center providing services and activities for people with mental illness. The sixty-five-year-old man was trying to describe the club when he suddenly announced, "I'm going to say something now. I suffered a stroke thirteen, fourteen years ago."

"I was going to ask you about that," Hedlund said. "We've talked about that, correct?"

Massengale fidgeted. "I don't know but, yeah, yeah, I did and I'm giving you all the answers. I just have to concentrate and try to do the best I can."

"So, actually you're a lot better now?"

"I'm a lot better but I wake up in the morning, take my pills and wonder if I . . . whatever."

He identified a photo of Perry taken around the time they met.

"That's when he was a man, I do believe," he said, adding that he and one of his brothers invited the defendant to stay with them until he got his affairs straightened out after he was released from prison. What they thought would be a day or two turned into two or three months.

The witness remembered buying guns for Perry but was thin on details. He thought it happened in Spokane until Hedlund showed him documents on a purchase made in Idaho.

"Yeah," he said. "I don't remember a whole hell of a lot . . . When I got hit with a stroke, I was unconscious for two weeks, this, that, and the other. I'm trying to give you the information. It is that way. I am trying. All I can do is try . . ." He finally said, "All I know is I . . . he handed me the money. I paid for the gun. I gave it to him . . ."

He said he only did that once, and he couldn't explain how more guns bought in his name ended up at Perry's house.

Hedlund asked if the witness knew Clairann Gallaway.

He nodded. "That was Donna . . . Douglas or Donna's streetwalker . . . And like I said, I believe she had six kids or whatever. I don't know what happened to her . . . I met her one time and that was . . . and that was at . . . he kept some very unusual hours. Like I said, when I was in bed at home, that he was out doing what he ever did."

Whitaker made sure the gun-purchase document from Idaho was still in front of Massengale before he began cross-examination. "Now, you said you don't remember ever going to Idaho to buy a rifle. Is that correct?"

"When I got the stroke . . . anything and everything that . . . I could remember the past, but I can't remember the future . . ."

At his seat in the courtroom, Dresback struggled to squelch a laugh. Massengale can't remember the *future*? The brothers had been a challenge to interview, but that line was on a whole different level of absurdity.

"So, this was the only time that you ever went with Mr. Perry to buy a gun?"

"Hey, I'm trying to do it. If I went more . . . I . . . I just remember one time, one time only. I am being honest, true, and that, and I am here, so that must mean something."

"It does. And you remember specifically that it was a Ruger 10/22?"

"If it says it's here, 10/22 or whatever. You know what I mean? I don't even remember the gun."

"OK. That's really what I was asking."

"Yeah. You should ask."

"You're right, I should have. Thank you very much. I don't have any further questions."

And then it was time for the second brother, Mark V. Massengale, to take the stand. When he spelled his name for the judge, he added, "Oh, don't forget to put the V in there." The judge responded with a friendly, perhaps amused, "OK."

Hedlund delved into Mark's relationship with Perry.

"Do you recall meeting Donna Perry, who was then Douglas Perry?"

"Oh, yes. Very nice person, very private, didn't say a lot, but very private."

"OK. Now, when you met her, were you aware of any girlfriends that she had?"

"No. No, not really . . . She did have somebody named Clairann I met one time and that was it."

"What do you remember about Clairann?"

"She had a lot of problems."

Hedlund pressed for details.

"I'd say she needed some mental health services very badly. It was pretty severe . . . Her general behavior was just a little, you know, very . . . not . . . just not right," Massengale said.

He testified he heard Clairann took a bus to Seattle and disappeared.

"Do you remember how Douglas reacted to that?" Hedlund asked.

"Well, a little upset, which I don't blame him. I don't blame him at all."

Massengale said Clairann was arrested many times, and Perry always found a way to get the money to bail her out of jail. That couldn't have been easy for a man living on Social Security disability payments, but somehow his buddy managed.

Hedlund asked, "Now, have you maintained contact with Mr. Perry since he had his gender reassignment and became Ms. Perry?"

"Oh, gosh. Oh, boy. That's another good one. I can't remember what year that was."

Massengale said he didn't know that records showed he bought guns in his name that were seized from Perry's house in 2012.

Hedlund handed him a document from 2009 identifying him as the buyer of a Ruger 10/22 rifle that was found in Perry's home in 2012.

Mark V. Massengale said he didn't remember buying the gun. Whitaker passed on cross-examination.

Holed up in a Spokane hotel room, Chero Everson was a mess. She'd talked to her mom the night *and* morning before she was scheduled to appear in court. Though she knew that what she was doing was important—and necessary—she still found herself falling apart over the prospect of being in the same room with the monster who'd stalked her in the hall and around the exercise track at Carswell. Donna was not only looking for a partner in crime, another free-agent assassin to carry out a killing spree that had taken the lives of many more than the three victims in Spokane, she wanted much more. Donna Perry's feelings took the form of a distorted romance, far from the usual gestures like candy or flowers.

More like poison and razor blades.

"I'm scared," she told her mom.

"She's going to be locked up for a long time."

"What if she isn't?"

"She will be."

Despite her mom's assurances, Chero told her handlers from the prosecutor's office she didn't want to, *couldn't*, testify. It was too risky. Her health was failing. She couldn't take the stress. Lots of reasons came to her woolly mind.

The bottom line, however, was how could she testify when there was a chance Donna would make her prediction come true and get off on any charges?

Who would buy a cat-loving, little old lady as a serial killer?

If Chero testified and there was acquittal, she was convinced Donna would kill her.

The Donna Perry she knew thought that killing someone was akin to a walk in the park. Something easy. Something she just *did*.

CHAPTER
THIRTY-NINE

A contract killer who underwent sex-change surgery to disguise himself by becoming a harmless old woman confided to an inmate in a women's federal prison that he had killed twenty to thirty people, compared himself to a famous and fictional serial killer, wanted his young confidante to train as an apprentice assassin, and proposed marriage to her.

Who hasn't heard that story before?

It took some doing, but Chero Everson finally took the stand on the tenth day of trial, June 23, 2017, to deliver some of the most astounding and intriguing testimony ever heard in a murder trial anywhere. Chero testified that her relationship with Donna began in the Federal Medical Center in Carswell, Texas, in the spring of 2013.

Chero said she and Donna hadn't known each other more than a few days when Donna confided that she was a contract killer who had murdered nine prostitutes and then soon grew her grisly score to claim twenty to thirty victims. She admitted still having the urge to kill, and Chero began to fear that Donna would take more victims when she got out of prison, and perhaps would kill her.

Chero explained that, despite knowing the defendant had undergone sex-change surgery, she wouldn't refer to her as a woman, and had always used the male pronouns "he" and "him." That stood out deep into a trial where everybody else had been very careful to refer to the defendant as a woman. She refused to accept her prison pal as a woman partly because "he told me that becoming a woman was a disguise to get the heat, if you will, off of him, and that nobody would think that an elderly lady with mental illness would ever get caught."

"So, in your interactions with Ms. Perry, did you interact with her as a male?"

"Yes."

"Did Ms. Perry state whether she was raised as a male or a female?"

"A male," she said. "Well, he said that he was a hermaphrodite."

"What, if anything, did she tell you about the sex change that she underwent?"

"The sex change, like I said, was, I guess, a way to go into hiding, be disguised."

Defense attorney Bryan Whitaker challenged Chero on the transgender issue, asking, "When did you learn that Ms. Perry was a transgender person?"

"Well, it was very obvious, for one, and for two, he described the steps that he went through to become a woman."

"So, it wasn't until after you met Ms. Perry and started speaking to her that you realized there had been a gender change?"

"No. I don't want to disrespect, but just looking at him, you can obviously tell that he's a man."

Under direct examination by Curtis, Chero continued to describe how Donna confided in her. She said Donna told her he was schizophrenic and a sociopath who lacked a scintilla of remorse for the murders he had committed.

"What, if anything, did she say about whether she dated anyone prior to the sex change when she was a male?"

"That he had dated a lady by the name of Claire," Chero said, letting her words trail off while she searched her memory. "That she had been a prostitute and that she had escaped to California."

"Did Ms. Perry say whether she had ever interacted with any other prostitutes besides Claire?"

"That he'd had interactions with them. He had a few, I guess, regulars, if you will, and he would take them home and feed them or cuddle and let them sit on his lap."

"Did she describe these prostitutes that she claimed she had killed?"

"Yes . . . They were nothing. They were nobodies. They were pond scum."

"Did she explain why she believed that?"

"Because they could breed, they could have families, and that was something that he was jealous of."

Chero said the defendant told her he killed the prostitutes "in a vehicle, by a river . . . around Spokane."

"How did Ms. Perry say she killed these prostitutes?"

"Firearm."

"Did she name any specific handguns that she favored?"

"PPK. A nine-millimeter Beretta . . . That's what I can recall."

"Other than guns, what, if anything, did she say about other types of weapons?"

"That you can . . . you don't even need a gun to kill somebody. You can go to a hardware store and get a saw blade, take it home, file it down so that it's sharp and when you slit somebody's throat, it cannot be stitched up."

"What other ways did she mention it could be possible to kill someone?"

"Bare hands, saw blade, firearm, pencil."

"Who, if anyone, did she compare herself to?"

"Hannibal Lecter."

"What did Ms. Perry say to you about a river and how that related to the killing of these prostitutes?"

"That's where he left a lot of bodies. There were times that he said when he shot them, the bullet or casing, I guess, would stay in the vehicle, but he would, I guess, kick them out and so wherever, you know, he kicked them out, he left them there, left them that way."

"Did he bury them?"

Chero shook her head. "No, that was somebody else's problem."

Curtis asked if the defendant expressed any fear about getting caught.

"Yes . . . That Spokane was hot and that he needed to get away."

The lawyer asked why Donna Perry confided to Chero, nearly a stranger.

"He initially felt like I was an advocate for him and then a few days passed, completely trusted me, and that I was an experiment."

"What do you mean when you say, 'an experiment?'"

"Because, you know, the declaration of being a sociopath, that he felt only rage and shame and so I asked him, 'If that's all you feel, then, you know, why are you . . . why do you trust me or want to marry me or any of that,' and he said 'Because I was an experiment.'"

On cross-examination, Whitaker asked the witness to confirm most of the comments she made on direct examination, but his tone suggested he thought her story was too fantastic, too ridiculous, to believe.

"So, you basically believed everything you were told?" Whitaker asked.

"For the most part, yes, sir."

Whitaker seemed to become more skeptical, asking, "It seemed reasonable to believe you were being recruited to become an assassin?"

"Yeah."

"Because you have what skill set? What skills do you have that would make you a good killer?"

"Mental illness."

"That's it?"

"I don't, I guess, really have a skill set to kill people, but I'm a very good listener."

CHAPTER FORTY

Spokane County Sheriff's Detective Jennifer Sutter took the stand to testify about the flight she shared with the defendant when escorting her from Texas to Spokane. How Donna was convinced she was never going to be free again.

She chatted up the detective about her love and knowledge of guns and ammunition.

"She told me that she liked guns and ammunition and she seemed to be pretty knowledgeable about the subjects," Sutter said. "Didn't like Glocks and I believe I was carrying one at the time."

The detective said Donna told her that she had spent time at Eastern State Hospital for mental health issues.

"And she said, 'You want to know something?' And I said, 'Sure.' She said, 'By the time I learned how to control myself, it was too late.' And then she went on to explain that she didn't have the money for her medications. And she also asked me about if I had seen the movie *Sling Blade* and told me that 'That's going to be what happens to me.'"

Observers in the courtroom took that remark to be a reference to the main character spending the rest of his life in a mental hospital.

Sutter concluded her testimony by telling the jury that Donna also asked if serial killer Robert Lee Yates got the death penalty in Spokane.

Barbara Byington was next. The Spokane city police detective testified how Donna talked about her childhood and recalled how the police had once taken "a bunch of her cats."

Byington also testified that Donna told her she hoped she'd be sent to Eastern State Hospital instead of prison.

"She said, 'You know, I'm on medication now,' and she says that 'I'm not violent now,' which kind of made me think she was violent in the past."

Dr. Nathan Henry, the forensic psychologist who evaluated the defendant at Eastern State Hospital and specialized in forensic mental health assessments for the courts, told the jury Donna Perry suffered from personality disorders, but he found no mental illness. It was true, he said, that she might be a malingerer, someone who feigns "symptoms of a mental disorder or impairment—in this case, both—for the purposes of some type of secondary gain."

Donna, he said, often contradicted herself when talking about symptoms with various people conducting the evaluations. Sometimes she said she heard voices, and other times she said she didn't. She sometimes described symptoms that "just simply don't occur in genuinely psychotic people."

"When I gave her the brief IQ measure," Dr. Henry testified, "she obtained the lowest possible IQ score which, if that were accurate, you would be seeing a person whose impairment was blatantly obvious to a professional such as myself or even a nonprofessional . . . a person whose functional abilities were extremely poor, highly dependent on the assistance of others for basic needs and functioning. So, clearly that presentation was not consistent with her observable behavior and functional history."

He administered a test on basic legal knowledge that asks questions with a fifty-fifty chance of getting the right answer. Donna scored significantly below the average result for choosing answers by chance, which, he said, "means that she could have done better on the test by randomly guessing the answers."

Dr. Henry said his goal was not to conclude whether Donna Perry was guilty or innocent, but whether she was competent to stand trial—meaning whether she understood the charges against her and could participate in her defense. To reach that conclusion, he had to determine whether she had a mental disorder.

"My ultimate conclusion was that she was feigning both cognitive impairment and psychopathology," he told the jury.

Treppiedi asked, "Did you believe she had a serious mental disorder?"

"That's actually a complicated question in her case. My ultimate diagnostic conclusion was that she does not have a serious mental disorder apart from a serious personality disorder . . . In my opinion, she does not have a long-term documented history or recent documented history of a serious psychotic disorder such as schizophrenia . . . It was the opinion of the treatment team and the psychiatrist that she did not have a psychotic disorder and I agree with that."

On cross, the doctor said he had not seen the reports from the Social Security Administration finding that Perry was disabled or from her treatment at two federal medical facilities.

Whitaker asked if his client had been uncooperative during the evaluation.

"I wouldn't even necessarily say she was uncooperative. She was actually fairly cooperative and pleasant in my interactions with her . . . When I conducted psychological testing with her, she did intentionally poor on the testing. So, you could describe that as uncooperative. But like I said, in terms of my interactions with her, there wasn't a kind of oppositional or negative or uncooperative nature to her interactions."

On redirect examination, Treppiedi asked, "Have you found that people feign mental disorders in order to gain some advantage for themselves?"

"It happens."

"Could that include being housed at different facilities?" Treppiedi asked, obviously referring to Donna's statements that she hoped to go to Eastern State Hospital rather than prison.

"Well, malingering is by definition feigning impairment for some secondary gain. So, examples of that could be affecting a person's housing, it could be affecting personal benefits, it could be avoiding culpability. There are many . . . as many examples as there are motivations to feign a mental disorder."

Charlotte Schell, the welfare-eligibility specialist for the Washington State Department of Social and Health Services, had remarried and was living in Idaho by the time she took the stand to tell the jury how Donna Perry casually dropped a comment about shooting people into conversations they had in her Spokane office. Charlotte stated that the defendant said her life had gotten "out of control and wild" before she underwent gender-reassignment surgery.

"And basically, at one point during the course of talking about that, she said something about shooting people, and that kind of brought me up a bit short."

Charlotte had asked what she meant, and the defendant reacted as if she realized she had said too much.

"She didn't deny shooting people but she immediately kind of made it clear she wanted to change the subject and talk about something else."

The witness also described how the defendant explained why she had the surgery.

"'My life was getting out of control, and I knew that I was either going to end up dead or in prison again if I didn't do something about it. So, I had the surgery, just like you geld a horse, and I got my life back under control . . . I became controlled and, you know, able to lead a pretty regular life.'"

Next, Charlotte recounted Donna's racially infused anger over the family of Somalian refugees who had moved next door.

"And this was becoming so upsetting to her that she was telling me that she could take aim from certain windows and viewpoints in her yard and that she could shoot them. And I said, 'But Donna, you've been in prison. You don't want to go back to prison. You don't want to do that.' And she just very calmly looked at me and said, 'Oh, I've been in prison before. It's not that bad.'"

The witness was concerned enough by Perry's comments about shooting people that she filled out a department incident report and talked to a social worker to "just basically let them know that I felt that the potential for violence there was very, very real and I was very concerned about it."

She also reported it to Detective Dresback after he was quoted in the media as seeking information about Douglas and Donna Perry.

On cross, Whitaker asked if his client indicated how many people she'd shot.

"No."

"Indicate if she'd ever killed anybody?"

"No."

"And this discussion about the Somali family, are you familiar with how paranoid people present . . ."

"Oh, yes."

"Would you qualify this as being one of those types of presentations?" Charlotte nodded.

"That's why it scared me so bad, yes."

The Spokesman-Review's headline the next day was accurate, but decidedly unkind.

INFORMANT RECOUNTS CLAIMS OF KILLINGS:

MENTALLY ILL INMATE TESTIFIES DURING PERRY MURDER TRIAL

Chero, who was gravely ill, had come forward to make her stepfather, a retired police sergeant from Nebraska, proud. She was mentally ill, but she wasn't crazy. Chero knew right from wrong.

What Douglas Perry had done to Yolanda, Nickie, and Kathy was all kinds of wrong.

CHAPTER FORTY-ONE

Despite the careful and conservative caveats that seem to come with scientific testing in criminal cases, the forensic scientist who matched Donna Perry's DNA to the blood under Kathy Brisbois's left middle fingernail was willing to give the jury a shockingly definite opinion.

After Lorraine Heath, the supervising forensic scientist in the State Patrol Crime Lab DNA section, put the chance that the DNA belonged to someone other than Donna Perry at 1 in 790 sextillion—that's 790 followed by twenty-one zeros, or 790,000,000,000,000,00 0,000,000. Prosecutor Sharon Hedlund asked, "So, does that number in and of itself prove that Donna Perry's DNA was underneath or on Ms. Brisbois's fingernail?"

Heath responded with unflappable confidence.

"To a reasonable degree of scientific certainty and barring an identical twin, yes. In my opinion, that is Donna Perry's DNA on that fingernail."

Heath was the first witness on the eleventh and last day of testimony in Perry's trial on June 26, 2017. She was the fifty-third of fifty-three prosecution witnesses, and it was her job to confirm all of the DNA tests connecting Perry to all three murders.

In addition to tests that confirmed Perry's DNA under Kathy's fingernail, Heath said she also matched Perry's DNA to a slide with a vaginal smear from Kathy Brisbois. The odds were not as great, however, since the DNA profile on that slide had been observed 7,364 times in the US population. Heath said it was not expected to occur more frequently than one in three males. She described it as "So, it's an association, but not super strong."

Heath said tests on a cutting from the blanket found near Yolanda's body produced a profile that was a mixture of DNA by two contributors. The profile for the major contributor matched Donna Perry. That profile was found once in the US DNA database and was not expected to occur in more than 1 male out of 3,300.

Heath also tested the lacy pink panties found in the closet at Perry's home on East Dalton Avenue. She did not recover semen, but she did find a DNA profile that was a mixture from two individuals. Again, Perry was the major contributor, and the other sample was too small to identify. But Heath said she was able to exclude Yolanda, Nickie, and Kathy as contributing to that sample.

Whitaker cross-examined Heath at length on the number of contaminations of samples and tests in the labs of the State Patrol Crime Lab network. Heath said the numbers were low, but some incidents were to be expected because of the large number of tests the lab conducts each year. She said only one of the eighteen incidents over several years that Whitaker cited was related to the murders in the trial.

"On average," Whitaker asked, "how many of these quality incidences is your lab involved in per day?"

"Zero, on average," Heath said. "We average two quality variances or less per scientist per year and some of those that count in that list are those that are outside of our control."

For the fifth time in the trial, and the last time in his career, Detective Jim Dresback took the stand to tie up one loose end—the fate of the Ruger 10/22 rifle that was seized from Perry's house by ATF in 1994, which could have been the murder weapon. Dresback explained to the jury that ATF property records marked the rifle as gone but didn't say whether it was destroyed, auctioned to the public, or donated to a police agency. There was no way to determine what happened to it.

Another Ruger 10/22 rifle that was purchased by Mark Massengale and seized from Perry's house by ATF in 2012 was manufactured after the date of the murders. It couldn't be the murder weapon.

Under cross by Whitaker, Dresback said he was still exchanging emails with an ATF agent about the rifles during the trial. Pushed by Whitaker, Dresback agreed he could have tried sooner to confirm the fate of the rifle that police had implied could have been the murder weapon.

Just after Dresback left the stand, Sharon Hedlund announced that the State would rest its case.

That seemed right to Dresback as the last act on his last day after thirty-three years as a cop. He hoped he was leaving on a high note—convictions of Donna Perry.

After the judge denied another defense motion for separate trials for the three murder charges, Whitaker said, "Over the course of the last three weeks, we've been making some decisions about presentation of our case . . . And we're going to close."

And then, just like that, without calling a single witness, the defense rested.

CHAPTER FORTY-TWO

Sharon Hedlund stood at the podium between the attorneys' tables and spoke directly to the jury box. She began her closing argument by reciting the three familiar names once more—the members of the Circle.

"Yolanda Anastasia Sapp, age twenty-six. Nickie Inez Lowe, age thirty-four. Kathleen Mewes Brisbois, age thirty-eight. This is not the last time that I will state their names and it's not the last time their names will be known. They live on in the memories of their families, their friends, their loved ones . . . They were women. They were daughters . . . They were friends. Mothers. Stepmothers. They were connected in life, and they were connected in death."

The prosecutor knew she had to make the jurors look past these women's identities as prostitutes and see them as real people with lives not all that different from the jurors' lives.

Hoping she had accomplished that, Hedlund moved quickly to an argument that the physical evidence, especially the DNA and the fingerprint, should overcome Perry's denials that the jurors heard in the interview with Dresback and Burbridge.

"You can see how many times she said that throughout the interview: 'I didn't do it. I didn't kill these women. I didn't even know these women.' Yet we have physical evidence connecting her in ways to each of these women."

Hedlund referred to Donna Perry's less-than-absolute comments about whether Douglas could have killed the women: "I don't know what Douglas did . . . Douglas didn't stop it; Donna did . . . Donna has killed nobody."

The prosecutor reminded the jurors how well the victims knew each other. "They worked in the same circles. They shared an area on East Sprague. They shared johns sometimes. They shared rooms at the Spokane Street Motel sometimes . . . They utilized the rooms there close to the strip."

Without a detailed explanation, Hedlund suggested a connection between the dates that Clairann Gallaway was in jail and the dates Yolanda and Nickie were killed, which could not have been coincidental. "One of those is the day before Ms. Sapp's body was found and one of those is the day that Ms. Brisbois's body was found. It is unknown where she was during the time frame in which Ms. Lowe was, in fact, found."

Hedlund said Clairann's connection to the three women also meant Perry must have had a connection to them, despite her denial of that.

Hedlund pointed to the most glaring similarity in the murders. All three bodies appeared to have been dumped roughly on the riverbanks but were posed naked or nearly naked. And firearms experts testified that the two bullets recovered from Kathy's body and the one from Nickie's were all .22-caliber long-rifle, rimfire bullets. The bullet from Nickie and one of the bullets from Kathy bore similar markings and could have been fired by the same gun. The second bullet from Kathy appeared to have been fired through a different gun barrel. The experts said that could suggest two guns were used or one gun with two barrels, like a two-shot derringer.

Next, the prosecutor turned to the DNA matches that connected Perry to the murders and noted that she was the only person out of hundreds investigated who had physical links to all three murders. "There's DNA and prints in each of these cases, one of each, that tie or connect in some manner to Ms. Perry." Hedlund pointed out the detailed testimony by Chero Everson about Perry's admissions while they were in prison, which Hedlund described as the place where criminals talk about their exploits. She recited the long list of admissions and claims of murder Chero quoted from her former prison pal, and asked how Chero would know about those things if Donna Perry hadn't told her.

Hedlund ran down a long list of incriminating statements Donna Perry made to others:

To Danielle Arndt at Eastern State Hospital: "The only reason I was caught was because they found DNA under a fingernail."

To Detective Barbara Byington on the plane: "I will never get out of this."

To Detective Jennifer Sutter on the plane: "By the time I learned how to control myself, it was too late. This is the last time I'll be outside of concrete walls."

To Charlotte Schell, the state welfare worker, Donna talked about being out of control and shooting people. She believed she had to become a woman to stop the violence, and that's why she had the sex change.

Hedlund quoted Dr. Nathan Henry's mental health assessment, which concluded Perry was a malingerer who had personality disorders but no mental illness. She was feigning mental illness, perhaps to avoid responsibility for the murders or to get sent to Eastern State Hospital instead of prison.

Hedlund suggested Perry hated Clairann's work as a prostitute and may have been trying to get her out of "the life" by killing the other prostitutes she associated with. Or perhaps Perry killed the women out of "downright hatred" for women who prostituted themselves.

She closed by asking the jurors to remember the women by convicting Perry of "the first-degree murder of Yolanda Anastasia Sapp . . . of Nickie Inez Lowe, and . . . of Kathleen Mewes Brisbois."

Detective Jim Dresback was cleaning out his office on his last day at the sheriff's department when Sharon Hedlund was making her closing argument at the courthouse. He had done his job and was finished now. He didn't see the need to sit through closing arguments, to wait out the jury's verdict, or to sit in the courtroom when the judge read the verdict. He was ending his last day on the job as quietly as possible. He was closing out his career not with fanfare but with the quiet resolve of a job well done. The end of this case wasn't about him. It was about the victims.

"Always had been," he would say.

Back in the courtroom, Bryan Whitaker shaped his closing argument as a story of a small community of people whose lives were endangered by their involvement in prostitution and drugs. The murdered prostitutes, their boyfriends, Douglas Perry, and Clairann Gallaway—they all knew each other and associated with each other, which Whitaker suggested could explain why Perry's DNA and fingerprints were found on the victims or their belongings.

Whitaker pointed the jurors away from Perry as the killer of Yolanda, Nickie, and Kathy by citing Gorden Lucas's suspicion that the women were involved in some criminal activity like a drug rip-off, and that was the reason they were killed. Lucas testified the women were afraid that something was going to happen to them, but they wouldn't give him any details. And after Yolanda was killed, Darrel Thomas said, "They killed my baby."

Whitaker cited Lucas's testimony that he wanted to kill the person who killed Nickie. But Whitaker reminded the jurors that Lucas never suspected Perry was the killer or linked her to the murders in any way.

"Why? Because he knows that neighborhood. He knows who the tough guys are. He knows who the drug dealers are. He knows who the people are that will rain on you if you make them angry. He knew that in 1990 when he saw our client and he knew it two weeks ago when he sat in that chair right there and looked at our client. He knew it then. Still not somebody that Gorden Lucas was going to worry about down there on Pacific and Sprague."

Whitaker turned his attention to the forensic evidence, suggesting that Clairann could have been the carrier that deposited Perry's DNA on the victims or their belongings, such as Yolanda's blanket. Clairann worked with and even partied with the victims while she was living with Perry. "Clairann was a friend of these women. They are part of the same community, so, suddenly, the whole idea that it's a match is not so overwhelming," he said.

Whitaker called the investigation of Perry after his DNA was matched to Kathy's fingernails a case of confirmation bias. "They would look for evidence, and if they couldn't find what they were looking for, they would stop looking. What are they looking for? They are only looking to connect our client with the case."

He also implied the tube of lubricating jelly that bore Perry's fingerprints could have been Clairann's. After all, several people apparently had thrown their trash in the dumpster where Nickie's belongings were found, including the welfare department envelope that bore another man's fingerprint and empty beer bottles. "All the evidence you have is, there's a fingerprint in a trash can down in the same area where Nickie and Yolanda and Kathy and Clairann and Gorden and Doc and Linda and Douglas threw their trash," Whitaker said.

With understated sarcasm, he said, "But because our client's DNA is on Ms. Brisbois, this means our client killed Nickie Lowe . . . There is absolutely no proof of anything, other than the following: Our client had contact with these people. The DNA people told you, you do not know who the last person was who had contact with any of them. You do not know who killed them as a result of DNA testing. The fingerprint puts our client's stuff in a trash can with Nickie's stuff. None of the DNA says our client was anywhere near Nickie Lowe. None of it.

Whose evidence was that? Theirs [the prosecutors]. They spent three weeks of your lives not proving anything . . .

"Then the argument is they were killed because they could breed . . . That whole theory falls on its face because our client had a sex-change operation in the year 2000, not in 1990. He would not have harbored the inability to breed in 1990 because he was a man . . . Nobody testified he couldn't have kids."

Whitaker took aim at the confused and confusing testimony by the Massengales. At first, they didn't remember and then they did remember buying guns for Perry. They agreed they bought a Ruger 10/22 .22-caliber rifle for him at his request in 1989—a rifle that a crime-lab expert said could have fired the bullet that killed Nickie Lowe.

Whitaker suggested the Massengales' testimony was of little value. "Let's say for a moment that it's absolutely true. What does it prove? It proves that a weapon that has statistically a three percent chance of being the firearm manufactured for one of the bullets was in our client's possession. That's what it proved."

Whitaker said Perry's interview with police was really an interrogation in which they violated her right to be represented by an attorney, which he said she requested six times. The detectives kept haranguing her for forty-five minutes until she agreed to talk to them. She denied killing the women repeatedly, only to be told sixty times that she was lying.

What about Chero's story? Whitaker didn't address everything she said, but he denied Donna Perry could have told her in 2013 about killing prostitutes because his client didn't even know then who was killed or how they were killed.

Without making a specific allegation, Whitaker seemed to dismiss much of the testimony and evidence because of the mental issues with the primary parties in the trial. "We have Chero; she's in a mental institution. We've got the Massengales; they hang out at the place for the disabled people downtown. Our client comes from a mental institution."

Whitaker referred once more to the application of reasonable doubt when a parent is deciding whether to open a thirty-year-old bottle of Tylenol for their child.

"You have to make sure that you're really confident before you break into that 1980s bottle of Tylenol and give it to your kids. Once you've eliminated all the reasonable doubt, that's when you can break into this. And reasonable doubt comes from the lack of evidence. We can sit here all day and give you theories, alternative theories at that. But every time you're given an alternative theory, you're undermining yourself. You're saying, 'I haven't proven this beyond a reasonable doubt, so believe this instead.' You can't open this bottle [if] that's what you're thinking."

The defender insisted the prosecutors had failed to prove their case.

"They've done nothing to overcome reasonable doubt. They've done nothing to prove that Donna Perry killed anybody . . . The burden is proof. The proof is nonexistent."

He asked the jury to find Donna Perry not guilty.

Sharon Hedlund was eager to make her rebuttal argument, and she began with the best answer a prosecutor can give a jury in response to defense criticisms of incomplete evidence, witnesses with spotty memories, and conflicting testimony.

"You know, I keep hoping for the perfect case where there's absolutely no issue whatsoever and all the witnesses are one hundred percent consistent and come in here like a TV show and present the evidence. But, unfortunately, that's for television and Perry Mason is not a resident of my office."

Hedlund attacked Whitaker's repeated argument that the DNA and fingerprints could have found its way onto the victims or the evidence because Douglas Perry associated with Clairann Gallaway, and both were part of the community of prostitutes that inhabited the Stroll.

"Now, much is talked about of this community . . . and the fact that Ms. Gallaway was recognized as being someone who was in that community . . . We had an indication that Mr. Perry . . . had, in fact, been down there. But down there apparently soliciting prostitutes, not down there in the community . . ."

Hedlund asked how Perry's DNA or fingerprints could have innocently gotten on anything, especially when she mostly denied even knowing the murdered prostitutes. Yes, she finally admitted she might have had sex with Nickie and Kathy. But that would have been during the times Clairann was living with the defendant, and by Donna Perry's own admission, Douglas never saw prostitutes while Clairann was with him.

While Prosecutor Hedlund agreed Clairann was "pretty firmly" a member of the community of prostitutes, she said that was not true of Perry. She noted that Gorden Lucas testified he had only seen Perry once and that was on the east side of town after the murders, not on the Stroll. Lucas's sole exposure to Perry had nothing to do with the prostitutes and never made Lucas suspicious of Perry.

Hedlund defended linking the defendant's fingerprints on the tube of lubricant found in the dumpster to Nickie's murder. She rejected Whitaker's suggestion that the tube could have been thrown in the dumpster by someone else.

Sharon Hedlund rejected Whitaker's implied criticism of the mental conditions of some of the witnesses and even his client. She specifically rejected the suggestion that the defendant was mentally ill by citing Dr. Henry's conclusion that Donna Perry suffered from personality disorders but was not mentally ill.

The prosecutor urged jurors to ignore the defense attorney's Tylenol example when gauging reasonable doubt. She recommended reading the explanation of reasonable doubt in the jury instructions they would take with them into their deliberations.

Hedlund closed her last chance to address the jurors with advice on how to reach a verdict.

"Think about the comments that were made to Chero Everson that she testified about. Think about the comments made to other people. Think about the comments she makes in the interview . . . Ms. Perry does not like prostitutes as Mr. Perry. She did not want her girlfriend to be one. She did not want to have anything to do with them. So how is it that she ended up with them so often, according to other parts of her interview? What was she doing with these women that her DNA and prints ended up so closely associated with them? I do, again, ask you to review all the evidence and return verdicts of guilty in all three counts and in the common scheme or plan aggravator."

And then immediately—at three o'clock on Tuesday, June 27, 2017—the trial was complete. Judge Price dismissed three women who were alternate jurors and sent the rest of the panel of ten men and two women to the jury room to begin deliberations on the evidence given over the last two and a half weeks by fifty-three witnesses and scores of exhibits.

Jurors deliberated for about two hours before breaking for the evening.

The jury returned to put in a full day of deliberations on Wednesday, June 28. The prosecutors knew the longer the panel deliberated, the better for the defendant. Many lawyers say a guilty verdict in an average murder case—which really doesn't exist—will take four to six hours. But there was nothing—absolutely nothing—average about this case. A woman who used to be a man was tried on allegations that she was a serial killer of three prostitutes twenty-seven years earlier when she lived with a prostitute. All the parties knew there was no "average" equation for the length of jury deliberations in that scenario. Still, nerves were beginning to fray when deliberations rolled over into Thursday, at least until word came from the jury that they had reached a verdict.

After everyone assembled in the courtroom—with Donna Perry as subdued and seemingly distanced from the event as she had been during the trial—the dignified and solicitous Judge Price turned the usually stern warning against any outbreaks in the courtroom after the verdicts into a gentle request.

"Ladies and gentlemen," he said, "I appreciate the fact that we've been here the better part of two or three weeks and there is a lot of emotions that are running high in this case, so can I respectfully ask if you're here and you feel that you can't maintain your composure or you're prone to outbursts, can I kindly ask you to step out? All right."

Then he turned his attention to the subdued defendant. "Ms. Perry, can you please stand?"

Dressed in an ill-fitting men's black suit and black shirt, Donna Perry stood slowly and kept her eyes downcast as the judge began to read the verdict. "We, the jury, find the defendant, Donna Rebecca Perry, *guilty* of the crime of murder in the first degree as charged in Count One [the murder of Yolanda Sapp]."

The word "guilty" seemed to reverberate through the courtroom as the family and friends of the three women hugged each other and some began to cry.

Without a trace of emotion in his voice, Judge Price repeated essentially the same words for Count Two—the murder of Nickie Lowe—and Count Three—the murder of Kathleen Brisbois. Guilty and guilty.

And then he read the three special verdict forms that said the jurors had answered "yes" to the question of whether the State had proven aggravating circumstances in addition to the defendant's guilt. The forms said the aggravating circumstances were "There was more than one person murdered and the murders were part of a common scheme or plan." The answer was "yes."

That sealed Donna Perry's fate. Although the judge set the sentencing for July 24, a conviction for premeditated first-degree murder with aggravating circumstances mandated life in prison without parole.

Donna wasn't wrong at all when she had told police she knew what was coming.

"I'll never see the outside of concrete walls."

As she was being handcuffed and about to be led back to jail, the judge turned to her. "Ms. Perry," he said, "I appreciate all your courtesy and dignity shown throughout this proceeding."

Family reunions were both rare and difficult for Kaishea Rain Kegley. To be fair, they were difficult for all members of the Brisbois family. Assembling the frayed edges of the ties that bound them together was complicated for several reasons.

Chief among them was that Kathy's sisters had gone in and out of the life that ultimately brought Kathy to the edge of the Spokane River. They'd worked the streets together—not because it was some manifestation of their singular brand of sisterhood, but because they needed the cash and prostitution was a straight line, albeit a risky one, to that end.

Whenever Kaishea was with her aunts, she found herself a bit of an outsider. She loved them, of course. She knew their troubles. She knew the guilt they carried for whatever part they held in the trajectory of her mom's life and death. Sometimes the air around the Brisbois women felt toxic and it was hard for Kathy's oldest daughter to breathe. Other times, like a rare reunion at her grandmother's house many years after the murder, Kaishea could feel that sisterhood that her mother surely felt, as the older women laughed, smoked cigarettes, and reminisced about growing up, stumbling, and their attempts at regaining their footing. It was true Kathy was long gone, but reminders of her were everywhere. Her high cheekbones were shared by her sisters. Her green eyes were the same as Kaishea's. And, most of all, their stories threaded memories that always included Kathy.

She should be here, Kaishea thought. *No one had a right to take her from her family.*

As Kathy's girls grew older, each felt the unrelenting sadness that came with the realization they'd either approached or passed the age their mother had been killed.

We're able to live, age, do things that she could never do.

When Kaishea received word there had been a verdict and she'd be needed to make an impact statement to the court, she—along with her father—packed up her youngest and oldest children for the six-plus hour's drive from Oregon for Spokane.

She was more than relieved by the verdict. She was also ready.

CHAPTER FORTY-THREE

Guilty.

For the survivors of the murdered members of the Circle, the verdict did little to mend the shattered hearts over the twenty-year period they'd waited for a resolution. It is only a word. Not a cure-all, a panacea. It didn't stem the sense of loss for a mother or daughter. Some would later say it brought a measure of relief, but that had more to do with the idea that at least they knew who was responsible. That the monster had been captured and finally contained.

It didn't make things nice or better. And it didn't seem to bring any sense of real closure for those who loved Nickie, Yolanda, and Kathy.

Neither did it bring contrition to the person who'd killed them.

Indeed, Donna Perry appeared relaxed and even smiled as she entered the courtroom for sentencing on July 24, 2017. For what seemed the first time, she chatted with her defense attorneys as they sat at the table.

"What do we got here?" Donna asked. "Bad news?"

She'd already been handed the bad news.

And then to open the hearing—in a move reminiscent of the Circle that formed in hopes of protecting Yolanda, Nickie, and Kathy—a new circle of their family and friends formed in the back of the courtroom. But its members were there to force Donna Perry to face the damage she had inflicted on so many by taking the lives of those three women. The witnesses who had lived for decades with the emotional and practical harm caused by the woman at the defense table lined up to deliver their own condemnations of the serial killer. Many of them had grown close while attending the trial, and now they stood together to seek justice for the three women and those they left behind.

Gorden Lucas, unable to attend because of car trouble, sent a brief note, which was read into the record by a woman from the prosecutor's Victim/Witness Unit.

"I'm so sorry I am unable to attend sentencing. Thank you all for all these years for all of your help. Judge Price, Sharon, attorneys, the jury, and the police department, with all my heart, thank you. Law has been exacted and rightfully so to Perry. May God bless you all. Amen."

But what followed in the comments from survivors was significantly more personal and forceful than Lucas's last-minute message.

Chilesa Patzer, who was an infant when her aunt Nickie was murdered, wished a long and agonizing life on the killer she insisted on referring to as a male.

"There will never be enough time in jail for him," she said. "He's over sixty and when he's facing three life sentences for first-degree murder, I don't believe that's even close to a fair and just punishment. I have been tortured by this for twenty-seven years. I doubt that he will even have to suffer for as long as I have. I would hope that he be placed in isolation for the rest of his life so that [he] has minimal contact with anyone . . . or that he is placed into a general population men's prison. Yes, I'm aware that he had a sex change, but we have heard testimony that this was only as a disguise. We have also heard that your DNA doesn't change when you have a sex change. So, technically speaking, he is still a man and will always be a man regardless of [if] he has a women's private area. I know that this will never make my aunt or any of these women come back, but I don't believe that he should be able to have a pleasant experience in prison for the rest of his life."

She said her aunt's murder was so devastating to her mother that she was unable to live a normal life for years, destroying their own mother-daughter relationship.

"I'm asking that, when you place the sentence on Mr. Perry, that you first think about how he's ruined the first twenty-seven years of my life, how he left me without any family, that my aunt was never able to follow her dreams."

Natasha Sapp was next. She told the court she had been angry about what happened to her mom as long as she could remember, but had no memories left of the woman who died when Natasha was only five or six.

"So, as I got older . . . you go to school and you see people have pictures with their moms and, you know . . . and you just kind of feel like you're just empty. You know, I don't have a hug to remember. Unless I look at a picture on my grandma's wall, I don't know what she looks like. I can't remember a conversation or anything and at times that has made me feel really crappy because I tried so hard to remember and I can't. But if she would have not been killed by a monster, then I would have had a memory . . . You're supposed to forgive, and I don't. And it's a daily battle that I have all this anger, and I can't forgive. I want justice, an eye for an eye. You kill, you deserve to be killed in the worst way. And it sucks that I have this anger and this hatred towards somebody that I've never even met."

Yolanda's other daughter, Marika Sapp, left her Tacoma home at 3:00 a.m. to get to court to represent her mother. If she was exhausted, she didn't show it. Marika was a fierce defender of her mother, pointing out that while Yolanda struggled with addiction, she was a mother first.

"No one had no right to take my mom away. She was a mom. She was a daughter . . . She had nieces and nephews, cousins. She was a sister. I don't know who thinks they're above God to even decide who gets to live just because—I don't know the reason why. I would like to know why he killed these three beautiful women. Years, I wondered and questioned, you know, when I went to school like my sister said, I see other people with their mothers and I'm like, why, God? Why was my mother taken away, you know? For years I was scared thinking maybe the person is going to come after me and my family."

Marika admitted wrestling with the concept of forgiveness.

"It's going to take me a while," she said, "but I do pray, pray for your soul and ask for forgiveness because there's no punishment going to be worse when you have to deal with God and he's going to set the final punishment for you for what the horrible things you have done. You destroyed families, you took away precious people, and I hope that you will sit in your cell forever and you think about the horrible things that you have done, and I pray to God that people won't show their anger out on you . . ."

Marika appeared to buy into what Chero had said about Donna becoming transgender as a ruse.

"And you disguising yourself to turn your identity in is a slap in the face, trying to make yourself, I guess, not get caught. But I thank the Lord, that God used this beautiful team to find justice and I thank them so much."

Kaishea Kegley, like others in her family, wore one of the T-shirts they'd made for the sentencing. A color photo of Kathy covered the front, and the back bore the words "In Loving Memory . . . Kathleen Ann Brisbois, Beloved Mother, Sister, Daughter, 1951–1990."

Kaishea gave Donna Perry a hard stare when she took the podium.

It was so weird, so disrespectful.

Donna, eyes cast downward, headphones on, seemed to be living in some alternate universe in which she'd done nothing wrong because, well, *Douglas did it*. It made Kaishea's blood boil. She wanted nothing more than to bolt over to the defense table and put her hands around the now-convicted killer's neck and show her just how tough she could be. How she could fight just as hard as her mom did.

She didn't do that, of course.

Neither did she ever really give up hope that someday, someone would be held accountable.

And now, in that Spokane courtroom, that was the day.

The eldest of Kathy's daughters painted a picture of who her mom had been.

"My mom was pretty," she said. "She was fashionable. And she loved her family. She loved spending time with her family. She was a doting aunt to her nieces and her nephews. Some are here today. She was a loving mother, a daughter, and a wife. She was a person with feelings with the will to live, so she fought for her life, May 15, 1990. She fought the fight of her life and that's how we ended up here today."

Kaishea stared once more at Donna and let the world know she didn't buy her story one bit either.

"I want to thank my mom for scratching up this man so that he could meet a real woman, Justice, who carries the scales of justice. She's here today. So is my mom. This whole event has been a nightmare for me. I was nineteen. I lost the person who loved me the most in the world. A piece of my heart was stolen: my support, my mother. My four kids, she has eleven grandchildren, two great grandchildren, so her fertility goes on and on, as it does in our family. My daughter here was just born before my mom was killed and my mom never got to meet her. He stole that from me that night and now justice is here to steal his freedom."

Next, Josiel Morton, Kathy's granddaughter, stood. She spoke of the loss she has felt all her young life.

"I never got to meet my grandma and always have that hole in my life," she said. "She was a beautiful woman from what I know. She lit up a room and I will never get to experience that. Thank you for all your hard work in bringing us justice today."

Kathy's sister Susan also offered a brief but heartfelt memory.

"Kathy was my younger sister, but she was the joy of my life . . . We always called her Wiggy. It's the name we'd given her, and she was a beautiful, beautiful woman. I used to always say she had Tina Turner legs. It's been twenty-seven years, but it's like it was just yesterday. And I miss her a lot."

The last two speakers had similar and specific hopes for Donna Perry's future.

Debbie Bailey thanked the prosecutor, the detectives, and "everybody that fought for these girls." Kathy's sister hoped the sentence would be fair, although she didn't know what that should be. And then she looked over at Donna.

"But I hope this person," she said, "that sits there and pretends like we're not talking to him rots in hell."

She also called Donna *him*.

Tabatha Mora, a lifelong friend of Kathy's, spoke directly to the convicted serial killer.

"Thank you for everyone that caught this monster. But to me, I hope you rot in hell. And I don't care if he got a sex change. Even if you go to a woman prison, they could be just, just as bad as a men prison, so, you know, I hope you get justice in all kinds of ways in my book."

When the judge turned to the prosecutor and defense attorney for comments, there wasn't much they could say. Sharon Hedlund offered her gratitude and respect for those who had been involved in the investigation, noting that many of the detectives who testified at the trial were retired and on their own time. She said many of the victims' family members had stayed involved in the case for such a long time. And she noted that there were several—such as Nickie's mother, Diane Matney, and Nickie's sister, Jackie—who had died. Hedlund noted that Yolanda's boyfriend, Doc Thomas, had been dedicated to assisting in the investigation until he died. She said everything she had learned indicated that Yolanda and Thomas had a genuinely loving relationship. She said sources had told her that, for years after Yolanda's murder, Doc "could be seen on street corners basically bawling his eyes out, so despondent about the fact that he would never be with Yolanda again, that he was never able to pull out of it."

"Obviously," Hedlund said, "the volume of material in this case was incredible but one of the things that really came through was the fact that these three women had an impact so far beyond just their deaths.

They had an impact in their home life, in their family life, you know, in the community."

When it came time to address the sentence Judge Price was about to impose, the prosecutor said there was no choice under the law. Convictions on first-degree murder charges with special aggravating factors mandated life without parole, with the sentences to be imposed consecutively. She called those sentences "appropriate."

Defense lawyer Bryan Whitaker acknowledged the mandated penalty, but said he was obligated to request the judge make the sentences concurrent instead of consecutive. He said he had to do that so the sentences could be challenged on appeal. He also noted that Donna had no family left to speak for her at the hearing since she had no contact with the sister who was her only living relative. And, Whitaker added, he had advised Donna not to make any statement to the court, although it was her right to do so.

As Judge Price prepared to begin his comments and the sentencing, he asked Donna Perry to give him her attention so he could ensure she understood her right to an appeal, which he was about to explain. Once he had done that, he asked if she had any questions about that.

When she shook her head, her lawyer told her to say it out loud.

"No," she said softly.

The judge took a few minutes to make some notes before he began by thanking the prosecutors and defense attorneys and complimenting them on their presentations and work during the trial. And then he began what would be a remarkable soliloquy about Donna Perry and her victims.

"In my fourteen years here in Superior Court, I've tried and presided over countless murder trials. But I have to say this case has by far been the most complicated criminal proceeding of any type that I have ever had, and I suspect it will be the most complicated case I'll have in my career as a Superior Court judge," he said.

"I think the reason we're all here is because law enforcement never dropped the ball. They kept up the search for all these years and they didn't stop until they put together every part or every detail in this case. And I have to say in a day and age where law enforcement officers seem to be subject to so much criticism—some of it justified, much of it not—I wish some of the critics could be here to see how diligent and hardworking law enforcement are."

He took a run through the kinds of homicide cases he had seen.

"I've had murder cases where that murder was," he said, "I'll call it a crime of passion. You know, a relationship that went bad. I've had murder cases involving drug deals that went sideways; somebody didn't pay somebody that they were supposed to pay and there's a murder. Or perhaps a murder case where someone was killed during a robbery, a robbery that went bad; shots were fired; someone dies. I've had murder cases where someone is killed where the individual is fleeing or attempting to flee the scene of a crime and shots are fired and someone dies. And I hope we would all agree that no one has the right to take another person's life, no one. But in the circumstances that I have just described . . . at least you can get your head around it as a judicial officer or a lawyer. Even citizens, maybe to some extent, can understand it . . .

"But this case is my first time, and I hope my last, addressing a horrible crime, murders seemingly committed just for the sport and no other reason.

"And I didn't know these three women, but I feel like I know them now after all these weeks in trial . . . during this trial I really felt like for the first time I got to know these three women. And all three of these women, now victims, they were all human beings. They had lives. They had families. They had significant others. They had people that cared about them. They had aspirations. There were things they wanted to do with their lives. Most of all, they wanted to live their lives and, despite living lives that are so difficult that most of us probably can't comprehend it, all three of these women managed to make the best of it. They managed to live their lives fully under the most extraordinary and difficult circumstances.

"So, make no mistake, all three of these women, they were courageous, they were caring, they were loving. And I say this because it has to be said. You know, these three wonderful women didn't work the streets because they wanted to. It's not a lifestyle they chose. And if you're addicted to drugs, you become a hostage to those drugs. You become a hostage to that addiction. Nobody, as I say occasionally during sentencings, nobody decides, I'm going to be a drug addict. It's not anything that a person would wish upon themselves. But it happens and when it happens, people become trapped. And all three of these women were trapped. They were trapped by their life circumstances, and they made the best of it and they did the only thing they could to try to live their life.

"And can you imagine for a moment the fear these women must have had every time they stepped into a car with a total stranger and they're wondering, 'Is this the guy that murdered my friend?' But it's not like they have a choice. It's what they have to do to survive. Imagine how brave you have to be to be able to do that—incredibly brave. That's what all three of these women were."

The judge took a breath and looked directly at Donna.

"And Ms. Perry, what you did was you selectively hunted these women down and you murdered them, not because of passion, not because they owed you money, not because it was all a mix-up and shots were fired or there was some sort of a deal gone bad and they didn't pay you something they owed you. You murdered these women purely for the sport of it. Maybe it's fair for the Court to say you killed these women for nothing more than the thrill of it. That's the part when I say this is my first experience ever having a case like this and I hope it's my last.

"And after killing these three women, each and every time, you selectively chose to display their bodies in the most humiliating way you could conjure up. And why did you do that? You did that to make sure that everyone knew that to you, to the person that had taken these women's lives, these women were garbage. They were nothing. They should be tossed aside. They didn't deserve to live life. That's the message you were trying to put forward when you killed each and every one of these women.

"So, Ms. Perry, would you please stand?"

Donna, expressionless as ever, put her palms on the defense table and lifted herself from her chair.

"As I indicated earlier, my discretion in this particular instance is essentially nonexistent. But I wanted to say, if the Court had discretion, I would have, in fact, implemented the sentence that the legislature mandates the Court impose. And indeed, the legislature here has mandated, Ms. Perry, that you be sentenced to a period of life in prison without the possibility of parole, and it's important to say for purposes of the statute, without the possibility of parole or early release. The three counts are to be served consecutive to each other."

The judge shifted his gaze to the defense lawyer.

"Mr. Whitaker," he said, "your request is well taken by the Court for a concurrent sentence—and is denied."

The woman with the blank expression and downcast eyes showed no reaction to a single word the judge said.

Rarely does a judge expose his own inner thoughts and feelings about a case to the extent revealed by Judge Price. The murders of these three women had obviously offended the judge's heart and soul.

After a quick check with the attorneys to ensure they had nothing else to bring before the bench, he turned to the families of the victims.

"And so, I don't neglect to say this, to the families of Ms. Sapp, Ms. Brisbois, Ms. Lowe, if you're here, I didn't want to neglect to say I'm so very sorry for your loss."

The women of the Circle, loved, missed, and remembered, were finally avenged in a judicial system that took twenty-seven years to do so.

JURY FINDS PERRY GUILTY OF 3 MURDERS

The Spokesman-Review

June 30, 2017

EPILOGUE

Donna Rebecca Perry, now seventy-four, continues to serve three consecutive life sentences at the Washington Corrections Center for Women in Gig Harbor. Those familiar with Donna say she has no visitors or communications with anyone outside the prison—just as it had been during previous incarcerations. Conduct reports indicate the inmate has been punished with temporary suspensions of privileges after a couple of minor violations of the rules. Donna once refused to relocate when she was assigned to a different cell. Another time, she tossed a milk carton at a guard when caught trying to leave the lunchroom with it.

Donna rejected multiple requests to talk about her life and the lives of the other women she left dead along the Spokane River so many years ago. Her only comment came in the form of a letter in which she declined an interview because the publication of the author's *If You Tell* had caused her friend tremendous pain. The friend was Michelle "Shelly" Knotek, the central figure in that book, who was also incarcerated at the women's prison. The letter, as it turned out, was a forgery. Shelly, ever the deceitful manipulator, had written the missive pretending to be Donna.

Two months after giving her testimony in Spokane, Chero Everson was found unresponsive in her home in Corpus Christi, Texas. She had been napping on the sofa when her daughter checked on her shortly after 11:00 p.m. There was no indication that her death was the result of anything but natural causes. Chero was just thirty-nine years old.

The only woman Douglas Perry truly loved—and perhaps the woman who unknowingly provided the motive for his killing spree—died on November 28, 2014, in a hospital in Arcadia, California, at the age of fifty-eight. Clairann Gallaway, who had been treated for debilitating mental illness in the final years of her life, died from complications from HIV/AIDS. She was survived by seven children and nineteen grandchildren, and her sister, Viola. Almost three months after her death, beautiful, talented, and deeply troubled, Clairann was remembered at a memorial service on the family's dairy farm, which had been converted to an events venue by her son and his family.

With the passage of time, the primary detectives on the Perry case have all moved on.

After thirty-two years in law enforcement, Mark Burbridge retired during the early days of the pandemic. In doing so, he traded long shifts and tough cases for golf in the summer, gardening in the spring, and being Grandpa all year long. Though some cases still haunt, he finds peace in the present: watching his three grandkids a few days a week, cooking dinner most nights—barbecue three times a week, chicken stir-fry on repeat—and leaning into the rhythm of life as a househusband of forty-one years, "mostly her doing, not mine." With the weight of the job behind him and his family in front of him, Mark has no doubt of what matters most.

These days, Jim Hansen spends his winters in Arizona, where he enjoys the sunshine and plays golf three to four times a week. Every Christmas, he and his wife return to Spokane to be with family, including his children and several grandchildren—ranging from a rambunctious toddler to a college senior. He and his wife celebrated fifty-five years of marriage last year. Back in the Lilac City, he keeps up with his old colleagues, meeting weekly to swap stories and stay connected. Retirement suits him well.

Jim Dresback is also happily retired. He's enjoying life with his wife, whom he calls the most wonderful woman God ever created. About six years ago, she got her own motorcycle—tired of riding behind him and giving "bossy directions"—and is now upgrading to a three-wheeler. They often ride with two other couples whose wives still ride passenger, but she prefers the independence of riding solo. On his last day at work, something symbolic happened: While talking and packing up, Jim flung his wrist, and his ten-dollar Timex flew off and landed neatly in the trash. He gave it a look, but never picked it up. After decades in law enforcement—where cheap, replaceable watches made sense—he decided he didn't need to track time anymore.

He hasn't worn a watch since.

AUTHOR'S NOTE & ACKNOWLEDGMENTS

Writing about a transgender person was challenging, and it took careful consideration and, yes, an extra measure of sensitivity. In the case of Douglas Robert Perry, who was responsible for the murders of three women and who later became Donna Rebecca Perry, there were additional complexities. I want readers to come away from this with the understanding that the murders of Yolanda, Nickie, and Kathy were not motivated by her being transgender. *Identity* is not Brian De Palma's *Dressed to Kill*, the film in which a psychiatrist played by Michael Caine slashes women with a straight-edge razor to quell his own gender identity crisis. Questions, however, remain, whether Douglas transitioned to Donna in order to stop the killings or simply as a tactic, a drastic one, to evade the police. We can't ever know for sure either way. What is clear is Douglas Robert Perry's life began amid ridicule, abuse, and shame related to his birth anatomy. At the same time, that's not an excuse for the murders that sent her to prison for what surely will be the rest of her life.

Books that delve into sensitive topics, like prostitution or gender identity, are notoriously challenging in terms of finding people willing to share memories and perspectives when criminal activity is involved. I understand completely. Indeed, none of Donna Perry's surviving family would talk about life in Omak or the events that happened later. No relatives of Nickie or Yolanda would speak either, letting the voluminous police reports, interviews, and court dispositions do the talking for them.

I want to extend my gratitude to the following individuals whose contributions made this book possible: Mark Burbridge, Amy Charles, Karen Denton, Jim Dresback, Viola Eberle, Debra Fecht, Toney and Virginia Fitzhugh, Dan Gallaway, Carolyn Gallaway, Barry George, Brad Gregory, Jim Hansen, Kaishea Kegley, Kris Lingle, Mariah Low, Glen Massengale, Greg Moses, Loreen Rendon, Kreg Sloan, Jennifer Sutter, Jim Williams, and Bonnie Worley. Your willingness to share your time, insights, and resources was instrumental in bringing this story to light. In addition, much appreciation for my researchers, led by Robbin Lassen, as well as Charles Bosworth, Chris Renfro, and Nora McSorley. Your commitment to uncovering the bits and pieces of the truth was invaluable. And finally, special appreciation to Nash Azarian for his counsel on sensitive aspects of this story.

AFTERWORD

No matter how bizarre or disturbing a case might be, I trust Gregg Olsen to deliver the facts and provide a full story. I was pleased to learn that he'd taken on the Perry case, which is among the most bizarre serial murder narratives I've encountered. As a new twist on the "some other guy did it" defense, the effort involved in skirting actus reus responsibility is both a conceptual and psychological puzzle. Does guilt lie in the body or in the soul?

In 1990, Yolanda Sapp, Kathleen Brisbois, and Nickie Lowe were all shot and left near the Spokane River. The cases went cold until some breaks led investigators to Douglas Perry. But there was a twist. Douglas had undergone gender-affirming surgery and was now Donna Perry. And Donna claimed she wasn't responsible; *she* hadn't done anything. She thought it shouldn't matter that she shared DNA with her former incarnation. She believed there were sufficient differences that erased her accountability. The female she is now should not be mistaken for the male who'd once inhabited her body. In fact, given the biological changes, the body in question isn't even the same body, and being female reduced her aggression. Thus, she does not pose a future danger.

Her argument is similar to those with dissociative identity disorder who claim that an alter personality committed a crime. Imprisoning the host body, which noncriminal alters also inhabit, will unfairly punish them.

We can take this dual personality argument back to Dr. Jekyll and Mr. Hyde: If Jekyll willingly drank a potion that he knew would enable Hyde to commit atrocities, then Jekyll should be held accountable for whatever Hyde does. But if Hyde acts in a way that Jekyll could not predict or control, then Jekyll is not responsible for Hyde's crimes.

Perry says she never killed anyone, and while she can't erase what Douglas did, she's not likely to repeat it. This stance might have played a stronger role in her legal case had Donna truly left Douglas behind. But she didn't. She couldn't. She still had the negative influences from his abusive family background, as well as his personality. She talked, a *lot*. She even offered to presumed confidantes a reason for why she'd shed her male form that had nothing to do with a yearning to be female. In addition, her ideas were mired in debunked notions about both gender and aggression.

There are three problems with Perry's proposed defense. First, she seems to think that reducing her aggression against others should give her a pass. However, imprisonment is as much a punishment as a means to protect the community. So, she addresses only one component of our corrections philosophy.

Second, Perry believes that a shift in hormones reduced her violent tendencies. While seemingly logical, this idea has little research support. Hormone therapy does not necessarily diminish aggression. There are more factors than biological makeup in a decision to harm others, and some have a strong influence. From Perry's controlling behavior since her gender shift, we still see signals of potential violence.

Third, Perry believes that a gender change is equivalent to a change in *personhood* and therefore releases her from the consequences of the "other" person's behavior. This remains unclear. In various news reports on Perry's crimes, prior to the trial, experts weighed in.

Dr. Jack Drescher, a New York–based psychiatrist, was asked to comment because he'd been part of the committee on sexual and gender identity disorders for the fifth edition of the *Diagnostic and Statistical Manual of Mental Disorders* (DSM-5). Drescher stated that viewing oneself as a different person after gender-reassignment procedures is more metaphorical than actual. "It's a certain way that they use the metaphor when transitioning for those who were very unhappy before and now are happy," he said. "But it's different when a person makes a claim that somehow they have no linkage to the person they used to be—that would be more of a disturbed presentation."

Transgender professor Jack Halberstam recognized the "multiple personality" line of argument. To clarify this connection, he described the concept of the physical body as a host that various personalities can take over. "It's an idea that we are simply competing personalities or selves," he said.

Perry's case might then be compared to that of Billy Milligan. He was accused of a series of robberies and rapes at Ohio State University in the late 1970s. By the time he faced a trial, ten of his twenty-three "alter" personalities had reportedly surfaced. One had a British accent and could write in Arabic. One was a protector, another a lesbian. Male and female identities had emerged from the same host body.

A psychiatric report for Billy Milligan indicated that one offending alter was a twenty-three-year-old Yugoslavian named Ragen. He had taken over Milligan's consciousness to rob some women. But before he could complete this, a nineteen-year-old lesbian alter supposedly grabbed control and raped the victims. Billy and his other alters had no memory of this incident.

Both sides agreed to acquit Milligan by reason of insanity. (Some follow-up reports state that he duped the psychiatric professionals.)

With Perry, the legal system likewise faced the tricky notion of identity, because it's germane to responsibility. Fact finders had to consider whether the male personality had a center of consciousness distinct from the female personality versus there being an embodied continuum that Perry could not escape. Despite her denial of any memory of the murders, she did recall other things from her time as Douglas. She experienced no mental barrier or disturbance of integration. Significant personal factors remained the same.

In truth, Perry didn't care about any of this. She wasn't striving to be the person she believed she was meant to be. As a female, she expressed no compassion for the victims and demonstrated no remorse for the murders. Her indifference tied her to Douglas, who murdered for petty personal reasons. Although we might sympathize with someone whose gender was arbitrarily assigned at birth due to a physical defect, Perry's gender-affirmation process wasn't about healing her violated sense of identity. Plain and simple, it was an escape plan. We can stand in awe of the considerable difficulty undertaken to achieve it. We can also recognize that her case is a poser for the legal system. However, the banality of her motivation eclipsed any opportunity for higher-order debate. This doesn't make the case less intriguing. In some ways, it makes it more so.

Olsen handles it well without getting into the philosophical weeds. Given how controversial some of these concerns can be, *By the River's Edge* remains a solid true crime narrative. Olsen adds one more to his impressive oeuvre.

—Dr. Katherine Ramsland, Anthony Award–winning coauthor of *The Serial Killer's Apprentice*

ABOUT THE AUTHOR

Gregg Olsen is the #1 *New York Times* and Amazon Charts bestselling author of more than thirty books, including *If You Tell, Out of the Woods, The Amish Wife, I Know Where You Live, The Hive, Lying Next to Me,* and *The Last Thing She Ever Did;* five novels in the Detective Megan Carpenter series; and *The Sound of Rain* and *The Weight of Silence* in the Nicole Foster series. His work has received critical acclaim, numerous awards, and prominence on the *USA Today, Wall Street Journal,* and *New York Times* bestseller lists. Washington State officially selected his young adult novel *Envy* for the National Book Festival, and *The Deep Dark* was named Idaho Book of the Year. *The Amish Wife* was a finalist for the Mystery Writers of America Edgar Award for Best Fact Crime. Born in Seattle, Olsen lives with his wife in rural Washington State and is already at work on his next book. Visit him at www.greggolsen.com.